Outlet Pipe

...nding parts are tinted ... with similar colour in order to shew more clearly the mode of connecting the Angle Iron, Struts & Diagonals.

Girder A at Inlets

Paxton Gutter

Outlet Pipe

Detail of Girder A at those parts marked b in General Draw.t shewing Bracket for supporting Gutter

Side   Elevation.   Transverse   Section

Section at G.H   Section at I.K   Section at L.M   Section at N.O.   Section at P.Q

Section at R.S.

...of Struts   in connection with Angle Iron of Girders B.C.D.E.

Sect.l Plan at L.

Sect.l Plan at L

Section Plan & at o.

M.F. 2...

Paddington Station

Its history and architecture

ENGLISH HERITAGE

Published by English Heritage, Kemble Drive,
Swindon SN2 2GZ

Copyright © English Heritage 2004

First published 2004

ISBN 1 873592 70 1

Product Code 50727

British Library Cataloguing in Publication Data
A CIP catalogue record for this book is available from the British
Library.

Brought to publication by Rachel Howard, Sue Kelleher,
   Andrew McLaren, René Rodgers and Robin Taylor,
   English Heritage Publishing
Edited by Rowan Whimster
Designed by Simon Borrough
Indexed by Susanne Atkin

Printed by Snoeck-Ducaju & Zoon

Front and back endpapers: Contract drawings for the station by
Fox, Henderson & Co, 1851.

Title page: A late 19th-century carriage door panel with the arms
of the GWR.

Frontispiece: 'The Gateway to the West', Paddington Station,
1933.

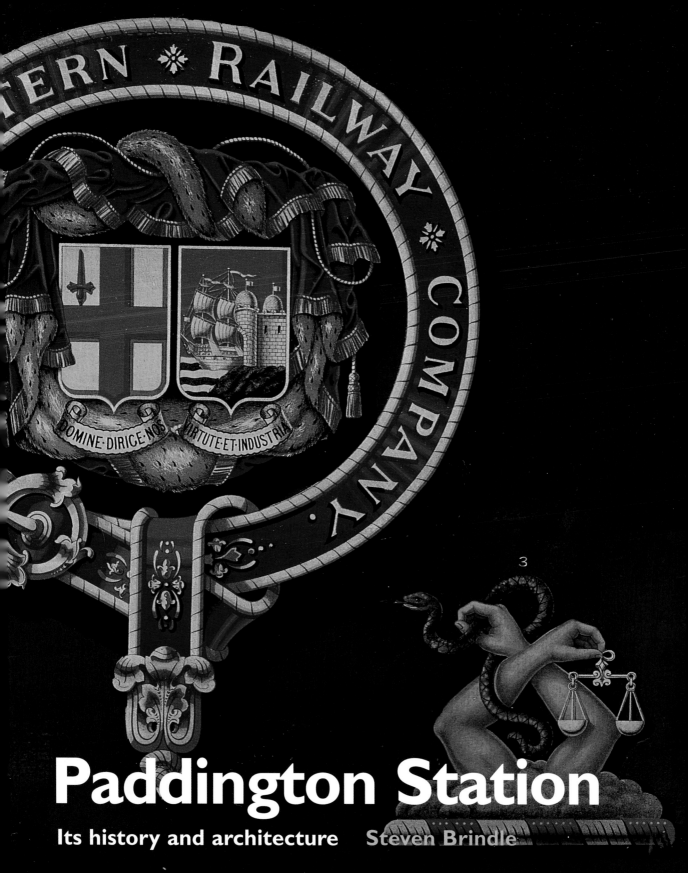

3

Paddington Station

Its history and architecture   Steven Brindle

CONTENTS

I am going to design, in a great hurry, and I
believe to build a Station after my own fancy;
that is, with engineering roofs etc. It is at
Paddington, in a cutting, and admitting of no
exterior, all interior and all roofed in…

Isambard Kingdom Brunel, in a letter to
Matthew Digby Wyatt, 13 January 1851

Railways represent a society, a community, in
motion; so it is perfectly reasonable to judge its
general health by its success or otherwise in
organising this, the most public of communal
activities…

Nicholas Faith, *The World The Railways Made*

PREFACE AND ACKNOWLEDGEMENTS

The best way to approach Paddington is from its Underground station. You struggle through the crowded, low-ceilinged anonymity of the subways, through a ticket barrier: stairs and an escalator loom ahead. Suddenly the ceiling ends and there is an arched roof high above and as you ascend that happily-placed staircase the whole tremendous interior reveals itself at once. You are standing in the middle of the broad central span with, on a fine day, light flooding in from the Lawn roof behind and, almost 215 metres away, light silhouetting the delicate tracery at the far end. The milling crowds, the long perspective, the waiting trains and the light in the distance produce an atmosphere of expectation: the experience of travel is heightened here in a way that few other British stations can match. It is a huge space, but somehow it never overwhelms; it is dark enough to have mystery, but at the same time you can understand at once where you are and where everything is. The proportions are perfect, with the inevitability of a great work of art. It is one of the great interiors of London.

Paddington, the Great Western Railway (GWR) and their principal designer, Isambard Kingdom Brunel, are at the heart of railway history. Railways were one of the defining phenomena of Victorian Britain and one of Britain's many great gifts to the world, so the story of the building of the GWR has a place in world history. This is why Paddington, together with the other principal elements of the main line to Bristol, is at the time of writing a candidate for inscription as a UNESCO World Heritage Site.[1] The name and memory of the GWR continue, however, to have a resonance which goes well beyond these matters of historical fact. Why? Certainly, the company built a superb railway network, but so did other companies. It provided the West of England with excellent train services, but they were not always so. It had a remarkable record of engineering excellence, but in some respects, in matters as important as electrification, it was rather slow. It was a reliable and safe, but unspectacular investment, usually yielding around 4 to 5 per cent, year after year, to thousands of middle-class investors.

In the 19th century the GWR was often controversial and occasionally unpopular, but in its golden age from c 1890 to 1914 and its silver age between 1921 and 1939, the company attracted a remarkable degree of loyalty and affection from its servants (as they were always called), passengers and shareholders. This is not just nostalgia: many people will remember that old GWR employees were still wearing their GWR uniforms and badges into the 1970s, in preference to the nationalised British Rail's offerings. The GWR achieved tremendous things, while maintaining a reputation for absolute integrity, honesty and competence, for over a century. It is difficult to think of any other vanished company, whose 'brand' remains so strong – and the GWR ceased to exist 55 years ago.

So, in writing a history of Paddington Station, one is uncomfortably aware that there is a great deal to live up to. The station has meant so much to so many people, and it embodies so many stories, that there is a certain presumptuousness about the whole business (especially if, like the present author, you come from Lancashire, in London, Midland & Scottish territory, and not from GWR country at all). I am therefore deeply grateful to the many people who have been so generous with their time and knowledge during the writing of this book, a task which began in 1992, was resumed in 2000 and carried to completion in 2002. I am particularly grateful to Robert Thornton, senior architect at Network Rail plc, for all his help and advice; to Ian Nulty, the records manager, and Mervyn Hellen, the senior conservator, and their colleagues at Network Rail's Western Region Plans Room, for all their help and kindness on numerous visits to this extraordinary collection; to Tim Bryan, Director, and Felicity Ball, Assistant Curator, at STEAM, Museum of the Great Western Railway; to Peter Rance of the Great Western Trust and Peter Treloar of the Great Western Society; to Alan Garner and John Spellar of the Broad Gauge Society; to Michael Richardson, archivist at Bristol University Library; and to Ed Bartholomew of the National Railway Museum. I have relied on the staff of the British Library, the Hulton Getty Picture

Library, the library of the Institution of Civil Engineers, the National Portrait Gallery, the Public Record Office (now National Archives), the Royal Institute of British Architects Drawings Collection, the print room at the Victoria and Albert Museum, and Westminster Archives. They have all responded with helpfulness and efficiency in the highest degree.

Various other friends have read drafts of the text and provided much help and advice: I am especially grateful to Alan Johnson, Michael Tutton, Andrew Saint, Gavin Stamp, James Sutherland and Robert Thorne. At English Heritage, I am grateful to Philip Davies for first proposing that the research might be turned into a book; to John Thorneycroft and Paul Velluet for their encouragement and tolerance of the demands on my time which it has involved; to Tim Jones, Keith Falconer, Val Horsler and Robin Taylor for their advice and encouragement; to Cathy Philpots and the Library staff for their remarkable helpfulness; to Nigel Corrie and Philip Sinton for providing the excellent new photography and graphics; to Rachel Howard, Sue Kelleher and Andrew McLaren for their help with the illustrations; and above all to the editorial team of Rowan Whimster and René Rodgers for all their efforts, their support and confidence on the road to publication.

The sources for Paddington's history are vast and complex, much has never yet been touched by scholars, and inevitably much that might have gone into this book has been left out, either from necessity or from ignorance. Any omissions and mistakes are, of course, the sole responsibility of the author and I would be grateful for any corrections and suggestions on these scores.

Finally, we are very grateful to Network Rail plc, who own and run Paddington, for all their help in the writing and production of this book.

Paddington Station – the contemporary passenger concourse.

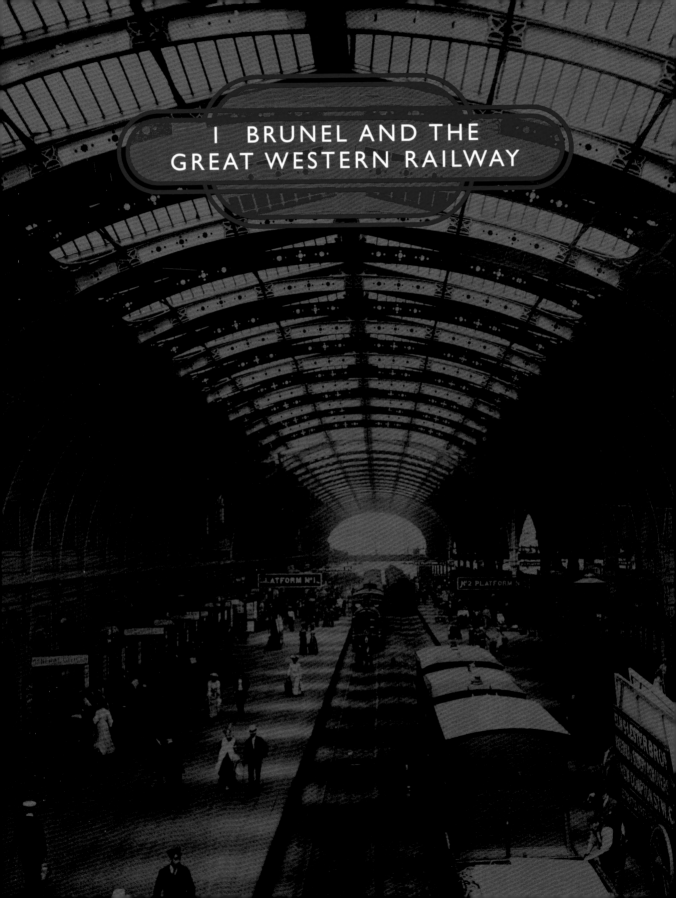

I BRUNEL AND THE
GREAT WESTERN RAILWAY

To understand Paddington Station one needs to understand the Great Western Railway. Isambard Kingdom Brunel, the Great Western's Engineer, called it 'the finest work in England' (Fig 1.1).[1] Many people since have regarded Brunel's line from London to Bristol as the greatest masterpiece of early railway engineering and the GWR as a whole has a special place in railway history. Yet today, when engineering is a mature profession, earth-moving and construction are mechanised and easy, and railways are rather taken for granted, it is difficult to grasp the physical and intellectual scale of the first railway builders' achievements.

In 1824 a group of Bristol merchants assembled to make the first proposal to build a railway linking Bristol with London, 110 miles (177km) to the east. It was unsuccessful, as were the next five.[2] However, Bristol needed a railway. In the 18th century it had been the busiest port in England after London and the hub of the Atlantic trade, but by the 1820s it had clearly been overtaken by Liverpool. Bristol's narrow and confined harbour was always silting up; it was linked to its hinterlands by poor roads and winding canals. The opening of the Liverpool & Manchester Railway in 1830 was a further blow. Outdoing the northern rivals with a railway to London seemed to be Bristol's best hope.[3]

In the autumn of 1832 another group of four merchants met in an office on the site of Temple Meads Station and formed a committee to build 'the Bristol Railway'. This time the venture took off. A company was formed, with representatives of Bristol's four corporate bodies: the City Corporation, the Bristol Dock Company, the Company of Merchant Venturers and the Chamber of Commerce. The Bristol & Gloucestershire Railway, a rather ambitiously titled 10-mile tramway for horse-drawn coal wagons, was also represented.[4] On 21 January 1833 they held their first public meeting and in February they raised funds for a survey. The job was offered to whoever would carry out the survey most cheaply and the company further stated that they would appoint whoever submitted the cheapest building estimate as their engineer.[5] There were already some local candidates in the picture, including William Townsend, the Bristol & Gloucestershire Railway's surveyor. Two others, William Brunton and Henry Price, had in May 1832 published a speculative proposal on their own initiative for a railway to London, taking a rather hilly route via Bath, Trowbridge, Devizes, Hungerford and Reading.[6] One of the directors, Nicholas Roch, however, put forward the name of a 27-year-old London engineer: Isambard Kingdom Brunel (1806–59), son of the celebrated French-born engineer Sir Marc Brunel (1769–1849).[7] The younger Brunel was already well known in Bristol, having won a competition for a bridge to span the Avon gorge at Clifton and served as the engineer to the Bristol Dock Company.

In 1833 the younger Brunel had never yet worked on a railway, but then very few people had: the only substantial railways using steam locomotives were the Stockton to Darlington (1824), the Canterbury & Whitstable (1825) and

Figure 1.1 Isambard Kingdom Brunel, a portrait by his brother-in-law, J C Horsley.

Figure 1.2 The Liverpool Road Station, Manchester – the simple façade of the office and booking hall, looking much like a terraced house, belied its status as the world's first railway terminus.

the Liverpool & Manchester (1830) (Fig 1.2).[8] In 1831 Brunel had travelled to the north of England looking for work; he visited the Stockton to Darlington Railway and on 5 December 1831 he took a journey on the Liverpool & Manchester Railway. This seems to have been the total extent of his experience of railways when he set about surveying and designing the Great Western. He had the benefit, however, of a peerless education in engineering, thanks to his brilliant father. In 1820 he went to school in Paris and became a pupil to a celebrated engineer and clockmaker, Louis Breguet. From the age of 16 to 19 he helped his father, carried out surveys and served an apprenticeship with the mechanical engineering firm of Maudslay, Son & Field.[9]

In 1825 Marc Brunel was appointed engineer to the Thames Tunnel Company and began work on that daring undertaking, the first tunnel ever driven beneath a significant body of water, using the 'tunnelling shield' which he had patented in 1818. From 1827 his 21-year-old son was the resident engineer on the project, keeping a horde of unruly labourers in check and struggling to keep the Thames at bay. The project was perilous in the extreme: the tunnel workings flooded in May 1827, and again in January 1828 with the loss of six lives and Isambard himself seriously injured. Work on the tunnel came to a halt. It was while convalescing from this accident that Brunel first went to Bristol. In 1829–30 he was making his competition-winning entry for the Clifton suspension bridge and looking for work. In the event, the Clifton Bridge Committee could not raise the money to start. However, Brunel had made valuable contacts in Bristol and in 1832 he was appointed as engineer to the city's

Dock Company. The docks were struggling with a perennial silting problem and Brunel designed several minor works in the city's Floating Harbour to tackle this.[10]

For Brunel, the chance to survey the new Bristol Railway was the greatest professional opportunity he had yet had. Nevertheless, he dealt very frankly with the directors, criticising their emphasis on cheapness: 'You are simply giving a premium to the man who will make the most flattering promises. The route I will survey will not be the cheapest – but it will be the best.' Many would have found such an attitude off-putting, but on 7 March 1833 the directors voted by a majority of one to appoint Brunel to make their survey in partnership with William Townsend.[11]

On 9 March 1833 Brunel and Townsend set out from Bristol to begin work on their survey. It was clear from the outset that this was no equal partnership. Townsend was gratifyingly deferential: he was happy to remain in Bristol, responsible for that end of the line, and to work to Brunel's instructions. Brunel made an initial survey of the whole vast area from horseback, hired local surveyors to assist him, opened discussions with landowners and produced the initial plans. It was arduous work. Brunel's son was to write:

> His diary of this date shows that when he halted at an inn for the night but little time was spent in rest, and that often he sat up writing letters and reports until it was almost time for his horse to come round to take him on the day's work. 'Between ourselves', he wrote to Hammond, his assistant, 'it is harder work than I like. I am rarely much under twenty hours a day at it.'[12]

In this way, he finished the survey in ten weeks flat. On 30 July 1833 Brunel explained his proposals at the Bristol Railway's first public meeting. He estimated that the line would be 116 miles (196km) long and cost £2.5 million, complete with stations and rolling stock (it turned out to cost two and a half times as much).[13]

A London committee was formed and the first joint meeting of the two committees was held on 19 August, at which the London & Bristol Railway renamed itself the Great Western Railway.[14] At the same meeting Charles Alexander Saunders was appointed secretary to the London Committee: he turned out to be one of the key figures in the creation of the railway and one of Brunel's staunchest supporters (Fig 1.3). The speed and efficiency with which Brunel had carried out the survey had impressed the new board and he was appointed as the company's engineer on 27 August.[15] His salary was £2,000 plus £300 in lieu of

Figure 1.3 Charles Saunders, the first company secretary of the GWR.

travelling expenses. This looked princely but Brunel was expected to find 'all personal charges for his general professional duties' from this, including the salaries for his assistants and draughtsmen. He was expected to devote himself to 'the general service of the company' and was naturally barred from working for any other railway without the permission of the board: in the event he was to be the chief engineer for several of the GWR's allied lines, such as the Bristol & Exeter and the South Devon Railway.[16]

With a whole railway to design, Brunel swiftly rented a London house at 53 Parliament Street and hired several assistants, though it was a while before he established a settled office. He commissioned a specially constructed britschka (a large four-horse coach), with sleeping accommodation. Brunel lived mostly on the road for several months, turning his survey into a full design, treating with landowners, writing all the correspondence, checking all the accounts and joining in the work of selling shares. By the end of the year, just nine months after Brunel had ridden out of Bristol with William Townsend, complete plans for the 116 miles (196km) of railway were deposited with the Parliamentary Bills Office. Apart from the London end, where Brunel showed a terminus near Vauxhall Bridge, the line was shown mostly as built. Brunel proposed a tunnel beneath Sonning Hill, where in fact a cutting was used, and between Bristol and Bath he had the line crossing the Avon four times: as built, it crosses the river twice.[17]

Raising the immense sums of money needed proved very difficult. As an interim measure the first bill was only for the construction of the outer sections of line, from Bristol to Bath and from Reading to London: opponents derided it as 'neither Great, nor Western, nor even a Railway'. The bill went through its committee stage in April 1834. Brunel was the most important witness and performed superbly during several days of questioning. The bill, however, was thrown out by the House of Lords in July, on the grounds that the company's financial security was inadequate. A new prospectus was issued, more shares were sold and a revised bill was entered in February 1835. Brunel was questioned for eleven of the forty days that the bill was before Committee and this time they were successful. The Great Western Railway bill received royal assent in August 1835: it had cost the company £88,710.[18]

Brunel and the infant GWR stood apart from the other railway companies. Railways began in the north of England, based on the experience and the technologies that had developed around coal mines, coal tramways and canals. Most of the early railway engineers were northerners,

'practical men' typified by George and Robert Stephenson, with little formal education but rich in experience. Most of the early railway entrepreneurs and financiers were northerners too, above all from Liverpool and Manchester. It is remarkable how little of the impetus for the first railways came from London.[19] The GWR was set apart by being a Bristolian venture: Bristol was probably the only southern English city other than London which would have had the means and the confidence to do something on this scale. Brunel was set apart by being a Londoner, half-French and well educated.[20]

In planning the Great Western, Brunel acted with remarkable boldness and originality. His rivals Brunton and Price had proposed a southern route, taking in as many significant towns as possible, including Bath, Bradford-on-Avon, Trowbridge, Devizes, Hungerford and Reading. This would have delivered the traffic of these towns, but at the cost of a winding route with steeper gradients, inevitably slowing everything down. Brunel instead chose a northern route, swinging north from Bath and across broad, level, relatively empty country from Chippenham to Didcot. From there his line followed the Thames Valley south to Reading and east to London (Fig 1.4). Brunel's line is remarkably straight: none of its curves have a radius of less than a mile. It is also remarkably level: the first 50 miles (80km) from London to Didcot rise at a gradient of 1 in 1320 (4ft per mile) and the rest is nowhere steeper than 1 in 660, except for two stretches of 1 in 100 at Wootton Bassett and the Box Tunnel.

Brunel conceived of the Great Western Railway as a complete system, 'the best of all possible railways' with all its interdependent parts, rolling stock and equipment designed together and executed to the highest standards.[21] His vision was of a trunk line from London to Bristol, level and straight and therefore fast. The branch lines could come later: what mattered was choosing the best route to provide the trunk for those branches. By comparison with Brunel's strategic vision, Brunton and Price's plan was a short-sighted join-the-dots exercise, but Brunel was nevertheless criticised for taking his line through so much empty country. To survey and plan so level a line over such great distances, working from horseback, using the simple maps and surveying equipment then available was in itself a remarkable achievement. To do this, and then design the whole railway in just nine months, was extraordinary.

Brunel's track design was equally original, departing radically from the 'Stephensonian' model. George Stephenson modelled his railways on the horse-drawn tramways of the

Figure 1.4 The Great Western Railway – the first London to Bristol route designed by Brunel in 1835 and the main routes that were open or under construction (shown as broken lines) by 1859. The following routes are represented by the coloured lines on the map (dates of opening are given in brackets):

1 Great Western Railway, London to Bristol (1841). Branch to Oxford by 1848.
2 The Bristol & Exeter Railway (1844)
3 The Cheltenham & Great Western Union (1840), merged with GWR in 1844
4 The Berkshire & Hampshire Railway (1848)
5 The South Devon Railway (1849)
6 The Oxford & Rugby Railway, only built to Fenny Compton (1852)
7 The Birmingham & Oxford Junction Railway (1852)
8 The Oxford, Worcester & Wolverhampton Railway (1854)
9 The Birmingham, Wolverhampton & Dudley Railway (1852)
10 The Gloucester & Forest of Dean Railway (1851)
11 The South Wales Railway to Swansea (1850). The line that was under construction to Haverfordwest and Milford Haven (1856) is represented by the broken line of the same colour.
12 The Wiltshire, Somerset & Weymouth Railway (1851)
13 The Cornwall Railway (1859)
14 The West Cornwall Railway (1859)

North-East where he grew up. Most of them had a gauge (that is, the breadth between the rails) of 4ft 8½in. (1.44m), and this is what Stephenson adopted for both the Stockton to Darlington and the Liverpool & Manchester Railways.[22] In 1833 the London & Birmingham Railway was begun with his son Robert Stephenson as engineer. In the same year work began on the Grand Junction Railway to link Birmingham to the Liverpool & Manchester Railway: this too adopted the 4ft 8½in. gauge. These Stephensonian lines were originally laid on stone blocks, which had a tendency to settle unevenly under the weight of the trains.

Brunel proposed a different system. His rails would be laid on longitudinal wooden beams, held down to a bed of tightly packed sand by being fixed to wooden piles driven into the ground.[23] Moreover, they would be 7ft (2.14m) apart. Brunel favoured a broad gauge for several reasons. He believed that vehicles with a wider wheel-base would be more stable, and thus safer, especially at high speeds. It would also allow for larger wheels, which would reduce friction with the rail and within the engine, achieving smoother running. A larger chassis could also allow for larger locomotives and rolling stock. There seems little doubt that the broad gauge made the Great Western more expensive: the lines had a 'maximum width of passage' of 13 feet (3.96m) as against 10 feet (3.05m) on the London & Birmingham, so all the bridges, tunnels and embankments had to be bigger.[24] Brunel believed, though, that the combination of the broad gauge with his level and relatively straight track would make the GWR's trains altogether faster.[25] The Stephensonian 4ft 8½in. gauge was already established, however, as the industry standard.

Brunel had not decided to rebel against the 4ft 8½in. gauge from the outset: the first Great Western Railway Bill of 1834, like most railway bills, had specified use of the standard gauge; had it passed, the broad gauge would probably never have existed. Brunel changed his mind between then and the passage of the second bill in February 1835.[26] He persuaded Lord Shaftesbury, who was overseeing the drafting of the bill, to omit the clause about gauge, leaving the GWR free to determine the matter for itself. On 15 September 1835, he wrote a long letter to the GWR's board of directors, setting out his arguments for a broader gauge in some detail. He considered the arguments against and said that, in his view, the only convincing one was the inconvenience that could arise in making a junction with the London & Birmingham Railway (as the company was considering having a joint London terminus with the London & Birmingham Railway at Euston, as discussed in the next chapter).[27]

The directors agreed to his proposal on 29 October 1835, though this was not publicly announced until August 1836.[28] A protracted public debate on the 'break of gauge' ensued during the construction of the line. Representatives of the northern railway establishment had bought shares in the GWR and secured places on its board. This group, known as the 'Liverpool party', lobbied against Brunel and the broad gauge. In July 1838 the GWR commissioned outside experts to advise them: they too were hostile. They found that the track was over-fixed: because of the timber piles there was no 'give' in it and the passengers had a very hard ride as a result. The board decided that the piles would have to be cut off and the track re-laid, at great extra cost. Worse still, the GWR's engines performed poorly in their first trials and between October and December of 1838 Brunel's career and the future of the broad gauge hung by a thread. Brunel and Daniel Gooch, his young locomotive superintendent, did not believe that the speed trials had been fair. They made adjustments to the *North Star* and this seemed to do the trick: further speed trials on 27 December were startlingly successful (Fig 1.5). The board believed that Brunel was vindicated and on 9 January a special meeting of the company voted to continue with his design by a majority of 7,792 to 6,145.[29]

In 1835 Brunel moved to 18 Duke Street, Westminster, where he set up an office under Joseph Bennett, his chief clerk, who stayed until Brunel's death in 1859 (Fig 1.6). Brunel seems to have borne the office costs of Duke Street out of his £2,000 salary, but in September 1835 the board authorised him to appoint three resident engineers 'at salaries not exceeding £600' to supervise work on the line.[30] By the time it was nearing completion, their number had risen to seven: G E Frere, George T Clark and T E Marsh for the western section; T A Bertram, John W Hammond and Robert P Brereton for the eastern section; and W Glennie for the Box Tunnel.[31]

Brunel was a difficult man to work for. He was loyal to reliable subordinates but he treated under-performers with great harshness, on occasion culminating in their abrupt dismissal.[32] He was not a good delegator. One of the great puzzles about the building of the GWR is the extent to which Brunel was responsible for designing it all, for he seems to have been very jealous of his primacy in this area and it is difficult to understand how far he shared this responsibility. Brunel certainly laid out the route and designed the track, and his sketchbooks contain great numbers of drawings for bridges, cuttings, tunnels, stations, cottages, sheds and machinery of every kind.[33] These seem

Figure 1.5 The *North Star*, the GWR's first reliable locomotive.

to have gone to assistant engineers, or occasionally to collaborating architects (as at Bristol Temple Meads), to be worked up: Brunel seems to have maintained a close interest in almost everything. Designs would be sent to the drawing office at Duke Street, corrected, redrawn and finally engraved on steel plates as contract documents.[34] Brunel was involved at every stage: he was notoriously unable to leave detail to others.[35] He handled most of the detailed negotiations with difficult landowners, on occasion varying the designs to suit their demands.[36] He wrote the draft contracts for every job and proof-read all the final contract documents, frequently noticing errors. He let the contracts and he supervised the contractors. The obverse of Brunel's olympian self-confidence and decisiveness was an unwillingness to recognise others as equals. The one famous exception, by his own statement, was his rival Robert

Figure 1.6 Brunel's office at 18 Duke Street, Westminster, probably photographed shortly after his death in 1859.

Stephenson, engineer to the rival London & Birmingham and champion of the 4ft 8½in. gauge.

In retrospect, Brunel's towering reputation is such that his appointment and his triumphant completion of the railway seem inevitable. At the time, he was a controversial figure, with many detractors. In 1887 a Bristol historian, J Latimer, summed up the view of those who thought that Brunel had been altogether too careless with Bristol people's money, lamenting 'the deplorable error of the original board in neglecting the sober-minded, practical and economical engineers of the North… and in preferring to them an inexperienced theorist, enamoured of novelty, prone to seek for difficulties rather than to evade them, and utterly indifferent as to the outlay which his recklessness entailed upon his employers'.[37]

This was not at all just: Brunel had constantly to keep economy in mind as it soon became apparent that his initial estimate of £2.5 million was far too low. He went to extraordinary lengths to get value for money out of his contractors, becoming famous, or notorious, for what F R Conder called 'an extreme and unprecedented insistence on excellence of work'. GWR specifications were unusually strict and Brunel insisted on them being carried out to the letter, often delaying payment and sometimes withholding it altogether. One result was that the contractors learnt to push their prices up, another was that on occasion it proved difficult to let the contracts.[38] Two of the contractors, William Ranger and David McIntosh, brought major lawsuits against the GWR, which were not resolved until 1859 and 1865 respectively.[39]

The work was on a huge scale, involving thousands of labourers. It is sobering to reflect that the great embankments, cuttings and tunnels, for which millions of cubic yards of earth and rock had to be moved, were all dug by hand by navvies, who were normally only equipped with spades, picks, shovels and wheelbarrows, assisted by hundreds of horses.[40] Such scenes of back-breaking labour were shortly to be seen all over Britain as railway mania took off.

From 1836 to 1838 the line grew westwards from London on immense embankments. Two major obstacles had to be crossed: the River Brent at Hanwell just west of Ealing and the Thames at Maidenhead. Brunel designed superb crossings for both. That over the Brent, later named the Wharncliffe Viaduct, was the place where work commenced on the GWR, in November 1835.[41] From there the track led west on broad embankments to Maidenhead. There, to span the 100-yard-wide Thames, Brunel designed a bridge with two immense brick arches 128 feet (91m) wide but only 24ft 6in. (7.5m) high, the widest arches that had ever been built (Fig 1.7).[42] The line opened between Paddington and Maidenhead on 31 May 1838, in circumstances of chaotic haste.[43] Further stages opened, reaching Twyford in July 1838, Reading in March 1840, crossing the Thames Valley to Steventon near Didcot in June 1840, and to Faringdon Road in July.[44] Meanwhile, the line had crept along the Avon Valley from Bristol to Bath. This was

Figure 1.7 An early GWR train crosses Brunel's Maidenhead Bridge in J M W Turner's painting *Rain, Steam, and Speed – The Great Western Railway, c* 1844.

more difficult terrain and this relatively short stretch only opened in August 1840: Bristol Temple Meads station was still under construction.[45]

This left a gap to the east of Bath, the most difficult part of the whole line: Box Hill rose in the path of the railway, at the point where the limestone ridge drops into the steep-sided Avon valley. Of the 13 miles (20.9km) of track between Bath and Chippenham, scarcely one mile of it is within 10ft (3m) of the natural ground level: it all had to be sunk in cuttings or raised on embankments. The most difficult task of all was digging the Box Tunnel, 2 miles (3.2km) long through solid rock with another mile through deep cuttings to the east. The construction of the tunnel was an appalling epic, lasting five years, with three main contractors in succession. A ton of gunpowder and a ton of candles a week were consumed, as a thousand or more navvies hacked their way through the rock. At the beginning of 1841 Brunel persuaded the contractor George Burge to raise his workforce from 1,200 to 4,000. At last, in April 1841, the Box Tunnel was finished (Fig 1.8). It is said to have cost the lives of over a hundred men.[46] In June the GWR's main line was complete from London to Bristol, at a cost of £6,150,000.[47]

In fact the Great Western's trains could already run a good deal further, to Bridgwater in Somerset. In 1836 the Bristol & Exeter Railway was established. Another Bristolian venture, it had many shareholders and two directors in common with the GWR. It also appointed Brunel as its engineer and was similarly laid to the broad gauge. The Bristol & Exeter company built a second station at Bristol Temple Meads, close by the GWR. Now, trains could either run into the GWR's original terminus, or through the Bristol & Exeter station on to the South-West. The Bristol & Exeter opened as far as Bridgwater on 14 June 1841, and to Exeter in 1844.[48]

In their wider context, the building of the GWR and the battle for the broad gauge were a chapter, almost the last chapter, in the contest between Bristol and Liverpool for dominance of the Atlantic trade. In 1835, before work on the railway had even begun, the GWR set up the Great Western Steamship Company, again with Brunel as engineer. He designed the *Great Western* for them: built in Bristol, launched in 1838 and fitted out in London, it was the first transatlantic steamship and an absolute success. The Liverpudlians responded with the *Sirius*, a hastily adapted steamer from the Dublin run and a much inferior vessel, and

Figure 1.8 The Box Tunnel – a lithograph by J C Bourne from his *History and Description of the Great Western Railway*.

for a while it seemed that Bristol had regained the lead; Jack Simmons has observed how the Liverpool party's campaign to oust Brunel and gain control of the GWR reached its height around the time that the *Great Western* was being completed.[49] The Great Western Steamship Company next commissioned Brunel to design the world's first large iron steamship, the *Great Britain*. This superb vessel, also built in Bristol's Floating Harbour, was launched in 1843.[50] When Prince Albert set off from Paddington to attend its launch, it really seemed as if Brunel's vision of a high-speed transport network from London to the Americas was about to become a reality. Paddington would have been the London terminus for New York. What let Bristol down was the smallness of its docks, 6 miles (9.7km) up the Avon, compounded by the sloth of its Dock Company and the complacency of its merchant class in comparison with Liverpool's entrepreneurial spirit. By 1850 the railway was complete and a triumphant success, but the battle for the Atlantic was lost. For the rest of the 19th century the big transatlantic steamships, including the *Great Britain* herself, sailed from the Mersey.[51]

In the railway mania of the 1840s, new lines were being planned and built all over the country in circumstances of feverish competition. Several new lines were proposed for tactical reasons, to 'spoil' a proposal from a rival company. The GWR was one of the three leading companies, in competition with the two great narrow-gauge empires, the London & North Western (formed by the merger of the London & Birmingham and the Grand Junction Railway in 1845) and the Midland Railway (also formed in 1845, by the merging of four companies). Like these two, the GWR was building up a network of smaller companies under its influence. In 1844–5, the GWR supported the establishment of, and bought large shareholdings in, the South Devon Railway; the South Wales Railway; the Cornwall Railway; the Wiltshire, Somerset & Weymouth Railway; the Oxford, Worcester & Wolverhampton Railway; the Berkshire & Hampshire Railway; the Oxford & Rugby Railway; and the Monmouth & Hereford Railway.[52]

These GWR satellite companies laid their tracks to the broad gauge. In the 1840s, a full-scale 'gauge war' broke out between the GWR and the big standard-gauge companies. The GWR fought hard, running broad-gauge tracks on its own lines and those of its satellite companies all over the South-West, the West Midlands and South Wales – for example to Exeter (1844), Oxford (1844), Gloucester (1845), Cheltenham (1847), Plymouth (1849), Birmingham (1852), Swansea (1852) and Wolverhampton (1854). The gauge war became the

subject of national controversy and long parliamentary battles. It is a very complex story. It must suffice here to say that, though the broad gauge's technical excellence was widely acknowledged, swift developments in locomotive and track design improved the performance of standard-gauge trains, eroding the advantages of the broad gauge.[53] In the long run the broad gauge's technical merits were outweighed by the far greater mileage of standard-gauge lines that had been built and by the obvious inconvenience of having two different railway gauges in one country.

Figure 1.9 A late 19th-century view of the Paddington train sheds. Note the mixed gauge with three rails, dating this photograph to before 1892.

The Gauge Act of 1846 recognised 4ft 8½in. as the national standard; thereafter the GWR found it very difficult to secure permission for new lines with the broad gauge. In order to expand northwards the company was obliged to buy or build standard-gauge and mixed-gauge lines itself. As a result the first standard-gauge track was run into Paddington, the citadel of the broad gauge, as early as 1861 (Fig 1.9). The GWR gradually converted the outlying reaches of its network to the standard gauge but the men who ran it were loath to abandon the broad gauge. At last in 1892 the company converted its remaining tracks over a weekend of gigantic and minutely organised effort.[54]

As the GWR's engineer, Brunel did not see himself as simply designing and building a fixed system of track and rails. From the outset he envisaged it as a functioning whole, designing his track with its broad gauge and generous curves to allow for smoother running and higher speeds. The stations were seen in the same way: his sketchbooks make it clear that Brunel started his station designs with track layouts to plan the movement of rolling stock, fitting the movement of passengers and staff around that, and in turn fitting the buildings around these interlocking functions.

Brunel also felt fully responsible for the locomotives and rolling stock, but he was not really a mechanical engineer and it was here that his commanding omniscience ran out. In 1836–7 he ordered the GWR's first locomotives from the Vulcan Foundry at Warrington, the Haigh Foundry near Wigan, and Mather, Dixon & Co in Liverpool, to be delivered by canal to Paddington.[55] Brunel laid down specifications for a number of engine designs, all very idiosyncratic and unlike any others, with small boilers to keep the overall weight down and very large driving wheels. The specification was so odd as to render it impossible for the makers to build satisfactory locomotives: they were underpowered and unreliable, and most historians have concluded that Brunel bore the main responsibility for this.[56] As a result, when the railway opened, the only really reliable locomotive it had was the *North Star*, built by Robert Stephenson & Co in Newcastle for the 5ft 6in. (1.68m)-gauge New Orleans Railway and converted to the 7ft (2.14m) gauge for the GWR after the American company went bankrupt.[57]

The GWR's mechanical reputation (and probably its business) were saved by Daniel Gooch, whom Brunel appointed as the company's locomotive superintendent at the age of 21 in August 1837, before the company actually had any engines to superintend. Gooch got Brunel's collection of freak locomotives running, but with great difficulty. As Charles Saunders, the company secretary, put it: 'At the opening in 1838 we found the engines were so inefficient that time-table working was hopeless; one or two engines might keep time, the other eight or ten were always out of time. So we suspended time-tables till the locomotive power became sufficient.'[58]

These problems caused great tensions between the board, Gooch and Brunel, who was anxious to maintain his primacy in the company.[59] By 1839 Gooch was effectively given his independence and was responsible for the second generation of GWR locomotives, commissioning a series based on the *North Star* and another series, the 'Firefly' class, from Stephenson & Co and other makers (Fig 1.10).[60] In September 1840 Gooch proposed Swindon in Wiltshire as the site for the company's main engine depot and workshops. New buildings, including a 'railway village', went

up there in 1841–3 and in 1845 the works were expanded to allow the GWR to build its own locomotives. The first engine was completed in February 1846, the start of 140 years of locomotive building at Swindon.[61] Here Gooch masterminded and produced the fastest and most powerful locomotives of the age, the 'seven foot singles' and the celebrated 'eight foot singles', named from the diameter of their great driving wheels. In its first years, the GWR's trains were not especially fast, averaging 33 miles (53km) an hour,

Figure 1.10 The *Firefly* – one of a new generation of GWR locomotives designed by Daniel Gooch in 1839.

rather better than the London & Birmingham's 27 miles (43km) an hour. Official criticism of the broad gauge in 1845 stung them into action. The company laid on express services travelling from London to Bristol in four and a half hours: between Paddington and Swindon their average speed was 59 miles (95km) an hour, twice that of any other railway's services. The combination of Brunel's track and Gooch's engines gave the Great Western Railway almost the fastest and probably the safest trains in the world.[62]

2 THE FIRST LONDON TERMINUS, 1835–50

Paddington was one of the first sites that the Great Western Railway considered for their all-important London terminus (Fig 2.1). When Brunel presented his survey to the first public meeting of the London & Bristol Railway (as it was still called) on 30 July 1833, his report said 'The total length of the Railway would be from 115 to 118 or 120 miles [185, 190 or 193km], depending on its termination whether at Paddington, or on some part of the Southern bank of the Thames.'[1]

Finding a viable route into London and persuading all the relevant landowners to sell was clearly going to be difficult. The prospectus issued at the time of the first board meeting in August 1833 showed two alternatives, one terminating in Paddington, and the other crossing the Thames below Kingston and curving up the south bank, ending between Westminster and Waterloo bridges.[2] The plans deposited with the first parliamentary bill in November, however, showed a third alternative: a line from South Acton through Hammersmith and Pimlico, ending at Vauxhall Bridge, between Vauxhall Bridge Road and the Kensington Canal.[3] The company engaged in inconclusive negotiations with Lord Cadogan, owner of much of the land required. The bill, as we have seen, was defeated in the House of Lords on 25 July 1834.[4]

The GWR went back to the drawing board. On 2 September 1834 the Directors discussed the question of a London terminus with Brunel and decided to approach the London & Birmingham Railway 'for the purpose of ascertaining and determining whether a junction might be made with their line at or near Harlesden Green'.[5] The next edition of the GWR's prospectus, in November 1834, said 'The line of railway… will be 114 miles [183km] in length from Bristol to the point of junction with the Birmingham Line near Wormwood Scrubs. The Station for Passengers in London is intended to be near the New Road in the Parish of St Pancras.'[6]

Figure 2.1 'Interior of the Great Western Railway Terminus Paddington', a print of 1843 showing the covered roadway between the arrival and departure platforms.

In other words, the site of Euston Station. In this period, before the Great Western and the London & Birmingham were in direct competition with each other, the idea of sharing the enormous cost of a London terminus doubtless had major attractions. The London & Birmingham were ahead of the GWR: their original Act of 1833 specified a terminus at Chalk Farm, but they secured more land running south to the Euston Road and obtained an Act of Parliament for an extension in 1835.[7] The GWR's directors were certainly serious about the idea. It was written into their new parliamentary bill, and when the Great Western Railway Act received royal assent in August 1835 it named Euston as their intended terminus.

Strangely, given the vital importance of the issue, the GWR and the London & Birmingham Railway do not seem to have started discussing the joint station in any detail until October 1835. From then until March 1836 they engaged in tortuous negotiations, ultimately fruitless, with something of the character of a poker game.[8] The GWR, understandably, wanted to own their half of Euston Station outright. This met with a point-blank refusal from the London & Birmingham board. The GWR then asked for a 21-year lease, the bare minimum they regarded as acceptable to protect their interests.

Around the beginning of November, Brunel and Robert Stephenson, the London & Birmingham's engineer, met to produce outline proposals for the joint station. On 19 November, Brunel explained these to the GWR directors. The Euston site was fairly narrow from east to west and could only accommodate the passenger terminus: everything else would have to be further north at Chalk Farm and Camden Town. The land at Euston Square would be divided longitudinally. The western half would be the Great Western's, the eastern half the London & Birmingham's. The 'façade or public front of the joint depot' fronting Euston Square would be designed by a 'joint architect appointed by both companies'. The site sloped downhill from Chalk Farm, south towards Euston Square, and this slope was too steep for the primitive locomotives then available. Stationary steam engines would be needed at Chalk Farm to tow the passenger trains up the inclined plane. The companies would have to share the inclined plane and the stationary engines, but the London & Birmingham would construct and maintain them. Land would be set aside at Camden Town for the GWR's engine sheds, goods depot and warehouse. Cattle yards and sidings, though, would be held in common and shared. Brunel concluded by expressing scepticism about the wisdom of any leasehold arrangements.[9]

It became clear, however, that 'a large and influential body of distant proprietors' – in other words the 'Liverpool people' or 'Liverpool party', the London & Birmingham's powerful northern shareholders – were lobbying for a shorter lease, perhaps as short as five years. The Liverpool party were buying GWR shares on a large scale and the Great Western's directors were becoming very wary of them. They were not sure whether the short lease was intended to give the London & Birmingham Railway control over the GWR, or whether it arose from concerns that the two companies would soon outgrow Euston.[10]

The gauge issue also stood between the two companies. Brunel seems to have been pondering the question from around the end of 1834. Surprisingly, he did not share his thoughts with the GWR directors until 15 September 1835, when he wrote them a long letter on the subject.[11] Brunel carried the board with him and on 29 October they agreed to the broad gauge. Yet at the very same board meeting 'Mr Brunel reported that he had had an interview with Mr Robt. Stephenson the Engineer of the London and Birmingham Railway Company, who expressed his impression that he would advise the Directors of the London and Birmingham Railway Company not to accede to the proposals to lay rails of a greater span on that railway.'[12]

On 21 November the GWR's London Committee heard unofficially about a private meeting of the Liverpool party. What they heard alarmed them so much that on the same day they ordered Brunel to proceed with surveys for a different route into London, to Paddington. Another meeting with the London & Birmingham's secretary on 26 November seemed to put the negotiations back on track: the GWR's London Committee advised that the Paddington route could be dropped again.[13] The day before, the London & Birmingham had let a contract to William and Lewis Cubitt for building their last section of line to Euston, which may have had something to do with this softening in their position. Through December and January into February, discussions circled around the capacity of the sites at Camden and Euston, the rates that the GWR would be charged for use of the line, designs for the carriages they would operate jointly and so on. But the London & Birmingham would still not finalise the terms of the lease.

Thus it was that the GWR secretly revived the Paddington idea. On 9 February 1836 Brunel reported that arrangements to acquire land there had been made: they would have to proceed with 'great precaution', as any money spent on the Paddington extension would be at risk until they got the necessary Act of Parliament.[14] On 10 February

Figure 2.2 Euston Station *c* 1838 – a wash drawing by J C Bourne.

1836 C A Saunders, the London Committee's secretary, wrote to the London & Birmingham board, repeating the GWR's request for a 21-year lease. The board met on 17 February: they offered five years. For the GWR this was completely unacceptable. A decision could not be put off much longer, as a half-yearly shareholders' meeting was already set for 26 February 1836. The GWR directors told the meeting that the London & Birmingham Railway would not concede the 21-year lease, but they believed that 'an excellent and independent terminus can be secured without much difficulty at latest in the next session of Parliament'.[15]

The Liverpool party, who were well represented amongst the GWR's shareholders, would have been in the audience. The negotiations collapsed. Saunders' letter to the London & Birmingham directors, rejecting the five-year offer, was read out at their meeting on 2 March.

Nevertheless, the London & Birmingham continued with their plans for Euston, almost as if nothing had happened. In 1836 their architect Philip Hardwick produced designs for a double station in line with Brunel and Stephenson's ideas. This was the origin of Euston's rather curious plan. The famous portico (or more accurately propylaeum) known as Euston Arch was to be aligned with a central roadway running northwards for the length of the station (Fig 2.2). Twin passenger stations would be arranged symmetrically on either side, the GWR notionally occupying the left (west) half, the London & Birmingham the right.[16] Hardwick's design for Euston has often been criticised on the grounds that the magnificent arch and façade bore no relation to the buildings and functions behind, but this is unjust.[17] His design makes perfect sense if understood as a grand entrance aligned with a central axis, with twin stations on either side.

It seems strange that the London & Birmingham went ahead and built Euston to this plan, well after the negotiations had broken down. Their London Committee considered the issue on 14 September 1836. Stephenson advised them that one half of the station, as originally planned, would suffice for all their present needs, so they resolved that 'the plan of a double passenger station of four lines to each wing, but of which only the East wing is to be constructed for the present, be approved and adopted' (Fig 2.3).[18]

On 5 December 1836 Hardwick went north to secure the approval of the Liverpool shareholders.[19] The contract for the Euston arch, lodges and gates was let to William and Lewis Cubitt on 7 December, and the contract for the arrival and departure stages, drains, boundary walls and paving on 5 April 1837.[20] The plans of Euston as it opened in June 1838 look bizarre, with the western half of the station left empty. It represented growth room, but it is also possible that the London & Birmingham Railway built Euston to this plan with a view to taking the Great Western Railway over, or at least installing a more pliable management. The cost of building the GWR was rising far beyond the initial estimates, the company had to raise more share capital, and in 1836–8 the Liverpool party were buying into it on a large scale. Through the second half of 1838 they used their voting power in the GWR to lobby against Brunel. In the crucial vote on 7 January 1839 they were only defeated by 7,792 votes to 6,145.[21] Had the Liverpool party been victorious, Brunel and

Figure 2.3 Philip Hardwick's original plan for Euston Station, showing its intended dual layout. The land to the west of the central axis was originally intended for the Great Western Railway.

Saunders would have been dismissed, the Great Western would have been converted to the narrow gauge, and its line might have been brought into Euston after all, as provided for in the GWR's Act of Parliament. Paddington Station might have closed almost as soon as it had opened.[22]

As it turned out, the London & Birmingham Railway filled Euston within ten years, and it would certainly not have sufficed for both companies. In 1845–6 the London & North Western Railway, as they had just become, filled the empty half of their station with P C Hardwick's 'Great Hall and Shareholders Room', creating an irregularity in Euston's layout which persisted until its demolition in 1961.

The GWR had a problem. Their Act of Parliament authorised them to build a line to Euston but they no longer wanted to do this, or at any rate, they had been unable to negotiate satisfactory terms. Work had already started on their line in November 1835 in the Brent valley just west of Ealing, where the resident engineer J W Hammond and the contractors Grissell & Peto began work on the foundations of the Wharncliffe Viaduct.[23] Taking their line to Paddington

instead of Euston would require a new Act of Parliament and the 1836 session of Parliament was too far advanced for them to start a bill that year. In the event, their Extension Act was not passed until July 1837.

The site Brunel had selected was next to the Paddington basin of the Grand Junction Canal which had opened in 1801: the prospect of establishing a direct link to the canal was doubtless an important factor in his choice (Fig 2.4).[24] Most of the immediate area belonged to the Bishop of London's estate. In 1836 London's western suburbs were spreading along the north side of Hyde Park and up the Harrow Road and in about 1828 the Bishop's surveyors, Samuel Pepys Cockerell and his successor George Gutch, began to lay out streets and building plots in the area.[25] The 'enormously high price' that the GWR had to pay the Bishop's trustees doubtless reflected the fact that the area was on the verge of being developed.[26] The GWR had to buy plots from several other owners, including the Grand Junction Canal Company, Paddington Parish Vestry and John Cockerell, owner of Westbourne Place, a large villa in

Figure 2.4 The Paddington area *c* 1829, from Crutchley's map of London.

extensive grounds which at the time was let to Lord Hill, who had been one of the Duke of Wellington's principal commanders.[27]

The Paddington Parish Vestry seem to have regarded the railway as a good thing, but they and the other vendors must have known that they were in a strong bargaining position and the negotiations took a long time.[28] The company only needed to buy a small plot of land from the vestry worth £1,200, but they also needed the vestry's consent to their scheme and this involved fulfilling several conditions. An outline agreement was reached with the vestry on 4 February 1837,[29] and with the Bishop's trustees on 16 February 1837.[30] The largest plot was an area of just over 44 acres (17.8 hectares) bought from the Bishop's estate for an initial payment of £30,000 and an annual rent of £2,366 12s.

The Great Western Railway never owned the freehold of the site of Paddington: the Church Commissioners, to whom the estates had passed, eventually sold it to the British Transport Commission in 1958.[31] The second major plot was bought from the Canal Company for £24,109. In 1838 the GWR estimated that in total they had spent £175,000 on purchasing property and compensating owners for the extension to Paddington, including the line, depot and station.[32]

The site at Paddington was in a shallow depression or bowl. This was probably the main reason that Brunel chose it in the first place, to allow for the easiest possible gradient out of London. This also suited the vestry, which insisted that the railway should be below street level and that two bridges be built spanning it.[33] The larger of these, linking

Spring Street (now Eastbourne Terrace) to the Harrow Road, became known as the Bishop's Road Bridge. A little to the west, another bridge carrying Black Lion Lane over the railway was labelled Lord Hill's Bridge, after the area's most distinguished resident. The GWR was obliged to build these bridges, which represented a large part of the total cost of the Paddington extension. In the event the Bishop's Road Bridge was used as the framework for the first 'temporary' station at Paddington.

This was certainly not Brunel's original intention. One of his surviving sketchbooks, dated 1836, contains a number of sketch plans and elevations labelled 'GWR Depot' for a terminus at Paddington (Fig 2.5).[34] They provide a partial

seem to be platforms. On the south side, one of the sketches has areas labelled '1st Class' and '2nd Class', which may be taken to represent the main 'departure platform'. The 'arrival platform', presumably, would have been on the north side.

Brunel sketched out two alternative designs for the main façade to Conduit Street. There would be a grand entrance to the road for private carriages, one version with a big central arch flanked by smaller arches, another version with a pair of identical arches. The arches would have been flanked by quadrant walls, arcades and five-bay buildings, all in an Italianate classical style. On these drawings Brunel quite carefully marked the tracks running right up to the rear wall of the buildings.

Figure 2.5 Brunel's first sketch for a station at Paddington, December 1836. A grand archway leads to a central roadway with platforms on either side, rather like the intended dual terminus at Euston.

picture of what Brunel intended and they represent a lost chapter in the history of railway station design. The general plan (Fig 2.6) shows the passenger terminus sitting on the present site and entered from Conduit (now Praed) Street, with a goods depot, on the site that it was eventually to occupy, planned around a new basin opening off the Grand Junction Canal. Where the passenger station is concerned, the sketchbooks show minor variations but all three versions agree on the main outlines. A broad central roadway marked 'private carriages' ran down the middle of the station with, in one version, stables alongside it. It runs into a turning-space with rounded corners: beyond this, the big plan shows several tracks running up to the platform edge. We can interpret this as being a loading dock, where the horses and carriages of wealthy passengers could be loaded onto horseboxes and carriage trucks. To either side of this central roadway are broad trackbeds and on the outer sides there

The implication seems to be that Brunel was planning to exploit the difference in level between the street and the tracks, which left him scope to run the tracks under Conduit Street and towards Central London in the future. This chimes in with a reference in 1845 when Brunel, in discussing the site of the goods depot, recommended leaving room 'in order to carry lines of railway farther into London hereafter'.[35]

When Brunel produced this first design, only two proper railway termini had been built (in Liverpool and Manchester): the building type was only just being invented. This scheme, with its grand entrance and tracks disposed to either side of a central roadway, bears a marked resemblance to Philip Hardwick's design for Euston, which of course had developed out of Brunel and Robert Stephenson's negotiations. This seems unlikely to be a coincidence.

Another striking point about the design is the prodigally generous provision that Brunel was making for the owners of

Figure 2.6 Brunel's first masterplan for Paddington, December 1836, redrawn from a series of contemporary working drawings.

1 Roadway for private carriages
2 Sidings for horseboxes and carriage trucks
3 Hotel and booking hall
4 Departure platform
5 Arrival platform
6 Goods depot

those private carriages who seem to have been the main (if not sole) beneficiaries of the grand entrance: it seems that all other passengers, whether first or second class, would have been directed to the more modestly scaled outer platforms. One cannot be certain but the implication seems to be that Brunel was envisaging that the private carriages would be loaded onto trucks and their wealthy passengers would travel in their own carriages, as indeed happened when the GWR opened. Brunel's design seems to be a vivid expression of the GWR's sense of social decorum and for whom it was really built: the grand entrance was for persons of quality, arriving and probably travelling in their own carriages, while everyone else could go round the side. In late Georgian Britain, after all, perhaps the most visible and important social marker was whether you kept your own carriage.

By July 1837, when the GWR obtained the Act of Parliament for their extension to Paddington, it had become clear that their main line was going to cost vastly more than the £3.3 million authorised by their original Act. Brunel was driven to economise in all directions and his plan for a grand London terminus was among the casualties.

Work on the line from London to Maidenhead was going well and the directors were keen (perhaps rather too keen) to push the work forward. At a half-yearly shareholders' meeting on 31 August 1837 they announced that the line would open as far as Maidenhead in November of that year. As for the terminus at Paddington, they reported that 'the space allotted for the Depot in London, for Goods, will for the present be employed as a Temporary Station for Passengers until the permanent buildings can be erected'.[36]

The company had already started excavating the site in April 1837. Michael Tutton has reconstructed the sequence of events from the GWR's account books.[37] Until September 1838, all the relevant payments come under the heading 'Paddington Terminus'. As Tutton argues, this seems initially to mean the embankments, retaining walls, bridges, drains and roadworks. The GWR used their directly employed workforce for the excavation works, spending £36,870 on wages in 1837 and another £33,903 in 1838–9. The brickwork of bridges, retaining walls and the station itself was divided up into contracts, which were let to two of the largest and most reliable contractors, Grissell & Peto (later to build the Palace of Westminster) and B & N Sherwood.[38] The two firms were paid £30,030 in 1837 and another £36,381 in 1838–9.[39] Considerable sums were also being spent on timber, rails, wheels, wagons, stone and gravel.

Brunel drove the work forward at a frantic pace, but the board's November 1837 deadline was completely unrealistic. The GWR only took delivery of their first locomotives in November, and at that point there was still not a single mile of track for them to run on. By Christmas, 1½ miles (2.4km) of track had been laid between Drayton and Langley. By 12 April 1838, there was still only 5½ miles (8.8km). Work must have speeded up greatly, for the line was finished from Paddington to Maidenhead, a distance of 22 miles and 43 chains (36.3km), by 31 May. On that memorable day the directors met at Paddington at 11am and travelled to Maidenhead in 49 minutes in a train pulled by the *North Star* at an average speed of 28 miles (45km) an hour. They then inspected work on the bridge over the Thames there, had a cold luncheon at Salt Hill a couple of miles back down the line, returning to Paddington at a brisk 33½ miles (54km) an hour. The Great Western Railway opened to the public at 8am on Monday 4th June 1838.[40] The company did not really have a station at Paddington, which was still a building site and would remain so into the 1840s, and it is not clear how the first services and the first passengers were accommodated.

On 15 August 1838, with the first stage of their line open, the board issued estimates for the cost of their extension from Acton to Paddington. They had spent £175,000 on land and compensation: 39 acres (16 hectares) for the station and its outworks, and 156 acres (63 hectares) for the 4½ miles (7.2km) of line. They had excavated 580,000 cubic yards (443,000 cubic metres) of earth for the track and its related embankments and roadworks, at a cost of £56,444. They expected to spend £62,508 on brickwork, including culverts and sewers. Another £83,366 came under the general heading of 'Paddington extension works'. The permanent way, which was already finished and open, had cost £41,178 (at £9,173 per mile). For buildings, including the passenger sheds, coach house, engine house and all the mechanical fittings, they planned to spend a relatively small £27,328. They expected the extension into London to cost a total of £450,224.[41] The accounts recorded a comparatively modest £5,439 spent on 'Paddington Station' between September 1838 and December 1839, referring to general construction costs, fitting out, ironwork, lamp-posts, laying pipes and machinery. Work began on the engine house in September 1839 (it cost £1,602) and on the merchandise station in October 1839 (which cost £3,802).[42]

By 1845 a fully functioning station was in place (Fig 2.7). Roads were made leading down from Conduit Street and London Street to the station approach and simple but dignified gates built at the entrance.[43] These led into a large,

Figure 2.7 Paddington Station in 1845, redrawn from a plan accompanying a series of historical articles in the *GWR Magazine*.

irregularly shaped yard on the site occupied by the present passenger station. Brunel had, indeed, planned to put his passenger station there, until the need for economy ruled this out. Instead, he put the temporary goods depot there: this was a wide, relatively lightly constructed shed, 330ft (100m) long by 120ft (37m) wide; early views show it having timber-framed and boarded sides (Fig 2.8).[44] The goods offices were off to the left, against the slope: they looked rather like a converted cottage (see Fig 2.12).

Directly ahead, spanning the low valley or cutting, was the Bishop's Road Bridge, which formed the station's principal façade (Fig 2.9). There were no fewer than twenty-six arches, with spans varying from 17ft (5.2m) to 20ft (6m), providing a fair amount of accommodation. The first nine arches were all skewed: reading from the left (south) side, tracks ran through the first three arches to the goods shed and a head-shunt; the next three arches also housed goods sidings; of the final three, two seem to have been blocked and the third was left open for carts taking luggage through to the departure platforms.

Beyond this point, the remaining arches were at a conventional right-angle to the façade. The first nine of them formed a symmetrical design: this is the part which Bourne concentrated on in his lithograph and which housed the station entrance. The first arch, with a veranda in front of it, housed the booking hall. The next two were waiting rooms, the fourth one the 'down' parcels office. The fifth and central arch of the nine was the carriage entrance, through which the GWR's richer passengers could drive straight onto the departure platform, to have their horses and carriages loaded onto a train. The sixth arch was the carriage exit, the next two were cloakrooms, and the last of this symmetrical group of nine was the entrance to the arrival platform. Further to the right (north), six more brick arches took the bridge up to the canal, and one more iron span crossed it.

On the other, western, side of the viaduct was a complex network of lines, with timber platforms covered by simple roofs carried on iron columns (Fig 2.10; see also Fig 2.1). It must have been rather confusing for the visitor and can never have looked very designed. The southern departure side had three lines of track served by two fairly narrow platforms.[45] Next there was a broader roadway for carriages, ending in a platform edge and a series of wagon turntables. These allowed wagons to be run close up to the platform edge, so that horses could be led onto horseboxes and carriages wheeled onto carriage trucks: this was an important part of the

Figure 2.8 (above) A design for the first goods shed, *c* 1838, longitudinal section.

Figure 2.9 (right) Paddington Station *c* 1846, by J C Bourne.

Figure 2.10 Inside the first Paddington Station: a watercolour of *c* 1840.

GWR's business (*see* Chapter 5). Further north still were platforms flanking the two arrival lines.[46]

A little to the west, just beyond the horse and carriage dock, was the main carriage shed. Measuring 180ft (55m) by 70ft (21m) and spanning four lines of track, it was added in July 1840 at a further cost of £2,446.[47] Off to the left and south was another carriage shed. On the southern edge of the site, lines ran through to the first three arches and the goods depot, as described above. There was also a long traverser, linking the goods sidings together. Traversers, or traversing frames, were fairly standard pieces of railway equipment, which Brunel had apparently developed during the construction of the GWR in *c* 1837–8. They comprised mobile sections of track, carried on wheeled iron frames and running on rails at 90 degrees to the fixed track, that allowed carriages or wagons to be moved sideways from one line to another. Traversers were certainly installed at Reading in 1839, and at Bristol Temple Meads between *c* 1841–4, and they subsequently appeared in many other GWR stations.[48] Most of them, including the Paddington example, seem to have been manually operated with capstans: they were meant for carrying carriages and trucks, which were still quite light.[49]

Further to the west towards Lord Hill's Bridge was the engine house, the main part of which was a polygonal, timber-framed shed (Fig 2.11). This was designed by Daniel Gooch, the young locomotive superintendent who had joined the company in August 1837: in his memoirs he wrote that, not yet having any locomotives to look after, his first task had been to design the engine houses at Paddington and Maidenhead.[50] Gooch therefore seems to

have a claim to have invented the 'roundhouse' design for engine sheds, the next example being Francis Thompson's polygonal shed at Derby for the North Midland Railway of 1840.[51] Gooch's engine house at Paddington was demolished in the 1850s; it is, therefore, known only from plans and one engraving.

Work on the passenger station, engine house, goods station and stables continued through 1840–41. Everything had been done in a hasty and rather haphazard way. It is not surprising that several improvements were soon needed. The engine house was extended in 1840–41 (one of Brunel's volumes of 'Facts' has an interesting sketch design for load-testing its roof trusses).[52] On 19 March 1842 the GWR board decided to improve the platform facilities and add a waiting room, and on 8 April they decided to roof over the whole space between the arrival and departure platforms, for which an estimate of £475 was duly approved.

Meanwhile the GWR had been reforming the way it ran itself. In 1841 the London and Bristol Committees which had overseen the construction of the main line were abolished and replaced with the Traffic and General Committees. The board itself was reduced in number from 24 to 18 (February 1842). The company briefly flirted with the idea of making Steventon in Berkshire its head office on the grounds that it was midway between London and Bristol, and a board room was fitted up in the superintendent's house there. This did not last long and early in 1843 they decided to move their headquarters to Paddington. On 4 March Brunel submitted plans for a building to go over the main carriage shed to house additional offices, at an estimated cost of £2,400, and work began on this in August.

Thus the first Paddington Station was a makeshift affair (Figs 2.12 and 2.13). Modestly sunk in its cutting, it could not compete architecturally with the London & Birmingham Railway's magnificent façade at Euston. J C Bourne, drawing it for his 1846 *History and Description of the Great Western Railway* (*see* Fig 2.9), managed to give it a certain simple dignity by concentrating on the symmetrical part of the Bishop's Road Bridge and by some judicious omissions. Other early views give a somewhat fuller picture. Only one view of the interior (to the west of the bridge) is known, showing the simple iron columns and roof covering the roadway between the arrival and departure platforms.[53]

Paddington Vestry had initially given the GWR a guarded welcome, but like other communities, they had probably reckoned without the problems that started to arise, with this new centre of activity suddenly planted in the middle of their neighbourhood:

Figure 2.11 The engine house designed by Daniel Gooch, probably the first to be built on the roundhouse plan.

Many and heavy complaints have been made to the Vestry of the Nuisances which are daily and hourly committed on the Bridge over the Canal, and at the corner of North Wharf Rd, principally by Passengers to and from the Station, owing, as the Vestry conceive, to the entire want of proper conveniences on the Premises of the GWRC, and I am to suggest the necessity of such conveniences being immediately erected, to remedy the evil complained of, the Boards recently stationed on the Bridge by the Vestry proving ineffectual…

They also complained of 'the seeming unnecessary and protracted duration of the whistles of the engines, which it is hoped can be suppressed'.[54]

When the GWR opened their line to Maidenhead in June 1838, they can have had little idea of the level of demand. In the first week 10,360 people passed through the makeshift terminus and the company took £1,552 (see Table 1).[55]

The company started running goods trains in 1839, operated by carriers, who also took third-class passengers in the goods wagons. From 1840, the GWR began offering this rather uncomfortable service themselves: 'the Goods Train Passengers will be conveyed in uncovered trucks by the Goods Trains only'.[57]

By 1840, the company had enough of Gooch's reliable new engines to introduce proper timetables and also to start running a night mail service. They had also made their first experiment in providing 'special trains' when they laid on a locomotive with a single carriage to take the Duke of Lucca to Windsor in January 1839, at a cost of £10.[58] They carried the new Prince Consort between Windsor and London a number of times, and in 1840, anticipating further royal

	First Class		Second Class	
	Posting Carriage	Passengers Coach	Coach	Open Carriage
West Drayton	4s 0d	3s 6d	2s 0d	1s 6d
Slough	5s 6d	4s 6d	3s 0d	2s 6d
Maidenhead	6s 6d	5s 6d	4s 0d	3s 6d

Table 1 Fares when the line to Maidenhead opened[56]

patronage, they commissioned a royal carriage 'most magnificently fitted by Mr Webb, the upholsterer, of Old Bond Street'. On 13 June 1842 Queen Victoria made her first railway journey, from Slough to Paddington. It seems to have been a success and before long the Queen was a regular passenger on the GWR.[59]

In 1843 the company surveyed their operations with a view to cutting their costs. They counted 213 employees at Paddington, plus 4 conductors, 42 passengers guards and 10 goods guards based there –

Figure 2.12 Paddington Station *c* 1840, a view looking south towards the Prince of Wales' Hotel, with the cottage-like goods office in the foreground, emphasising the informal quality of the first terminus.

a total of 269. Among these was Mary Coulsell, the first woman to be employed by the company, appointed as the 'female attendant at Paddington' in May 1838.[60]

One important development on the GWR in these early years was the installation of the first electric telegraph line to be laid and used over any major distance, in 1838–9. The invention had only been patented in 1837. Its inventors, William Fothergill Cooke and Charles Wheatstone, had made experiments on the Liverpool & Manchester Railway, but that company had already committed itself to a pneumatic system. They offered their invention to the London & Birmingham but their board would not accept it.

Brunel was enthusiastic and persuaded the GWR board to lay telegraph lines for the 13 miles (21km) from Paddington to West Drayton. The line cost £2,817 10s and was an immediate success, carrying general messages and information about the running of trains.[61] The telegraph attracted immediate interest, and on 24 August 1839 Seymour Clarke, the traffic superintendent, wrote to C A Saunders, the company secretary: 'The Duke of Wellington, Lord Bathurst, Lord Fitzroy Somerset, and some ladies and afterwards Lord Howick came. The telegraph worked capitally. Mr Sims and Mr Gibbs (GWR directors) were here. The Duke appeared much pleased.'[62]

Figure 2.13 The first terminus at Paddington – an oil painting of *c* 1840.

In 1845 the GWR's telegraph system achieved still greater fame, by being instrumental in helping the police to catch a murderer. Cooke and Wheatstone sold their patents to the Electric Telegraph Company, which ran the GWR's system to Slough in 1843, but removed it after a dispute in 1849. In 1852 the telegraph was reinstalled over the whole distance from Paddington to Bristol.[63]

The GWR's network and traffic grew apace in the 1840s and the board soon found themselves faced with the inadequacy of their temporary station. On 6 November 1845 they discussed the building of a 'permanent goods station' at the end 'nearest Conduit Street' (towards the site of the present hotel). Brunel supported the idea but advised that space be left 'in order to carry lines of railway farther into London hereafter in case such measures be adopted'.[64] He was instructed to prepare plans, but nothing seems to

have been done.[65] The board returned to the subject in July 1846 and asked Brunel for plans. On 3 August he presented two options. One was to 'widen and lengthen' the existing station and replace the 'merchandize station' on land adjoining Spring Street (now Eastbourne Terrace, so on the site of the present station). The other plan was to build a new passenger station on the Eastbourne Terrace site and convert the temporary station for goods. Again, neither proposal was taken up. An undated plan in Network Rail's collection shows a different scheme for improving the station by adding an entrance building alongside the bridge, to house a round entrance hall, waiting rooms and a booking hall at bridge level, with stairs down to the platforms.[66] It would not have increased the station's real capacity and this too was never carried out.

Brunel's first station was demolished in c 1853 (Fig 2.14). One part of the original station survived until 2004, little noticed.[67] This was the five northern arches of the original Bishop's Road Bridge. The southern section of the bridge, spanning the tracks, was removed and replaced in 1906–7. Rather concealed from the surrounding roads, these arches represented the last fragment of the GWR's first terminus. At the time of writing they too are to be cleared, to make way for a further replacement of the Bishop's Road Bridge.

Figure 2.14 The earliest known photograph of Paddington, half of a daguerrotype 'stereo pair'. The photograph seems to record the demolition of the first station *c* 1853, with the first goods shed still standing on the far side of the bridge.

3 BUILDING THE NEW STATION, 1850–55

The Great Western Railway's network and traffic grew steadily through the 1840s and so did the pressure on the temporary station at the Bishop's Road Bridge: the company was obliged to make additions and alterations to it every year. In 1847 it was new carriage shops and sheds, in 1848 a large new engine house, and in 1849–50 it was new grain stores, the re-laying of a timber platform, roof repairs and repairs to the engine house and stables.[1]

By 1848 work was under way on the Oxford & Rugby Railway, the Birmingham & Oxford Junction Railway and the Birmingham, Wolverhampton & Dudley Railway. These GWR satellite companies, between them, would take the broad gauge to Birmingham and beyond, putting the Great Western in direct competition with the London & North Western Railway. This promised a huge further increase in the volume of traffic to Paddington. Yet still the company moved very cautiously. On 18 April 1850 the board of directors wrote in their six-monthly report to shareholders that the station was indeed inadequate, but 'to provide such accommodation before the immediate necessity arises would, as the Directors think, be imprudent, and they merely refer to it now, to guard themselves against cavils or reproof'.[2]

The tone of extreme caution and the reluctance to make a major decision can readily be explained. The whole railway industry had gone into financial crisis in the late 1840s. The boom in railway shares orchestrated by the 'railway king' George Hudson had come to a dramatic end, all the main companies' shares fell in 1847–9, and in 1849 the GWR was obliged to tell an angry shareholders' meeting that it was reducing its dividend from 4 per cent to 2 per cent.[3] The board would have been aware of the lavish new board room and great hall which Philip Charles Hardwick had built for the London & North Western at Euston at a cost of around £150,000 (1846–9), arousing a storm of criticism from shareholders.[4]

Over the second half of 1850 the board changed their mind; the formal decision to go ahead was taken on 21 December, by which time Brunel was making sketch plans for a new station. In their half-yearly report of February 1851 the directors said: 'It has been maturely considered whether any temporary additions to the present buildings at Paddington could have been usefully made, so as to postpone the construction of a permanent station, but every enquiry has proved that such expenditure would neither secure the main objects in view, nor be consistent with economy.'[5]

It was not just the Great Western who found that their first buildings soon became too cramped. The extreme case was Liverpool, where Crown Street Station had opened in 1830, to be replaced by Lime Street Station in 1836, which had to be rebuilt in 1846–51 and again in the 1870s.[6]

Most stations built in the 1840s were two-sided; that is, they had platforms and buildings on either side of the track, to serve the traffic going in each direction. When it came to planning a terminus, as at Paddington, this meant dividing the station between the departure side and the arrival side. However, for a terminus a third kind of plan, the 'head plan', was possible, in which the station was approached end (or 'head') on through a single concourse, opening into both the departure and the arrival sides.

Brunel's first real terminus at Bristol Temple Meads had been a curious variation on the head plan, in which the departure and arrival sides were indeed kept separate, and the five lines of track ran through to the engine shed, which occupied the head of the station, a very unusual arrangement (Fig 3.1).[7] In his initial 1836 sketches for Paddington he had considered a different kind of head plan, with a central roadway separating the trackbeds for the arrival side and the departure side. Since then, two superb head-planned stations had been started in Paris, Léonce Reynaud's first Gare du Nord (1845–7), and François Duquesney's Gare de l'Est (1847–52).[8] In both cases, the tracks were all united in a single wide bed, with a departure platform and an arrival platform on opposite sides, accessed commonly from a concourse across the head of the station. The Gare de l'Est, which was and is particularly admired, still stands.

Figure 3.1 Bristol Temple Meads, from J C Bourne's *History and Description of the Great Western Railway.*

In 1850, across London, Lewis Cubitt was designing Kings Cross Station for the Great Northern Railway, an elegantly planned compromise between the two-sided plan and the head plan. Unlike the French examples, the arrival and departure sides had separate trackbeds under twin train sheds, given heroic expression in the giant arches of the south façade.

At Paddington, Brunel was limited in what he could do by his site, which lay well below street level. Late in 1850 he began to draw layouts for the new station in his sketchbooks, preserved at Bristol University Library (Fig 3.2). An initial sketch simply hints at a wide separation between the arrival side and departure side.[9] Two rather more developed sketches show a remarkable plan, unlike any previous station in Britain.[10] This picked up the theme of Brunel's unexecuted 1836 design, with its central roadway. As then, he planned a grand entrance from Conduit (now Praed) Street. A roadway 58ft (17.7m) wide would have led down a ramp to a central concourse, about 125ft (38m) wide and 400ft (122m) long.[11] On either side are the tracks for the arrival and departure sides. The more developed of these two plans shows the position of the stables and of a hotel.

In the 1836 scheme the central roadway seems to be left uncovered. However, the 1850 sketch plans seem to show the whole station roofed in. One of the sketches shows the column positions around the central concourse at 10ft (3m) intervals; another outline seems to represent the edge of the covered area, and some tiny vignettes show Brunel's first thoughts for a wide segmental-arched roof. Two sketches, close by in the same sketchbook, show an end elevation for the train shed. The central span has a broad segmental arch, with two smaller spans on either side: it is not clear how these five roofs relate to the sketch plan. Brunel was experimenting with different designs for the openings in the end elevation: in one version he seems to be experimenting with horseshoe-shaped arches of an almost Moorish character.[12] The dimensions of this plan are not very clear, but the whole building seems to be 347ft (105.8m) wide.

Brunel clearly had an iron and glass roof in mind, but he had never actually built such a thing. His most ambitious roofs to date had been at Bristol Temple Meads

Figure 3.2 Brunel's sketch plan for a new station at Paddington, 1850, with a thumbnail design for the wide-span roof he envisaged over the central concourse.

Figure 3.3 Decimus Burton's Palm House at Kew Gardens of 1844–8.

(72ft (21.9m) wide) and Bath (50ft (15.2m) wide), both of timber and both of c 1840–41. That at Bath has disappeared without adequate record, but the original train shed at Bristol survives and has been studied in detail by John

Binding.[13] There, Brunel started with a daringly experimental design: the roof would not be carried on conventional trusses at all, but on 22 pairs of crane-like cantilevered beams facing each other. Each crane balanced on a column at its fulcrum: the heavier outer section was tied back to the wall, while the long inner arm reached halfway across the shed: the point seems to have been that if the two cranes did not meet in the middle, they would not exert any outward thrust on the walls. Nothing like this had ever been built before and the problem seems to have been that a timber roof simply could not have the stiffness that Brunel's design would require. It had to be modified during construction, with crown-pieces added to join each pair of cranes together, turning them into portal frames of a rather unconventional design. So many wrought iron straps were added that, as Mr Binding says, the roof could be described as a composite timber and iron structure.[14]

The Bristol Temple Meads roof was a brave attempt to push engineering in timber rather further than it would really go. By 1850 it must also have looked something of a design cul-de-sac when compared to the glass and iron roofs of unprecedented width that had recently gone up. This leap in building technology, which had seized the imagination of

architects, engineers and public alike, began with garden glasshouses and with slipway roofs in naval dockyards.

A series of increasingly ambitious greenhouses were built at Chatsworth for the 6th Duke of Devonshire to designs by his head gardener Joseph Paxton, a remarkable self-educated prodigy. These culminated in the Great Stove (1836–40), an iron-framed building 277ft (84.4m) long and 123ft (70m) wide, with a central nave 70ft (21.3m) wide spanned by laminated timber arches. Around the same time a Dublin engineer and iron-founder, Richard Turner, was also building superb glasshouses in Belfast (1839) and Dublin (1843). In 1844–8 Turner and the architect Decimus Burton collaborated on the Palm House at Kew Gardens, 362ft (110.3m) long, 100ft (30.5m) wide and 63ft (19.2m) high at the centre, at that date the finest iron and glass building in the world (Fig 3.3). Equally important in engineering terms, though less publicly known at the time, were a number of spectacular roofs over slipways in the naval dockyards at Portsmouth, Chatham and Pembroke. From around 1815 some very wide timber roofs had been built in the dockyards; in 1845–7 the Board of Admiralty had a series of magnificent iron roofs, with spans of c 80ft (24m), built by two firms of contractors: George Baker & Son of Lambeth and Fox, Henderson & Co of Smethwick. The latter firm will reappear shortly as the builders of the new Paddington Station.[15]

In the mid-1840s railway planners saw the advantages of wide-span roofs that allowed them greater flexibility to rearrange the tracks and platforms beneath. The new building techniques, developed in glasshouses, began to be applied to railway stations. In 1845 the architect John Dobson designed the curved train shed at Newcastle with three parallel arched-truss sheds each 60ft (18.3m) wide (Fig 3.4).[16] In the same year Eugene Flachat began the Entrepôt des Marais in Paris, with a single-span arched truss 118ft (36m) wide. These were immediately eclipsed by the second Lime Street Station in Liverpool for the London & North Western Railway, begun in 1846 with a single span roof 153ft (46.6m) wide and 374ft (114m) long. The Lime Street roof was made by Richard Turner, who was building the Kew Palm House at the same time: the responsibility for its design seems to have been shared by Turner and the London & North Western Railway's engineer Joseph Locke, with another engineer, William Fairbairn, advising them. It was carried on 'sickle girders', with upper and lower members of wrought iron tied together by cast-iron struts. This was pushing iron-founding to new limits and the first experimental ribs failed when tested at Turner's foundry in Dublin. Lime Street Station was nevertheless completed in

Figure 3.4 Newcastle Central Station, by John Dobson and the engineering contractors Hawks Crawshay – an early photograph.

Figure 3.5 The Crystal Palace, a general view of the transept.

1850 with the widest single-span roof in the world, wider than the Pantheon.[17]

In 1850 the new 'glasshouse' technology found even more spectacular expression in the Crystal Palace in Hyde Park, the most revolutionary building in the world. Brunel was closely involved in this as a member of the Building Committee for the Exhibition of 1851: the Crystal Palace is the key to understanding his rebuilding of Paddington (Fig 3.5).[18]

The idea for an 'Exhibition of the Manufactures of all Nations' came about in 1849 through the alliance of Henry Cole, Secretary to the Society of Arts, and the Prince Consort. At New Year 1850 a Royal Commission for the Exhibition was established under the Prince's chairmanship. An executive committee was formed, driven by Cole and meeting every day. On 5 February 1850 the Exhibition's building committee met for the first time. It numbered two aristocrats: the Duke of Buccleuch and the Earl of Ellesmere; three architects: Charles Barry, T L Donaldson and C R Cockerell; and three engineers: William Cubitt, Robert Stephenson and Brunel. They met about every four days for

the next six months. It seems clear that the leading voices on the Committee were Stephenson's and Brunel's.[19]

A competition was announced and 230 entries were received in April 1850. They represented an extraordinary range of 'radiating' and 'parallel aisle' plans, built of iron and glass. Two were singled out for special praise, one by Richard Turner whose Palm House at Kew was then rising, and another by a French engineer, Hector Horeau. Both were costed at around £300,000, however, against the exhibition's overall budget of £100,000. It was also a moot point how quickly they could be built: the Commission had already announced that the Great Exhibition would open on 1 May 1851. The building committee were alarmed. On 16 May 1850 they told the Commission that they could not recommend any of the competition entries. They wrote a more detailed brief for the Exhibition building and set to work producing their own design. On 22 June this was published in *The Illustrated London News* (Fig 3.6). It was in effect a massive, brick-walled, triple-span railway shed; in the middle was a giant iron and glass dome 200ft (61m) in diameter, contributed by Brunel. There is something rather

Figure 3.6 An *Illustrated London News* picture of Brunel's unsuccessful proposal for the Great Exhibition, 22 June 1850.

characteristic about the fact that Brunel, in his first attempt at designing an iron-framed roof, envisaged what would have been the widest single span in the world.[20] The Committee invited tenders from contractors, but the design caused a furore for its permanence and ugliness. It would have required 17 million bricks and there was much doubt as to how long it would take to build. By the first week of July the future of the Exhibition hung in the balance.[21]

Joseph Paxton, the Duke of Devonshire's brilliant head gardener had, however, started to take an interest. On 11 June 1850 he made his famous sketch design on a blotting pad during a disciplinary hearing of the Midland Railway, of which he was a director. Paxton contacted the Commission, let them know of his interest, and worked his design up in eight days. He met his friend Robert Stephenson by chance (on a train, of course) and showed him his design. Stephenson was encouraging. Paxton then went to visit another friend, Charles Fox of the engineering contractors Fox, Henderson & Co, and persuaded him to enter a tender for the Exhibition building on the basis of his design.[22] The building committee's rules required Fox, Henderson to enter a tender to build the 'official' design, as well as their own.

By early July the tenders were in for the official design. None of them came below the £100,000 limit: Fox, Henderson offered to build it for £141,000 for six months' use, if they could retain the materials. Paxton's rival design, however, was by now published and known, and Fox, Henderson offered to build this for what seems the extraordinarily low sum of £89,950, again retaining the materials afterwards. They guaranteed that the shell would be complete by 1 January 1851. There was then a last crisis over the Exhibition's lack of financial guarantees. On 26 July the Commission finally decided, choosing Paxton's design and accepting Fox, Henderson's tender. The sequel was a miracle

of organisation. The vast building, 1,848ft (563.3m) long and 456ft (139m) wide, the largest enclosed space in Britain and probably the largest in the world, was built in less than five months. On 1 May 1851 the Exhibition opened as planned. It was the most remarkable and public demonstration of what British engineering, iron and glass were capable of, and one of the most extraordinary chapters in the entire history of engineering.

The official design for the Exhibition had been well and truly defeated, but Brunel seems to have been too impressed by Paxton's work to feel resentful. He became an ardent supporter of Paxton's design, and as a member of the building committee was closely involved in its construction. Thus, while Brunel was planning the new Paddington Station in late 1850 and early 1851, he was also attending weekly meetings for the Exhibition and visiting the site in Hyde Park.

Brunel's first design for Paddington, as has been shown, was based on an entrance from Conduit Street leading down into a central concourse 450ft (137m) long and 125ft (38m) wide (see Fig 3.2). In December 1850, however, there was an abrupt change of design. This seems to have arisen from the board's decision to have a grand hotel at Paddington. The idea came from one of the directors, J St George Burke, whose letter urging the case for a hotel was read out at a board meeting on 21 September 1850.[23] The board were probably influenced by the fact that their new line from Oxford to Birmingham, then under construction, would put them in direct competition with the London & North Western for the first time (the line opened in 1852). In 1839 the rival company had opened a pair of hotels at Euston, designed by Philip Charles Hardwick and framing his father Philip Hardwick's monumental Doric arch.[24] Thus on 5 December the GWR board resolved to build a hotel too, observing that this amenity could 'decide passengers to adopt either one line or another', and setting a budget of £40,000 for it.[25] On 19 December 1850 Brunel attended another board meeting and 'submitted ground plans of an intended passenger station at Paddington such as he considers to be necessary, in order to determine the most eligible position for building the proposed Hotel'.[26]

The evidence of Brunel's sketchbooks suggests that he took a version of his 'central concourse' design to this meeting. One of the sketch plans, discussed above, has a rectangular block marked 'hotel' occupying part of the façade towards Conduit Street, much like his original scheme of 1836.[27] It would seem that the board rejected the central concourse scheme in order to give the whole of the Conduit Street frontage to the hotel, for it was only after this date that Brunel made the first sketch plans of the station as built.

Around this time Brunel chose T A Bertram, one of his assistants who had been the resident engineer for the eastern half of the main line, to help him with the designs for Paddington. On 20 and 21 December Brunel had meetings with Bertram 'concerning enlargement of Paddington Station'. For the next three months the office diaries record Brunel and Bertram having frequent meetings on the subject.[28]

On 21 December 1850 Brunel attended another board meeting with plans showing the 'future appropriations' of land that were needed for the goods yard and engine house. He was asked for estimates of the cost of the passenger station. The board then took the formal decision to go ahead. They did not want to make another temporary arrangement and felt it essential to decide on 'a permanent system of building', an interesting choice of words.[29] There was a problem, however, in that the existing goods station occupied part of the intended site. For this, as well as for financial reasons, the board ordered that work should start on the departure side (the south or Eastbourne Terrace side) and on the new goods facilities, so that there should be the minimum disruption of goods traffic.[30]

Three plans on consecutive pages of one of Brunel's sketchbooks represent the origin of the design for Paddington as built.[31] On page 11 there is a very approximate plan dated 26 December 1850, with a few key

Figure 3.7 Page 11 of Brunel's 'Large sketchbook 3', with the first of three successive sketches in which he developed the plan of Paddington Station. The rectangle at the bottom of the sketch represents the site of the hotel.

33

dimensions written in, all of them relating to the width of the building (Fig 3.7). The plan reverses the previous central concourse design in having the departure side and arrival side separated by a broad central trackbed. The cross-hatched rectangle at one end must represent the site of the hotel, greatly enlarged from the previous scheme.

On page 12 there is a much-developed but undated version of this. Many more dimensions are marked in. The train shed is marked as 750ft (229m) long (it is actually 700ft (213m)). The site for the hotel is shown in outline and marked as 70ft (21m) deep. The area directly behind it is given over to the track-heads and turntables. The Eastbourne Terrace buildings are roughly marked in. Brunel has also marked out the curvature of the tracks as they bend southwards to go under the Bishop's Road Bridge.

On page 13 is a variation of page 12, also undated. Brunel has written several dimensions in but a lot have been crossed out and changed, and there are several columns of calculations: he was evidently thinking straight onto the paper (Fig 3.8). For example, he was trying to decide whether to make the Eastbourne Terrace buildings 30ft (9.1m) deep (page 12) or 22ft (6.7m) (page 13); this related to the decision whether the adjacent cab road should be 56, 58 or 60ft (17.1, 17.7 or 18.3m) wide. On page 13, he defines the site of the hotel as 290ft (88m) long by 70ft (21m) deep. The sketches are in pen but, wonderfully, on page 13 Brunel added the outline of three arched-span roofs in pencil as an afterthought. These swiftly scribbled lines are the origin of Paddington's famous roof. On New Year's Eve Brunel and Bertram spent five hours looking at Waterloo and Euston Stations.[32] On 2 January 1851 Brunel presented his revised plan to the board, which seems to date the three sketch plans to the last week of 1850.[33]

Brunel's initial scheme for a grand central entrance from Conduit Street, with departure and arrival platforms on either side of a great concourse, thus seems to have been scotched by the board's wish to provide a larger site for the hotel and to make it an architectural statement in its own right, rather than a subsidiary element of the station façade. Thus the station came to be concealed behind the Great Western Royal Hotel. Having started designing a sophisticated variation of the head plan with a central concourse, Brunel was forced back to a two-sided plan, with a broad central trackbed (Fig 3.9). It was, in fact, much like a larger version of his terminus at Bristol Temple Meads of 1839–41, with the hotel in the place of the Bristol office building and the track-heads in the place of the Bristol engine shed.[34]

Figure 3.8 In the last of the three sketches, the plan of the station is largely worked out as built. As an afterthought, Brunel has roughly drawn in the profile of the celebrated triple-span roof, again essentially as built.

Bishop's Road

Eastbourne Terrace

Departure side approach

Goods depot approach

High-level goods yard

Staff hostel

Milk platform

Arrival platform for
horses and carriages

Movable platform bridge

Movable platform bridge

Departure platform

Departure side

Arrival side

Position of descending
platforms

Position of descending platforms

Line of subway and
lamp room beneath tracks

Royal waiting room

Traverser

Second-class waiting room

Departure side
approach and cab roof

Loggia or clock arch

Movable platform bridge

Arrival side roadway

Island platform

Island platform

Arrival platform

Booking hall

Position of descending
platforms

First-class waiting room

Position of descending platforms

Movable platform bridge

Traverser

Horse arch

Loading platform for
horses and carriages

London Street

Elevated passageway
from hotel to platforms

Parcel office

Narrow-gauge track
to bring luggage from hotel

Sector table for
incoming locomotives

Turntables

Great Western Royal Hotel

Conduit (now Praed) Street

0   100   200   300 feet

0   50   100 metres

Figure 3.9 Paddington Station in 1854 (based on MacDermot 1964a, 172).

35

Over Christmas 1851 the board had engaged Philip Charles Hardwick as architect for the hotel (Fig 3.10). His father Philip Hardwick had designed Euston Station, originally intended as the GWR and the London & Birmingham Railway's joint terminus, and Hardwick Junior added the 'Adelaide' and 'Victoria' hotels (1839), and the great hall and board room (1846–9).[35] He too attended the GWR's board meeting of 2 January 1851. It was held at Paddington, so they went to inspect the site of the hotel. Hardwick was commissioned to prepare plans and estimates: the hotel was to include rooms for third-class passengers and to house a subscription club.[36] He must have worked as fast as Brunel, for on 9 January he presented the board with a ground plan and elevation, which they approved on the same day as they accepted Brunel's general designs for the departure platform and offices. The secretary, Charles Saunders, was ordered to raise with Brunel the desirability of 'having the general offices as concentrated as possible'.[37]

It seems curious that responsibility for the hotel should have been taken from Brunel and that he should apparently have acquiesced in this so easily. He was an extremely capable architect and had designed numerous buildings in a variety of styles for the Great Western Railway, including Bristol Temple Meads and Bath Stations, both in a Tudor Gothic style. Furthermore, he was generally given a very high degree of freedom and responsibility by the board. Had the hotel been left in his hands, one can readily envisage how he might have integrated it better with his station, perhaps retaining the essence of his central concourse scheme.

The answer may be that Brunel had to delegate responsibility for the hotel to Hardwick as he was simply too busy to design it himself. His office diaries for these years show a frantic schedule, with Brunel attending anything up to ten different meetings a day, from seven in the morning until late at night, six days a week. In addition to designing Paddington, he was at this time working for the GWR and its allied companies on the Oxford & Worcester Railway, the Birmingham & Oxford Railway, the Vale of Neath Railway, the South Wales Railway, the West Cornwall Railway and the Chepstow bridge. He was also working for the Clifton Bridge Company and the Sunderland Docks Company. He had interests in the Galvanized Iron Company and the Vulcanized Rubber Company, and regularly attended meetings for them. He was attending meetings of the newly formed Eastern Steam Navigation Company (which was to build the *Great Eastern*). He was also regularly attending meetings of the Great Exhibition's building committee.[38]

It has been noted that Brunel was not in general a good delegator and that he had a marked tendency to try and control matters of detail, occasionally to the detriment of what he was doing.[39] That he was content to leave the hotel to Hardwick may reflect how hard-pressed he was. This would seem borne out by his decision, early in January, to engage some architectural assistance for the station itself. On 13 January 1851 Brunel wrote to the architect Matthew Digby Wyatt, who was secretary of the executive committee of the Great Exhibition (Fig 3.11). The letter is so important and so revealing as to bear being quoted in full:

Figure 3.10 Philip Charles Hardwick, a watercolour perspective of the design for the principal façade of the Great Western Royal Hotel.

I am going to design, in a great hurry, and I believe to build, a Station after my own fancy; that is, with engineering roofs, etc. It is at Paddington, in a cutting, and admitting of no exterior, all interior and all roofed in… Now, such a thing will be entirely <u>metal</u> as to all the general forms, arrangements and design; it almost of necessity becomes an Engineering Work, but, to be honest, even if it were not, it is a branch of architecture of which I am fond, and of course, believe myself fully competent for; but for <u>detail</u> of ornamentation I neither have time nor knowledge, and with all my confidence in my own ability I have never any objection to advice and assistance even in the department which I keep to myself, namely the general design.

Now in this building which, <u>entre nous</u>, will be one of the largest of its class, I want to carry out, strictly and fully, all those correct notions of the use of metal which I believe you and I share (except that I should carry them still further than you) and I think it will be a nice opportunity.

Are you willing to enter upon the work <u>professionally</u> in the subordinate capacity (I put in the least attractive form at first) of my Assistant for the ornamental details? Having put the question in the least elegant form, I would add that I should wish it very much, that I trust your knowledge of me would lead you to expect anything but a disagreeable mode of consulting you, and of using and acknowledging your assistance; and I would remind you that it may prove as good an opportunity as you are likely to have (unless it leads to others, and I hope better) of applying that principle you have lately advocated.

If you are disposed to accept my offer, can you be with me this evening at 9½ p.m.? It is the only time this week I can appoint, and the matter presses very much, the building must be half finished by the summer … Do not let your work for the Exhibition prevent you. You are an industrious man, and night work will suit me best.

I want to show the public also that <u>colours</u> ought to be used. I shall expect you at 9½ this evening.[40]

Brunel's invitation to M D Wyatt was not an isolated decision. He had already decided that he wanted the new station to be built by the great engineering contractors Fox, Henderson & Co, builders of the Crystal Palace. Later on Brunel followed up the hint in his letter to Wyatt about the use of colour by engaging the designer Owen Jones, who designed the colour scheme for the Crystal Palace, to do the same for Paddington. In effect, Brunel engaged the team who were building the Crystal Palace to build Paddington, with the obvious exception of Joseph Paxton. He may have consulted Paxton over the design, though this is not proven, but Paxton was a director of the rival Midland Railway and thus could not have worked formally for the GWR.

As it happened, Matthew Digby Wyatt was not available to come and visit Brunel at half past nine on 13 January. Instead, Brunel saw Charles Fox of Fox, Henderson that evening (Fig 3.12).[41] This is the first meeting with Fox specifically recorded in the office diaries, though Brunel must have met him many times at Great Exhibition committee meetings. On 14 January Brunel had three meetings concerning Paddington. At 10am he saw Bertram. At 5.40pm, M D Wyatt came round in response to the letter quoted above. At 8pm, Brunel saw Charles Fox again. Over the next few weeks he had frequent meetings with Bertram and Wyatt concerning the station. On 22 January,

Figure 3.11
Matthew Digby Wyatt.

Figure 3.12
Sir Charles Fox.

a particularly hectic day, Brunel met Fox, Henderson again, and Bertram (twice).[42] On 23 January he presented the board with plans for the buildings facing Eastbourne Terrace and the southern of the three roof spans, as well as a schedule of prices from Fox, Henderson.[43] There is no evidence that any other contractors were invited to tender.

It was most unusual for the Great Western Railway, which was under great financial pressure, to accept a single tender from one contractor for such a large piece of work. Brunel must have explained this to the board as an exceptional measure, justified by Fox, Henderson & Co's outstanding abilities in iron construction, and in particular in view of their astonishing performance as builders of the Crystal Palace. His preference appears the more striking given that Sir Charles Fox was a well-known opponent of the broad gauge.

They were indeed a most remarkable company. Charles Fox, trained as a surgeon, had turned by the age of 20 to engineering, worked on the 'Rainhill Trials' of locomotives for the Liverpool & Manchester Railway and became a protégé of Robert Stephenson.[44] He worked on the London & Birmingham Railway, designing their extension into Euston and the train shed roofs there, which had the first all wrought-iron trusses made up of angles and tees (1836–9).[45]

Around 1839 he left the London & Birmingham Railway to form a partnership with the contractor and founder Francis Bramah, son of the more famous Joseph Bramah. They established a foundry at Smethwick near Birmingham, trading as Bramah, Fox & Co. In 1841 Bramah died and Fox was joined by John Henderson, a Scots engineer.

Fox, Henderson & Co were the first firm to produce the whole range of railway plant and equipment and also developed a capacity for major iron construction projects.[46] From 1843 the company won a series of contracts from the Royal Navy for iron structures in the royal dockyards, most notably five wide-span iron-framed roofs covering slipways, two at Pembroke (1844–5) and three at Woolwich (1846–7). It has been established that Fox, Henderson themselves designed the remarkable Pembroke slipway roofs, which had clear spans of over 80ft (24.4m), though other works were undertaken in partnership with the Royal Engineers.[47] Their business developed fast and they added the GWR to their list of clients, supplying wrought iron roofs 45ft (13.7m) and 55ft (16.8m) wide for the smiths' forges and the paint shop at Swindon in 1846–7.[48] By 1850 Fox, Henderson & Co employed between 800 and 1,200 men, their smiths' shop with its 70 forges was claimed to be the largest in the world, and they turned out about 300 tons (305 tonnes) of castings a week.[49]

Through their work on Pembroke Dock and the Crystal Palace, Fox, Henderson developed great expertise in designing and building structures themselves, and for organising the logistics of large prefabricated buildings. They took on Brunel's contract for Paddington in January 1851 while still working on the Crystal Palace. At the same time they were building a smaller station for the Buckingham Railway at Oxford (Fig 3.13), of particular interest because its iron columns and beams were very similar to those of the Crystal Palace and because it survives to this day, albeit moved and reconstructed at the Buckinghamshire Railway Centre.[50]

In the same year Fox, Henderson also contracted to build a new smithery in the Royal Dockyard at Portsmouth (October)[51] and the immense Birmingham New Street Station for the London & North Western. The last-named was comparable in size to Paddington, with the widest single-span roof anywhere in the world: a tied truss 212ft (64.6m) wide.[52] It is little wonder they became over-stretched. This seems to explain why their work on

Figure 3.13 A 19th-century view of Rewley Road Station, Oxford, built by Fox, Henderson & Co in 1851 for the Buckingham Railway.

Paddington became so badly delayed, damaging their relations with the GWR as a result.

Throughout January, February and March Brunel was meeting Bertram two or three times a week to plan Paddington. Half way through February another assistant, Charles Gainsford, was called in to help with the work. Brunel was certainly directing the effort but day to day control of work was handled by his assistants. It is interesting to find that in 1889, from a GWR staff point of view, both the passenger and goods stations were remembered as having been 'built under the direction of Mr Gainsford, assisted by Mr W Jacomb, afterwards chief engineer of the GWR', without any reference to Brunel, Fox or Wyatt.[53]

Brunel met Charles Fox and M D Wyatt more irregularly. The office diaries, Brunel's sketchbooks and the drawings in Network Rail's plan room give a fairly clear idea of how the responsibility for the work was divided. The whole of the planning was Brunel's work, as was the outline design of all the buildings except the hotel. The sketchbooks contain well-developed plans for the Eastbourne Terrace range of buildings (see Fig 7.17).[54] Brunel was responsible for the outline design of the train sheds, but his sketchbooks do not contain any detailed drawings for them. Elsewhere, the sketchbooks contain numerous detail drawings for roof structures, castings, girders and so on, but not for Paddington. The surviving detailed drawings for the roof structure were all produced by Fox, Henderson. That, after all, was the whole point of engaging them. A copy of the specification for their second contract, which was closely modelled on the first contract, is known, and gives us detailed information about the materials used.[55]

Fox, Henderson were probably responsible for a crucial change to the shape of the arched trusses. Brunel's sketches all show the train sheds spanned with segmental arched trusses, which would probably have needed tie-rods in order to be stable: these would have interrupted the long vista

Figure 3.14 Fox, Henderson & Co, a cross-section of the station to accompany their first contract, 1851.

(see Fig 3.2).[56] Instead, the roof as built has beautiful five-centred arched trusses, which give the design more visual 'lift' (Fig 3.14; see also Fig 7.6).[57] There may be a parallel here with Bristol Temple Meads: when it became clear that Brunel's original cantilevered timber roof would not work he, or one of his team, produced a design for strengthening it with tie-rods, but this was not carried out: the roof was strengthened in other ways, leaving its beautiful profile intact.[58]

Matthew Digby Wyatt's role, and the degree to which he shares Brunel's responsibility for the design, has attracted a good deal of scholarly attention.[59] Brunel may have delegated 'detail of ornamentation' in his letter to Wyatt, but this did not mean either that he disliked architectural ornament, or that he was incapable of designing it himself. Brunel's previous designs for the GWR demonstrate his

Figure 3.16 (right) An extract from Brunel's sketch designs for the new Paddington station – 9 January 1851.

Figure 3.15 (below) Brunel's sketch designs for the new Paddington station – 7 January 1851.

clear understanding and judicious use of ornament: the handsome façade to the Box Tunnel may stand as an example. Furthermore, the sketchbooks provide abundant evidence that Brunel had a half share in designing Paddington's remarkable decoration.

Pages 5 and 10 of 'Large Sketchbook 3', discussed above, have sketches for the end façade of the first central concourse scheme. Brunel was experimenting with the segmental arch shapes for the shed roofs, framing semicircular or horseshoe arches carried on slender columns (see Fig 3.2).[60] On 7 January, by which time he had moved on to the revised plan, Brunel was again sketching architectural treatments for the end wall, generally similar in character (page 22). The same sheet has sketches for the long elevation of platform 1, one with round-headed windows, one with thin columns and flat lintels. Another tiny sketch shows columns and a girder, with a decorative pendant (Fig 3.15). On page 24 Brunel develops these ideas for the platform 1 façade, and for the column and lintel. This is the origin of the curious column capitals and of the decorative pendants hanging from the longitudinal girders (Fig 3.16). Page 28 has a swiftly dashed-off sketch for the platform 1 façade overlooking the two transepts (see Fig 7.9). On pages 33 and 34 are his first thoughts for the roof and railings of the departure side approach road, off Eastbourne Terrace. On page 37 is a cross-section of the main train shed. Despite its fairly late position in the book, this still shows segmental-arch trusses, by this time with straight lines indicating the 'Paxton glazing' as used at the Crystal Palace. Brunel's sketches would have been developed into working drawings by Wyatt, who was assisted by Charles Fowler Junior.[61] Thirty-nine full-size detail drawings for ornamental cast-iron for the roof are listed in Network Rail's catalogue of plans but unfortunately seem to have been lost.[62]

Matthew Digby Wyatt had actually designed very little before 1851, but he had worked on the short-lived but influential Journal of Design (1849–52). Here he had made several contributions to the debate, then very current, about the use of new materials and technologies, and the role of ornament in architecture. In 1849 Wyatt had reviewed John Ruskin's Seven Lamps of Architecture, the most influential work of artistic criticism in a generation. Ruskin's passionate hatred of industrial culture drove him into some contradictory attitudes. In 'The Lamp of Truth' he could write 'the time is probably near when a new system of architectural laws will be developed, entirely adapted to metallic construction', while adding, over the page 'the iron roofs and pillars of our railway stations are not architecture at all'.[63]

Wyatt admired Ruskin and his review praised 'this thoughtful and eloquent book' for its 'eloquent denunciation of shams'. He criticised Ruskin, however, for his emotional resistance to industrial culture:

Instead of boldly recognising the tendencies of the age, which are inevitable, instead of considering the means of improving these tendencies, he either puts up his back against their future development, or would attempt to bring back the world of art to…[what it was] four centuries ago…[64]

In 1850 Wyatt had written another article for the Journal of Art, on 'iron work and the principles of its treatment'. In this, he wrote of Brunel:

His independence of meretricious and adventitious ornament is as great and as above prejudice as his engineering works are daring in conception and masterly in execution. From such beginnings, what glories may be in reserve, when England has systematised a scale of form and proportion, a vocabulary of its own, in which to speak to the world the language of its power…[65]

To modern eyes there may be something of a contradiction between this condemnation of 'meretricious and adventitious' ornament and what Brunel and Wyatt ended up building together at Paddington, but this would be very much a late 20th-century reaction. Brunel and Wyatt both assumed that a building of Paddington's status required ornament: the point was to ensure that it was seemly and appropriate to its purpose. The 'correct notions of the use of metal' which Brunel referred to in his letter of 13 January to Wyatt can be deduced from the station itself. In the end elevations Wyatt substituted the beautiful tracery of vaguely Arabic shapes for Brunel's horseshoe arches. For the column capitals he developed Brunel's sketch into geometrical figures, with no historic antecedents (Fig 3.17). For the arched trusses he devised the applied tracery, reminiscent of leaves, or of gothic window tracery: it is possible that it plays a role in stiffening the arches. For the long platform 1 façade, he turned Brunel's sketch into a full design. The fat roll mouldings, rather appropriately, are made of cast-iron

Figure 3.17 Paddington – a view along the arched trusses showing Matthew Digby Wyatt's decorative cast-iron tracery.

Figure 3.18 One of Brunel's designs for the goods station showing details of the granary roof, *c* 1851.

sections and on some of them the scratched foundry marks are still visible: they could quite literally be halved sections of iron pipe, pressed into ornamental use and embedded in a general covering of cement render. For the façades overlooking the two transepts, Wyatt worked Brunel's little sketch up into the design for the delicate oriel windows, with their fantastic filigree and 'cut-out' ornament that we see today (see Figs 7.9 and 7.10).

Doubtless Wyatt had various historical sources for his contributions to Paddington, but the context and his handling of them effectively transforms them into something new, into what Henry-Russell Hitchcock called the 'High Victorian' style. There seems little point in pinning any historical label on Paddington other than 'Victorian', and that, presumably, was exactly what Brunel and Wyatt were aiming at.

On 17 April 1851 tenders for the hotel were opened: all were substantially higher than the board's estimate of £40,000. That of Messrs Holland, for £43,750, was

accepted.[66] Fox, Henderson & Co, perhaps because they had taken on too many commitments and were over-extended, were slow with the first deliveries of ironwork. As early as 15 May 1851 came the first of a long series of complaints by the board about their tardiness and a request for Brunel to investigate.[67] On 28 May 1851 he was instructed to threaten Fox, Henderson with the withdrawal of their contract.[68]

The GWR needed to demolish the old goods depot, as it occupied part of the site for the new passenger station. The new goods depot would go just to the north-west. Brunel started to think about it in January, with a cross-sectional sketch showing his idea for a 'transferring bridge from platform to warehouse'.[69] On 12 June 1851 he wrote to the board to say that the plans and specifications were ready (Fig 3.18).[70] Tenders for this were opened on 26 June 1851. They covered a disconcertingly wide range of sums, from £17,000 to £27,000, where Brunel's estimate had been £24,124.[71] Messrs Sherwood's tender, for £24,432, was accepted on 10 July.[72]

Work must have been proceeding on the departure side, but in October the board again complained of Fox, Henderson's 'insufficiency of means'.[73] On 20 November 1851 Brunel brought ground plans of goods buildings and warehouses.[74] On 27 November Fox, Henderson wrote to the board with a statement of progress, giving assurances that the existing contract would be completed by the end of March, as long as they were provided with the necessary drawings. Brunel stated that the outstanding drawings were for the gable end of the shed, the bow window (doubtless the windows overlooking the transepts of the train shed) and the entrance from the hotel.[75]

Right through the first half of 1851 Brunel's office diaries show that he attended several meetings a week, sometimes two or three in a day, concerning Paddington. Most of these were with his subordinates Gainsford and Bertram, but numerous meetings with Wyatt are recorded, and a few with Sir Charles Fox. On 3 February he had the first of several meetings with Sir William Armstrong, later Lord Armstrong of Cragside, the celebrated engineer and manufacturer. Armstrong was already celebrated as a designer and manufacturer of hydraulic machinery and Brunel was commissioning the machinery to power the cranes, turntables and 'traversing machines'. The evidence for this is patchy, but it suggests that Brunel had a vision of Paddington as a fully automated station, unlike any that had previously been built, with systems of traversers, dropping platforms, platform bridges and turntables, all integrated, to secure the most efficient movement of locomotives, carriages and wagons from line to line. This is discussed in more detail in Chapter 5.[76]

On 27 November 1851 the board discussed the arrival side for the first time and asked Brunel for a report and drawings. They instructed him to devise penalties to protect the company against further delays.[77] On 4 March 1852 the unfortunate Mr Wilder of Fox, Henderson appeared before the board. He promised that the approach road to the Eastbourne Terrace buildings would be completed in ten days and that 400ft (122m) of slating (out of a total of 600ft) would be done in a fortnight. Work had begun on stuccoing the exterior.[78]

Despite the board's strictures about Fox, Henderson's slowness, they instructed Brunel in March 1852 to obtain a tender from the firm for making and building the rest of the main roof, to be completed within a given period for a fixed sum, subject to penalty clauses. Brunel presented summary estimates of the total cost of the work then in progress (the departure side, the goods station, the engine house, coal sidings and roadways, but not the hotel), of £221,350.[79]

At this point the makeshift organisation of work and the rather haphazard chain of command was graphically revealed. On 17 March 1852 Brunel wrote to Charles Saunders stating that he had been obliged to spend large sums on draughtsmen's work and on employing Matthew Digby Wyatt – £650 for drawings of the station in the previous quarter, and £624 to Wyatt for his fee and for his draughtsmen. Brunel argued that by making this private arrangement with Wyatt he had saved the company money:

… if I had requested the Directors to call in an architect, as all other Companies have done for their stations, their charges would have been doubled and tripled, and I may safely refer to the Great Northern and the Euston Square and Camden Town stations as proofs that the building of railway stations by architects instead of engineers involves an excess of (illegible) in works which in our case would have not have been less than £20- or £30,000. The employment of an architectural assistant, entirely under my own control, I took upon myself …[80]

The board gave him £1,000 on 23 March but denied any responsibility for Wyatt's employment, or for any further remuneration:

The Board will appoint an architect, if absolutely necessary, to superintend buildings for stations etc., but they cannot agree to payment for the services of any architect employed by him to assist or advise him in designing portions of that work such as Mr Brunel admits to be comprised in the Agreement entered into for the three years, 1850–52.[81]

The clear implication was that the board did *not* accept that an architect was 'absolutely necessary', expecting Brunel to take care of this kind of thing himself. The directors had been kept in the dark about rather a lot. Apparently they were also unaware that Matthew Digby Wyatt had consulted the designer and writer Owen Jones (Fig 3.19) over colour-schemes for the train shed, following up the hint in Brunel's original letter to him of 13 January 1851.[82] Jones designed a rather elaborate scheme, and a trial area of the roof was painted in April 1852, when the board came to inspect. They profoundly disapproved and directed Charles Saunders to write to Brunel that 'The Directors … beg you will not introduce any ornamental or coloured tiles, but will have the ordinary stucco … under the roofs of the sheds. There is very decided objection on their part to any sort of decorative ornament to the passenger platforms or offices, which they wish to have as plain and inexpensive looking as possible.'[83]

No reference to Jones' work has been found in the GWR's records (presumably because he was paid by Brunel and Wyatt, not by the company). His involvement is confirmed by a magazine article about William Powell Frith's famous painting *The Railway Station*, in which reference was made to the directors having 'removed Mr Owen Jones' decorative colour from the roof and columns of the station'.[84]

Wyatt had also consulted the sculptor Alfred Stevens over the decoration of the octagonal royal waiting room, planned as part of the departure side buildings. Stevens produced a number of sketches for a magnificent decorative scheme in an Italian *cinquecento* style, which would have been immensely expensive (Fig 3.20). Again, there can have been no prospect of the board sanctioning this kind of thing.[85]

Messrs Holland had made swift progress on the great hotel, which was nearing completion in April 1852. A restaurateur, Monsieur Dethier, was negotiating to take a lease of it and the board considered whether to advance him a loan of £10,000 for the purchase of furniture; his surety was the Corsican hotelier Vantini who ran the Euston Station hotel and also the 'North Euston' at Fleetwood. On 27 May 1852 Hardwick submitted an inventory and estimates of furnishings needed: Dowbiggin, Holland & Co offered to furnish the hotel for £11,543. The board demanded a lower estimate, and the same firm obliged with a reduced version at £7,049 excluding carpets, curtains and bedding (3 June 1852). By October, though, Dethier had withdrawn from negotiations and the board were once more looking for a tenant operator. At the end of the year they gave up trying to find a tenant and resolved to form a subsidiary company of their own to run the hotel, endowing it with capital of £15,000.[86] In February 1853 the hotel was said to be 'in a very forward state, and can be finished for occupation as soon as the Passenger business shall be transferred into adjoining buildings'.[87]

The total cost of building and furnishing the hotel was a comparatively modest £49,134.[88] Brunel himself chaired the hotel company from 1855 until his death. According to his son 'he found attendance at the meetings of the Directors and the supervision of the management of the hotel a very agreeable relaxation from the more important duties which took him to Paddington'.[89]

The first stage of the goods depot was nearing completion in June 1852. Mr Sherwood, the contractor, was summoned before the board on 25 June to explain delays

Figure 3.19 Owen Jones, a portrait by H W Phillips. Jones, the leading theoretician of colour and ornament of the age, is shown against part of his 'Moorish Court' at the rebuilt Crystal Palace in Sydenham: Matthew Digby Wyatt drew on this kind of design from his friend Jones' *Grammar of Ornament*, for the decoration of Paddington.

Figure 3.20 Alfred Stevens, design for the royal waiting room, 1853.

manufacture the ironwork for the rest of the station roof, including the 'Lawn' area behind the hotel, keeping their unit costs the same despite a rise in iron prices. The offer was accepted, and on 22 July the contract price was settled at £35,199, to be completed within six months. Oddly enough, their specification for the work is dated 8 November, over four months into the contract period, which may be evidence of Fox, Henderson's slowness.[91] At the same time the contract for the rest of the passenger station works (earth moving, foundations and masonry construction) was let to Messrs Locke & Nesham for £10,998, and the contract for the engine house was let to the same firm for £14,130.[92]

Work presumably began on this next phase of construction in the late summer of 1852 but continued not to run smoothly; on 25 November 1852 the board were again discussing delays to the work. They found that Brunel had not been receiving regular reports from the clerk of works, Charles Gainsford. Henceforth he was to send regular reports to Brunel, and to themselves.[93]

Fox, Henderson's slowness remained a key theme in the directors' discussions. By the end of 1852 there had still been no deliveries of ironwork from Smethwick. Gainsford was sent to investigate, and on 17 February 1853 he reported that progress there was unsatisfactory.[94] The following week Sir Charles Fox came in person to explain the delays.[95] On 10 March 1853 Brunel attended a board meeting, bringing plans for the extension of the goods station; a second goods shed, similar to the first, coal drops, and facilities for stone traffic were to be added, at a further cost of over £50,000. At the same meeting Brunel submitted plans for the first-, second- and third-class booking offices, with tenders for furnishing them from Messrs Holland. The departure side was still not finished, however – a year after Fox, Henderson's promised completion date.[96]

Relations with Fox, Henderson reached crisis point in April. On 3 April there had still been no ironwork delivered, and work appeared to have stopped dead on the departure side as well. Brunel was said to be away pursuing 'other avocations' and the board were almost frantic with exasperation.[97] They instructed Saunders to write to Brunel on 4 April 1853, expressing their disappointment that they had not heard from him for some weeks and demanding that he send an inspector to reside near the Smethwick works and make daily reports on Fox, Henderson's progress. Saunders concluded the letter with the fear that 'we shall again lose this summer the occupation of the new building'.[98]

The board's criticism of Brunel does not seem fair. They were surely aware that at this time he was supervising the

and vowed that it would be finished in two months. The same meeting resolved that all the conventional construction work to complete the passenger station should be let as a single contract, which was to be advertised for competitive tender. A second contract would be let for the rest of the train shed. A third contract was to be let for the engine house and other works for the locomotive department. Brunel submitted drawings for all of these works, which were approved. He was asked to set about getting 'the whole Passenger Station under construction' immediately.[90]

The decision to separate the earth moving and masonry construction from the iron construction was presumably influenced by the board's dissatisfaction with Fox, Henderson's performance to date. Nevertheless their services were retained, and on 1 July 1852 they offered to

Figure 3.21 Brunel's Royal Albert Bridge at Saltash, nearing completion in *c* 1859.

construction of the GWR's allied lines, the South Wales Railway and the Cornwall Railway. In January 1853 he had been awarded the contract for the Royal Albert Bridge at Saltash (Fig 3.21), also for the Cornwall Railway, and he was within a month of completing the remarkable Wye Bridge at Chepstow for the GWR (opened fully on 18 April 1853). He was also designing the *Great Eastern*, the huge ship whose construction would dog the last years of his life.[99]

The directors had stronger words for their contractors. On the same day, 4 April, Saunders wrote to Fox, Henderson stating that the board 'felt compelled to … employ proper persons to enter upon and finish the work which has so long remained untouched and unfinished, within the new Buildings erected at Paddington for the General Offices and the Traffic Department at the intended Passenger Station'.[100] He threatened that the GWR would take work on the new roofs into its own hands as well if the contractors did not respond immediately.

This ultimatum seems to have been effective, for the work speeded up greatly. In August Brunel could report that:

… the works at Paddington Station for the passenger trains are still much in arrear, but are advancing towards completion. The alteration of the main lines … has been effected, and the engine house is in course of construction upon the site of the original line … As soon as it is completed, the old engine house may be removed and the extension of the goods department, so much needed, may be commenced.[101]

In August the size of the platforms was still being discussed. In October the decoration of the royal waiting room was ordered from Messrs Holland.[102] On 8 October 1853, *The Illustrated London News* could report that:

The vast work in progress at … Paddington are proceeding with very great rapidity … The new shed for the outgoing trains, being entirely roofed with glass, presents a light and handsome appearance, with separate entrance and reception rooms for the Queen and the Royal Family, and all the other requisite accommodation

Figure 3.22 A house for the locomotive superintendent, *c* 1853–5. The exact site, presumably near the sheds at Westbourne Park, has not been located.

for the general public, which are of the most appropriate and complete character, are finished, and the foundation of the arrival sheds, with extensive offices, is now proceeding with great rapidity.

On 27 October 1853 the board directed that traffic should be run out of the departure side from 27 December. Severe frost and snow prevented this and the first train was run out of the new station on 16 January 1854. Work on the main roof was nearing completion, but substantial elements of the arrival side remained to be done. In March 1854 Messrs Holland's offer to build the second-class waiting room on the arrival side for £987 was accepted.[103]

The board pressed for the arrival side to be opened on 18 May 1854. Brunel pressed for a delay of a week, as the roadway down to the platforms was still unpaved. In the event, the first train was run into the new arrival side on 29 May. The new Paddington Station was open and running, if not quite complete. The hotel opened on 9 June 1854 and

was visited the following day by the Prince Consort and the Prince of Wales.

In January 1854, *The Builder* ran a short piece on the new station, remarking that 'Colour is sparingly introduced – red and grey. Each vault is covered at the sides, about half way up, with corrugated iron: the remainder is glazed.'[104] In June 1854 *The Builder* ran a longer article, with a plan and a full-page view of the train shed, saying:

> The station may be called the joint design of Mr Brunel and Mr M D Wyatt, the former having arranged the general plan and all the engineering and business part … the latter the architectural details in every department. The principle on which they set out was to avoid any recurrence to existing styles, and to try the experiment of designing everything in accordance with the structural purpose or nature of the materials employed – iron and cement.[105]

On 17 June *The Builder* carried more technical description,

Brunel recommended that Paxton employ Fox, Henderson to build the water towers as well as the Palace, in terms which make an interesting coda to their collaboration at Paddington: 'With all their faults, and no man I believe has had much greater experience than I have of the faults of Messrs Fox Henderson as contractors, yet I am bound to state that if properly looked after they have the ability and the desire to execute excellent work.'[110]

The delays in the construction of Paddington suggest that Fox, Henderson & Co were, indeed, becoming over-stretched. As railway-building in Britain passed its peak, they like other firms were looking for work overseas and an ambitious contract to build the Zealand railway in Denmark proved their undoing. Fox, Henderson lost £70,000 on the job and became insolvent. In October 1856 the firm was declared bankrupt with liabilities of £360,000, causing 2,000 people to be thrown out of work.[111] Sir Charles Fox recovered from the crisis and went on to form a celebrated firm of consulting engineers in partnership with his sons. Sir Charles Fox & Sons later became part of Freeman Fox, now part of Hyder plc.

Matthew Digby Wyatt revived his association with the Great Western Railway when they appointed him as architect for the reconstruction of Bristol Temple Meads station begun in 1871, where he carried on the Tudor Gothic style established thirty years before by his friend Brunel. This time Wyatt was in partnership with Francis Fox, son of Sir Charles Fox.

By the time the new station was complete Brunel was stepping back from some of his responsibilities as the GWR's engineer. He had already delegated responsibility for maintenance of the line to deputy engineers and in July 1854 he established a permanent engineering department at Paddington under Bertram to carry out this function. Brunel

in particular of the train shed, with an elevation of part of the departure side façade overlooking one of the transepts.[106]

In July T A Bertram was appointed as the resident engineer.[107] The passenger station and the hotel may have been open, but to the west work was still in progress on many other departments. The northern part of the huge goods depot was finished, but the southern part and the high-level coal yard were still under construction, as were the staff hostel, the engine shed, the locomotive department offices and the locomotive superintendent's house (Fig 3.22). The wagon sheds, carriage sheds and stores were even further behind. All of these buildings have long disappeared: a summary description of them is given in Chapter 7.

It would be difficult to say at what point the rebuilding of Paddington was really finished – work continued on fitting out the station and its various dependencies right through 1857. By the end of that year the GWR had spent £668,790 on the new station, hotel, goods depot and associated works.[108]

A short post-script concerning the station's main authors seems in order. As work on Paddington neared completion Fox, Henderson & Co were at full stretch, building the 212ft (64.6m)-wide roof of Birmingham New Street Station for the London & North Western, the widest single-span roof in the world (Fig 3.23).[109] They were also rebuilding the Crystal Palace to a modified design, again by Joseph Paxton, in Sydenham. Paxton asked Brunel for advice about the 200ft (61m) water towers, a request which led to the towers being demolished and rebuilt to Brunel's design in 1854–6.

concentrated on new works, notably the great Royal Albert Bridge over the River Tamar at Saltash (1853–7).[112] Around 16 February 1855, Brunel was asked by the government to help plan a prefabricated hospital building, to be sent to Turkey to alleviate the desperate conditions amongst the British wounded from the Crimean War. He responded even faster and more energetically than usual, producing designs and placing contracts for a 1,000-bed hospital in six days. A little over three weeks later, in mid-March, he had a prototype ward built at Paddington Station for the War Office to inspect. The resulting hospital opened at Renkioi on the Dardanelles in July 1855. [113]

More and more of his time was being taken up, however, by the *Great Eastern*, the largest ship that had ever been built, which had been begun by Scott-Russell and Company on the Isle of Dogs at the end of 1853. The building of the *Great Eastern* was immensely traumatic and difficult, and it wore Brunel out. The ship was at last ready in August 1859 (Fig 3.24). On 2 September Brunel collapsed of a stroke on board the ship. The *Great Eastern* sailed on its first voyage on 7 September. The same day there was an explosion on board. It did only minor damage to the ship, but the news of this probably hastened Brunel's death on 15 September at the age of 53, prematurely aged and exhausted by his labours and achievements.[114] Daniel Gooch, his friend and colleague, wrote:

> By his death, the greatest of England's engineers was lost, the man of the greatest originality of thought and power of execution, bold in his plans but right. The commercial world thought him extravagant, but although he was so, great things are not done by those who sit down and count the cost of every thought and act. He was a true and sincere friend, a man of the highest honour, and his loss was deplored by all who had the pleasure to know him.[115]

Brunel was succeeded as the GWR's chief engineer by T A Bertram, his deputy for the building of Paddington.

Figure 3.24 Brunel at the launching of the *Great Eastern*, Isle of Dogs, 1857.

4 MATURITY, 1855–1947

It is a tribute to Brunel's foresight and the quality of his design that it was 50 years before Paddington Station needed significant expansion, despite tremendous growth in the GWR's network and passenger numbers. In the years after Paddington opened, the GWR experienced a generational change. Charles Russell, the chairman who had championed Brunel and the broad gauge, resigned in August 1855. He had been very highly regarded by the staff, and in 1852 1,700 of them had subscribed to the cost of a full-length portrait of him by Sir Francis Grant (Fig 4.1). Always known simply as 'the Picture', it hung in the company's board room at Paddington. For generations of GWR employees, being summoned before the directors was known as 'going to see the Picture'.[1] Sadly, Russell's mental health was in decline and he died by his own hand in May 1856.[2] In 1862 Charles Saunders, the company secretary who had done more than anyone apart from Brunel to create the GWR, resigned: he was 66 and suffering from heart trouble. By this time, only one of the directors had been on the board in the days of the gauge war in the 1840s. In 1864 Daniel Gooch, the locomotive superintendent since 1837, resigned also, to take a part in the venture to lay a telegraph cable across the Atlantic. This seemed like a final break with the GWR's origins, but in 1865 Gooch returned as the company's chairman.

In 1860–62 Paddington itself became the subject of one of the most famous of all Victorian paintings. The artist William Powell Frith was commissioned to paint *The Railway Station* by Louis Flatow, a major picture-dealer (Fig 4.2). The progress of the work aroused great public interest, as Frith was already a celebrity from the popular success of his earlier crowd-paintings *Ramsgate Sands* (1854) and *Derby Day* (1858), and there were regular reports on it in the press. There was also much speculation about the sum Frith was paid for it (£4,500, though Flatow claimed that the sum was 8,000 guineas). Flatow induced Frith to waive his usual right to display the picture at the Royal Academy and it was instead the subject of a one-painting show at the Haymarket Gallery from April to September of 1862, visited by over 21,000 people in seven weeks. A short book was also provided, describing the action of the painting to the visitors. Flatow sold the painting with the reproduction rights to the publisher Henry Graves for £16,300, again to a flurry of press interest: Graves published the superb engraving by Francis Holl, which also proved very popular. In 1883 the original picture was bought by the 'patent pill' magnate Thomas Holloway for just £2,000 and it remains in the gallery at the Royal Holloway College, Egham.[3]

Figure 4.1 Sir Francis Grant's portrait of Charles Russell, chairman of the GWR.

The Railway Station, one of the great Victorian icons, is also a valuable record of Paddington's appearance when it was newly built. Frith had commissioned the photographer Samuel Fry to take a series of pictures of the station for him to work from, though the architectural background was actually painted by William Scott Morton. The painting looks diagonally across the train sheds from the departure platform, where a train is drawn up ready to leave behind one of Gooch's 'Iron Duke' class locomotives (labelled the *Great Britain*, though Frith's actual model was the *Sultan*). Over sixty figures crowd the canvas, including Frith, his wife and two of their children (as the family sending their sons off to boarding school, left of centre). Officers of the Metropolitan Police and the GWR's Railway Police are also represented. Frith accurately depicts the GWR porters' livery of dark green with scarlet stripes. The GWR, naturally enough, were very interested in Frith's immortalisation of their station, though due to their financial plight they could not have contemplated buying it. They instead bought several

Figure 4.2 William Powell Frith, *The Railway Station*.

copies of the engraving and later commissioned Frith to
paint a copy, which was presented to George VI on the
nationalisation of the company in 1947.

The 1860s were very difficult years for the Great
Western. Because they were no longer able to gain
parliamentary permission for significant new stretches of
broad-gauge track, they had to expand by buying hundreds
of miles of standard-gauge lines in the West Midlands, which
almost amounted to a separate railway system, based on
Wolverhampton. To run efficiently they also had to extend
their standard-gauge services southwards: hundreds of miles
of track were thus converted to the mixed gauge on which
both kinds of train could run, imposing a huge extra financial
burden. The first standard-gauge train entered Paddington
itself on 14 August 1861, an ominous moment for the
company.[4]

Years of expansion and the need to build mixed-gauge
lines had left the GWR with a huge floating debt of more
than £13 million, the servicing of which was a great burden:
of the major companies, probably only the London, Chatham
& Dover was in a worse condition.[5] In 1858 profits dropped
almost to nothing and only some vigorous shareholder

Figure 4.3
Sir Daniel Gooch.

lobbying secured a dividend of 1.25 per cent, the lowest that the company ever paid. Worse was to come in May 1866, when the bank of Overend, Gurney & Company collapsed, causing a run on the banks and a general financial crisis. The GWR could no longer meet its debenture obligations. An attempt to raise £2.5 million in new shares was a fiasco and a request for a loan from the Bank of England was turned down. Sir Daniel Gooch (Fig 4.3), by now Chairman of the GWR, approached the government for support and was turned down there as well. In the first half of 1867 the company teetered on the verge of bankruptcy.[6] It recovered quickly, returning to profit in 1868, but the company remained short of money for several years to come. This, and the conservatism of Gooch's management, delayed full conversion to the standard gauge for another generation.

Paddington has never been thought of particularly as a commuter station. For most of its history the GWR seems to have assigned a fairly low priority to suburban services, remaining true to Brunel's initial vision of the GWR as a long-distance network. In this, as in much else, they had much in common with their greatest rivals, the London & North Western Railway. Southern companies, such as the London, Chatham & Dover, the London, Brighton & South Coast and the South Western Railway, knew that their long-distance business was never going to match the GWR's in scale, and probably for this reason they attached far more importance to developing suburban lines. This was a major factor in the development of south London, with its dense network of overground suburban lines fanning outwards from London Bridge, Cannon Street, Charing Cross and Waterloo, still the quintessential commuter stations. The Great Eastern Railway, hemmed in to its East Anglian territory, likewise spent much effort developing its network of suburban services: the historian Robert Thorne has written that 'when the Great Eastern built Liverpool Street it had its suburban services most in mind', and showed that these services and the Great Eastern's deliberate policy of serving working-class people were important formative influences on the development of east London.[7]

The GWR opened what might today be described as suburban lines to Windsor (1849), High Wycombe (1854), Uxbridge (1856), Henley (1857), Marlow (1873) and Staines (1885), but they hardly compare to the great networks in south London and it is worth considering why. The GWR certainly knew that there would be a demand for what we now call commuter services and by 1865 they had introduced season tickets between Paddington or Farringdon and stations as far as Windsor, Reading, Hungerford and

Oxford: a season ticket from Paddington to Ealing cost £10 in first class, £7 10s in second.

During the railway mania of the 1840s and into the 1850s the GWR was at full stretch, running broad-gauge lines and staking out its territory as far and as fast as possible. By the time the new Paddington was opened in 1855 the company was paying the price for this hectic expansion, with huge debts and a falling share price. Despite its difficulties, the GWR invested in the Metropolitan Railway when it was established in 1852. The Metropolitan was the first true underground railway in the world and in the 1860s it formed the basis of the GWR's suburban services.

There was a story, or myth, that Brunel had built Paddington in a cutting because he foresaw the building of underground railways.[8] This may seem far-fetched and is unlikely to have influenced his choice of site in 1836. Paddington nevertheless turned out to be at just the right level to be linked to the underground Metropolitan Railway: on 2 November 1852 Brunel attended his first meeting on the subject, rather tellingly referred to in the office diary as 'City Extension to Paddington'.[9] This is interesting, as this was well before the Great Western Railway had become formally involved in the Metropolitan: perhaps Brunel was investigating on the GWR's behalf.

The Metropolitan did not obtain its Act of Parliament until 1853 and then it had trouble raising money. A sharp lawyer, Acton Smee Ayrton, joined the board and persuaded the Great Western to invest £175,000 by proposing to link the new railway to the GWR lines at Paddington. Opposition in Parliament and financial difficulties delayed matters and work did not begin until February 1860.[10] The GWR's large shareholding meant that they could insist on the laying of mixed-gauge track and the linkage of their lines just north-west of the new Paddington train shed (Figs 4.4 and 4.5). Here they built the new Bishop's Road Station, which was the Metropolitan's original western terminus.[11]

When the new railway opened in January 1863 it was worked by the Great Western with broad-gauge rolling stock. This arrangement did not last long, but the new line enabled the GWR to run services through to Farringdon (1863) and later to Moorgate (1866).[12] The GWR's early relations with the Metropolitan were fairly stormy but nevertheless opened the way for them to develop what might be described as a small suburban network by proxy. The Great Western and the Metropolitan both bought shares in the Hammersmith & City Railway (now the Hammersmith & City Line), which opened in June 1864, again worked by the GWR. Trains could now run from the

Figure 4.4 Paddington Station and its environs from the first edition 25in. Ordnance Survey map.

Metropolitan Line through the new Bishop's Road Station at the north-west corner of Paddington, along the GWR's tracks to Westbourne Park, and then 2½ miles south to Hammersmith Broadway, thus winning traffic from the new suburbs of Notting Hill, Shepherd's Bush and Hammersmith.[13]

Another of the Hammersmith & City's attractions was that it could be linked to the West London Railway, till then one of the less successful legacies of the 1840s. The West London, which ran south to Kensington from the junction of the GWR and the London & North Western Railway at Willesden, was the only section of the ambitiously titled Birmingham, Bristol & Thames Junction Railway to have

been built. It had opened in 1844, but its passenger services were so unsuccessful that they closed a few months later, and the GWR and the London & North Western Railway took a joint lease of the moribund line the following year. It was little use to them, carrying only the occasional goods train. In 1858 the bill for a railway to Victoria Station was passed and the GWR and London & North Western were spurred on to try and make better use of the West London. They each put in £100,000, secured £50,000 from both the London, Brighton & South Coast and the South Western Railways, and obtained an Act to extend the West London south through West Brompton and Chelsea, over the river to Clapham Junction. From being a cul-de-sac it was now a

link between the lines of four great companies. The
extension opened in March 1863 and in April the GWR
began running broad-gauge services into Victoria Station,
where a new wooden terminus had been rushed up.[14]

In 1864 the Metropolitan Railway was extended from
Paddington to South Kensington. The new branch headed
southwards just to the east of Conduit (now Praed) Street
and involved the construction of a new station opposite the
Great Western Royal Hotel. Praed Street Station was
designed by Sir John Fowler, the Metropolitan Railway's
engineer, and opened in 1867.[15] Like the Metropolitan's other
stations it was built in a cutting lined with massive retaining
walls of yellow stock brick and covered with an iron and
glass shed roof. Praed Street Station was linked to
Paddington by a subway in 1877 and survives as the Circle
Line platforms (Fig 4.6; see also Fig 7.31).

Between 1852 and 1866 the company had been brilliantly
inventive, making strategic alliances and investments and
drawing in other companies' money, so they could run
broad-gauge trains to the City of London, to Hammersmith,
Clapham Junction and Victoria. The GWR only ran broad-
gauge trains on the Metropolitan Railway until 1869.[16] In
every other respect the policy nevertheless seemed to be

Figure 4.5 'Junction of the Metropolitan and Great
Western Railways at Paddington', an engraving from
The Illustrated London News.

Figure 4.6 The Metropolitan Railway Station on
Praed Street, opposite the Great Western Royal Hotel.

successful and a report of the same year on suburban traffic towards Reading and Wycombe showed that passenger numbers had risen from 513,018 in 1861 to 859,849 in 1867.[17]

The GWR also ran a 'Middle Circle' service from Moorgate, via Earls Court to Mansion House, around what we would now call the Circle Line, from 1872 until the Metropolitan Railway was electrified in 1906. In addition they rather briefly ran suburban services over lines belonging to the London & South Western Railway to Richmond in 1870 and after 1894.[18]

One may wonder why the company did not do more to develop suburban services, after their initial burst of activity in the 1860s. The answer may be to do with their financial difficulties: the Overend & Gurney banking crash of 1866 had brought the GWR to the brink of insolvency. The company recovered slowly: this and the heavy financial burdens of building the Severn Tunnel and converting the network to the standard gauge kept it short of cash for the next twenty years or so.

The GWR built two more lines in the London suburban area, though it is doubtful whether either of them can really be regarded as suburban lines in the true sense. In 1860 they opened an extension from their main line at Southall to the dock at Brentford on the Thames, but this seems to have been intended primarily for goods. Much later, the company built a new line from Ealing, via Greenford, to High Wycombe, in partnership with the Great Central Railway. This opened in 1904–5 and would probably be more accurately regarded as part of a new direct line to Birmingham than as a suburban line.[19]

By 1900 much of the traffic of the western suburbs had been picked up by the Metropolitan District Railway, which ran its lines from South Kensington to Hammersmith (1874), Richmond (1877) and Ealing Broadway (1879). Later, the Central Line ran out to Shepherd's Bush (1900) and Ealing Broadway (1920). By this time it was too late: Paddington would never be a great suburban terminus and the limited business it had was coped with by the relatively small Bishop's Road Station.

Brunel's great shed proved large enough to absorb half a century's growth in traffic. As railways became part of national life, however, so they changed society and generated new demands for travel. Railway excursions were born and the GWR found that their business for August Bank Holiday week rose by 20 per cent in the five years between 1876 and 1881.[20] More platforms had therefore to be added, colonising Brunel's broad central trackbed, in 1873, and in

1883, and another in 1889.[21] Between 1878 and 1882 a new 'milk platform' was added at the north-east corner of the train shed.[22] A couple of other alterations only require brief mention: a first-class waiting room added to the arrival side in 1875 has long gone.[23] The subway beneath Praed Street to the Metropolitan station, opened in 1877, remains as the access to the Circle Line platforms.[24]

The company's network and its bureaucracy were growing steadily and in the 1870s and 1880s the GWR had to expand their office accommodation. A proposal of 1872 to fill the gap between the Eastbourne Terrace offices and the hotel was not executed,[25] but in 1876 the gap between the offices and the isolated wing to the west was filled in, at a cost of around £28,369. This made space for the finance, engineers', estate and solicitors' departments.[26] In 1878–80, a further programme of rebuilding and enlargement was carried out. A second storey and a loft were added to the whole length of the range: the big skylight over Brunel's booking hall was sacrificed and built over, in the interests of making more room (Fig 4.7).[27] The Eastbourne Terrace range was extended eastwards over the carriage entrance to the departure platform. Beyond this, going towards the hotel, another nine-bay extension was built by Kirk & Randall of Woolwich for a comparatively lavish £37, 827.[28] This paid for a richer architectural treatment, with a facing of Greenmoor stone, window aedicules and a bracketed cornice. Only half the building remains, the rest having been destroyed in the Second World War. A further scheme of 1881, to build more offices with a 60ft by 40ft (18m x 12m) shareholders' room and a 100ft (30m) tower was abandoned for financial reasons.[29] Meanwhile, inside the station, the track-heads and turntables in the area now called the Lawn were curtailed, providing a wide paved area for horse-traffic (see Fig 7.25).[30] All of these works seem to have been designed in house by E Olander, the GWR's engineer, and Lancaster Owen, their architect.[31]

Still there was not enough space. The GWR took over several houses on the opposite side of Eastbourne Terrace as overflow office space: by the time of nationalisation in 1947 they had occupied most of the terrace.

In December 1880 electric light was installed at Paddington, one of the very first permanent installations anywhere in the world. Between 1878 and 1883, electric light developed from an entertaining laboratory experiment to a practicable alternative to gaslight: the very first proper installation seems to have been a run of arc lights along the Embankment in 1878. Within the GWR the initiative came from the chairman, Sir Daniel Gooch. He asked his chief engineer, Dean, and telegraph superintendent, Spagnoletti, to report on the options and they reported to the board on 10 November. The Brush system seemed to be the best: they tabled a plan for 34 arc lights for the passenger station and a quotation from the Anglo-American Electric Light Company for £1,953. Another £447 would be needed for a boiler and a shed to house the dynamo. With the brisk decisiveness of Victorian industry at its best, the directors agreed and the system was in by Christmas.[32]

These early arc lights were too bright for domestic use; they were also smoky and not entirely reliable. The inventor Joseph Swan had just invented the incandescent filament light bulb. This was first installed by Lord Armstrong (formerly Sir William Armstrong) at his house, Cragside, in Northumberland in December 1880, but it was some while before it was commercially available.[33] The GWR's arc-light system was dogged by difficulties, and in February 1884 the company signed a contract with the Telegraph Construction

& Maintenance Company, who offered to re-equip and supply the whole of the station and offices for three years for £4,200 per annum. A generator house was converted out of a carriage shed behind Gloucester Crescent. Two 90ft (27m) chimneys were built. Two dynamos, each weighing 4½ tons, were installed, with a third in reserve: the magnet wheels were 9ft 8in. (2.9m) in diameter. Each dynamo was driven by a pair of tandem compound engines of 600 horsepower. Three smaller Crompton dynamos, powered by Willans engines, supplied current for the magnets of the main machines. The system supplied 4,115 of the new incandescent lamps in the offices and hotel and 98 arc lamps in the passenger and goods stations. It was in operation by February 1885, but immediately there were bitter complaints from the neighbours about the noise, vibration and smoke. Injunctions were served by the Bishop of London's estate, the dynamo had to be shut down pending experiments to dull the noise and the GWR and the Telegraph Construction &

Figure 4.7 An early 20th-century view of the south flank of the station towards Eastbourne Terrace with the GWR's offices.

In the 1870s the Great Western Railway recovered financially, thanks to Sir Daniel Gooch's careful stewardship and a general upturn in the economy. It merged with its old partners the Bristol & Exeter Railway (1876), the South Devon Railway (1878), the West Cornwall Railway (1878) and the Cornwall Railway (1889).[37] It had the second largest network of any British railway (after the London & North Western Railway) and had returned to steady profitability, but the broad gauge, its most distinctive feature, now looked like an anomaly. The company had mixed-gauge lines across most of its network and a majority of its services were now standard-gauge trains. Substantial sections of the network

Maintenance Company got into contractual difficulties.[34] The new system may have caused problems, but this was probably due in part to its pioneering status. *The Electrician* described it as the 'first effort to be made in England to give a continuous supply of electric light on a very large scale' (Fig 4.8).[35] The system was replaced and a new generating station built out at Park Royal in 1907.[36]

Figure 4.9 The end of the broad gauge: the 10.15am Cornishman Express pulled by the locomotive *Great Western* leaves for Penzance, 20 May 1892.

were converted in 1872 and 1874 and by 1878 only seven out of forty-eight daily departures were of broad-gauge trains.[38] Sir Daniel Gooch resisted conversion of Brunel's trunk route, and only after his death in 1889 did the company brace itself for this break with the past. The last broad-gauge through-train to Penzance, the Cornishman Express pulled by the locomotive *Great Western*, left Paddington at 10.15am on Friday 20 May 1892 (Fig 4.9). Broad-gauge trains left for Plymouth at 1pm and 3pm, and at 5pm the last broad-gauge departure left for Bristol pulled by the *Bulkeley*, which returned to Paddington with the 'up mail' at 5.30am on Saturday 21 May, the last broad-gauge service of all. *Bulkeley* steamed back with an empty train to Swindon and over the following two days the remaining 171 miles (275km) of track were converted from the broad gauge to the standard gauge.[39]

It was the end of a great engineering vision, but the broad gauge had been holding the GWR back, and the immense costs of gradual conversion had been diverting resources away from improvements to service. The company's reputation for high speed was a thing of the past. The slowness of many of its services in the 1870s and 1880s had saddled 'God's Wonderful Railway' with the derisive tag 'the Great Way Round'.[40] From 1892, the company entered a phase of vigorous innovation, which its historian E T MacDermot called 'the Great Awakening'.[41] The period up to 1914 is often regarded as the GWR's golden age. In 1902 a new locomotive superintendent, G J Churchward, was appointed. Over twenty years he was to develop engines of almost unrivalled quality, in the 'City', 'Saint' and 'Star' classes. Churchward's work improved the GWR's standard locomotives too; he replaced the old clerestory coaches with a more modern design, lit the coaches with electricity and experimented with rail-motors, a petrol-electric railcar and a steam-powered 'auto-train' that could be driven from either end.[42] Meanwhile a new traffic superintendent, N J Burlinson, was raising the speed of the GWR's services generally. The Welsh coal trade came into its own, with millions of tons pouring through the Severn tunnel every year. The main line to

Devon and Cornwall was thronged with new holiday services and an inspired slogan, 'the holiday line', sketched out a new image for the GWR that was later developed in hundreds of specially commissioned posters.[43]

By the 20th century, Brunel's great train shed was used to capacity. The south or departure side of the station, with the cab road and Eastbourne Terrace immediately beyond, was lined entirely with offices and could only have been enlarged with great difficulty and at immense cost. The GWR's traffic was growing fast. In 1856 Bradshaw's guide had listed 20 trains leaving Paddington each day; by 1907 this had risen to 300 every twenty-four hours, not including excursions, empty stock and 'specials'.

Around 1903 the GWR's Traffic Committee began to plan accordingly. The 'up relief' line was extended into the train shed as a stop-gap measure.[44] In June 1904 the general manager placed a plan for major alterations to Paddington costed at £96,950 before the Traffic Committee, which was

Figure 4.10 'Paddington Station as it will be', a 1906 cutaway view showing the planned arrival side improvements.

swiftly authorised by the board.[45] It was designed in-house, probably by W Armstrong, the GWR's new-works engineer (not to be confused with Sir William Armstrong, who supplied the original machinery for the station). The plan provided three more tracks and platforms, each over 800ft (244m) long, two for passenger trains and one for milk traffic. A second line would be laid alongside the existing platform 9. All this would require radical reconstruction, including the digging out of London Street, the construction

Figure 4.11 The fourth span under construction, *c* 1915.

of a massive new substructure and the addition of a new fourth span to the main train shed (Fig 4.10). New footbridges would link the enlarged station with the Bishop's Road Station (the present Metropolitan Line and Hammersmith & City Line platforms). On 8 August 1906 the general manager presented revised plans costed at £115,500.[46] These were approved by the board the following day, a testimony to the GWR's efficient management style.

Several phases of enabling works were required. The first major step was the building of a huge new engine shed at Old Oak Common, three miles out from the terminus: this opened in March 1906.[47] In 1906–7 the Bishop's Road Bridge, Lord Hill's Bridge and Westbourne Bridge (all of 1835–7) were replaced with long-span steel girder structures to allow greater flexibility in planning the permanent ways beneath.[48] At about the same time new goods offices were built flanking the Bishop's Road Bridge to the south, a long four-storey block, 220ft (67m) long and

40ft (12m) deep, in a Victorian classical manner which stylistically could have been built in the 1850s.[49] A new stationery department was built on Porchester Road at the south end of Lord Hill's Bridge with a reinforced concrete frame, faced in red brick with Patent Victoria stone dressings. The building also housed a new electric sub-station for the Metropolitan railway.[50]

In 1908 the main departure platform (now platform 1) was lengthened westwards to provide a new milk platform. The main thrust of the new work, though, was on the arrival side. In 1908 the old high-level coal depot between the station and Paddington Basin was closed, together with London Street, the oddly named thoroughfare running along the north side of the passenger station. Brunel's arrival side and the near end of the Mint stables were demolished, the whole area excavated down to platform level, and a massive new concrete retaining wall built towards the canal.[51] In April 1909 a contract for £22,500 was let to Messrs Jackaman of

Slough for erecting the steel columns and superstructure to carry the re-routed London Street.[52]

A major element of the work was rebuilding the near (south-west) wing of the Mint stables as the new 'up' parcels depot. The site was dug down by another 7ft (2.1m) to platform level to allow a large basement to be built of reinforced concrete on the same Hennebique system as had been used on the Porchester Road building. François Hennebique had developed his ideas for using steel reinforcing bars to give tensile strength to concrete in France and Belgium in the 1890s.[53] By 1900 several patented systems were in use, but Hennebique's became the most successful, partly thanks to his marketing techniques and flexible licensing arrangements. The first British application of it was at Messrs Weaver & Co's provender mill in Swansea in 1897.[54] Hennebique's principal agent in Britain was the French engineer Louis-Gustave Mouchel. L G Mouchel & Partners designed numerous buildings using the Hennebique system in Britain and also arranged for the system to be licensed to other contractors.[55] The GWR were one of the first licensees and their engineers' department was designing buildings using the system from c 1905–6.[56] Most early examples of the Hennebique system have been demolished and the basement of the Mint stables is a notable survival.[57] At platform level, a large circulation area to receive parcels and a sorting area were made; lifts linked these to a road depot at street level, where six loading docks allowed the parcels to be put straight on to the GWR's wagons.[58]

A contract for renewing part of the high-level coal viaduct was also let in August 1909.[59] There followed further contracts for excavating the site of the new goods and cab ramps (December 1910),[60] the diversion of London Street (February 1912),[61] construction of a retaining wall (April 1912),[62] the new cab ramp and cellarage (January 1913)[63] and widening the arrival side approach (April 1913).[64] In November 1913 the contract for the new steel roof over platforms 9, 10 and 11, the 'fourth span' itself, was let to Messrs Holliday & Greenwood, for £28,969.[65] As a preparatory measure the northern row of Brunel's cast-iron columns was replaced in riveted steel.[66] The new roof was also designed by the GWR's engineering department. It was closely modelled on Brunel's three spans but wider than any of them at 109ft (33m). The steelwork was manufactured by the Horseley Bridge & Engineering Company (Fig 4.11; see also Fig 7.24).[67]

The new roof was nearing completion in June 1915. At this point the GWR board asked their engineer and new-works engineer to report on the train sheds generally.

This was prompted by the collapse of Charing Cross Station's roof (designed by Sir John Hawkshaw and dating from 1863). The engineers did not think that the Brunel roof was in any danger but assumed that at some point it would be renewed. They noted, though, that the northern row of Brunel's columns was being pushed out of true because of the difference in width beween his old north span and the new fourth span. They recommended adding tie-rods to the fourth span to remedy this.[68] They further recommended that the remaining original cast-iron columns be replaced in steel 'as a stage in the direction of the ultimate complete renewal of the roof'.[69] The existing octagonal columns of riveted steel were installed in 1922–3.[70] The new arrival side was brought into use gradually: the new platform 13 from November 1913, platforms 11 and 12 from December 1915, and platform 10 early in 1916.

The GWR was heavily engaged in the First World War (Fig 4.12), though not in so visible a way as the South Eastern & Chatham Railway, which took all the troop trains from Victoria to the Channel ports. The GWR hauled coal from Wales to feed the industrial war effort and 25,000 of the company's servants (about a third of the total) were called to the colours. At the same time, surprisingly, the company had to cope with booming passenger numbers. Britain was not mobilised for war in 1914–18 to anything like the same extent that it was in 1939–45 and it is strange to reflect that, in the terrible summer of 1916 while the battle

Figure 4.12 The Forces' canteen at Paddington, 1919. Note the abundance of flowers, the portrait of the king-emperor and the absence of alcoholic refreshment.

Figure 4.13 Demolition of Brunel's goods depot, 1925.

of the Somme was raging, three Cornish Riviera expresses carrying a total of 1,400 people were leaving Paddington every day.[71]

During the First World War, 2,524 GWR employees lost their lives. The company commissioned the very fine memorial on platform 1, designed by Thomas Tait, with the life-size bronze figure of an infantryman sculpted by Charles Sargeant Jagger. It was dedicated by Viscount Churchill, then the chairman, on Armistice Day 1922.[72]

In August 1914 the Government had taken overall control of Britain's railways, in order to manage war mobilisation. This control outlived the war and led to the Railways Act of 1921, which merged all the railway companies in Britain into four big groups with effect from 1 January 1923.[73] The Great Western Railway was the least affected of all the companies, being the only one to retain its original name and to maintain its identity largely undiluted.[74] It absorbed a whole

family of railway lines and docks in South Wales that added only 560 route miles (900km), but another 18,000 employees. This cemented the company's dominance of the Welsh coal trade, although that trade, like many of the Welsh coalfields themselves, was already in decline. For the time being, the GWR recovered strongly from the upheavals of war and reorganisation, to return an 8 per cent dividend in 1923, the highest in 75 years.[75]

At Paddington, Brunel's goods depot was filled to capacity, with 900 road vehicles passing through it a day and 900,000 tons of general merchandise being handled each year. The goods depot was demolished in stages during 1925 and 1926. In 1925 the 1854–8 buildings were demolished and replaced with a huge single shed measuring 625ft (191m) by 353ft (108m), with a seven-span steel-framed roof covering five double tracks (Figs 4.13 and 4.14; see also Figs 7.36 and 7.38). In the 1920s the company were still using horses for

Figure 4.14 Goods are transferred from the old goods depot to the new, March 1926: note the ubiquity and variety of hats.

all their short-haul goods traffic in London, but a motor transport department was being built up and in 1932 the company opened a depot for their 500 lorries at Westbourne Park.[76] The GWR were determined to compete with the road lobby on its own terms, but this was nevertheless an ominous sign for the future.

The war caused great disruption to the railway industry and the decade 1910–20 turned out to be the last period when it could generally count on rising revenues. In the 1920s road traffic grew steadily and the railway business stopped growing. The General Strike of 1926 gave the industry a bad jolt (Paddington was kept running through the Strike by 2,234 volunteers) (Figs 4.15 and 4.16).[77] Throughout the decade the GWR weathered the storm well. It had the benefit of an outstanding general manager in Sir Felix Pole, a latter-day Saunders, and in 1922 the great G J Churchward was succeeded as locomotive superintendent by C B Collett, who equalled Gooch and Churchward's achievements in producing the 'Castle' and 'King' classes, among the finest steam locomotives that have ever been built.[78] Thanks to them the Cheltenham Spa Express ran from Swindon to Paddington at 71.4mph in 1932, the fastest scheduled train service in the world.[79]

Although the GWR's business had peaked in the 1920s, Paddington was still under great pressure. In 1926 the general manager commissioned a report on its future,

and T S Todd of the engineer's department produced a remarkable document that set out a masterplan for doubling the size of the station. The Great Western Royal Hotel would have gone, Eastbourne Terrace with all its houses would have been cleared, the site would have been dug out and another three roof-spans added to match the existing four. The architect Sir Henry Tanner produced some rather bland classical designs in 1928, reminiscent of his work on Regent Street, for the immensely long façades which would be created on Praed Street and Westbourne Park Terrace (Fig 4.17). The new hotel, to the south, would have had a faintly American quality, like Tanner's Park Lane Hotel but on a bigger scale.[80]

It was a vision of Brunellian scale and thoroughness, but it came too late. Later the same year the General Strike represented a bad knock for the company. The last good year was 1929, when the GWR returned a dividend of 7.5 per cent, the highest amongst the 'big four' railway companies. The Great Depression of 1929–31 hit all the companies hard and their revenues fell alarmingly: for the railway industry as a whole, it would never be glad confident morning again.[81] The GWR was still capable of innovation, introducing colour light signalling on the main line from Paddington to Southall in 1932 and diesel railcars to British railways in 1933–4. It was also the first British railway company to introduce automatic train control, but in the

63

Figure 4.15 Volunteers handle milk churns during the General Strike, 1926.

mid-1930s it began to withdraw from the technological race; the kudos of having the fastest engines passed to Sir Nigel Gresley at the London & North Eastern Railway.

In 1930 the GWR embarked on another major round of improvements with the help of £1,000,000 in government loans under the Development (Loans, Guarantees and Grants) Act of 1929, but it was a scaled-down project, in keeping with the straitened times.[82] More powerful locomotives meant that longer trains were now in use, so a major element in the works was the lengthening of the main platforms, with lower shelter-roofs extending beyond the train sheds. The other main objectives were to modernise the Great Western Royal Hotel, to build new offices for the GWR, and to link the two sides of the station together more firmly. This last objective was to be achieved by converting the area at the back of the hotel, long known as the Lawn, then in use as a vehicle and loading area, into a pedestrian concourse.[83]

The works were designed by P A Culverhouse, the GWR's architect, and Raymond Carpmael, their chief engineer, and carried out between 1930 and 1935. Culverhouse and Carpmael were also responsible for a major remodelling of Bristol Temple Meads carried out at the same time.[84] As in 1906, there were extensive enabling works. To free the Lawn of vehicles, a new parcels depot was needed and a large new steel-framed building went up for the purpose on Bishop's Road with a separate access to platform 1. The hotel was given its own vehicle delivery entrance off the arrival ramp (at the north end of the hotel). To the south of the Lawn, there had remained a gap between the offices to Eastbourne Terrace and the south end of the hotel. Here, Culverhouse designed a new block of offices, steel-framed, eight bays wide and six storeys high, that filled about half the gap in a very restrained classical style, again faced in Patent Victoria stone. This was built c 1931–3 by Holliday & Greenwood.[85] The remaining gap between this

Figure 4.16 Some well-bred lady volunteers, working in the Mint stables during the General Strike, 1926 (their footwear rather gives them away).

building and the hotel was filled a few years later by a similar steel-framed building housing yet more offices, built by A D Dawney & Co.[86]

North of the Lawn, Culverhouse cleared the low 19th-century buildings which flanked the arrival side roadway.[87] Here he built another steel-framed office block in a distinctive art deco style, with shallow oriel windows incorporating ventilation vents. The name 'G.W.R. PADDINGTON' marched in bold letters across the top of the building and Culverhouse designed shell-shaped uplighters projecting from the façade to illuminate it (Fig 4.18).[88] On the east side of the Lawn the hotel was extended, with a Post Office sorting depot on the ground floor, offices for the publicity department on a mezzanine, a new drawing room for the hotel above that, and new bedrooms higher still.[89] At platform level, these new buildings had regular, simple classical façades of Patent Victoria stone

facing onto the Lawn, which was paved as a proper concourse. Finally, Culverhouse and Carpmael covered the Lawn with a new steel-framed glass roof, with laylights around the perimeter, glazed in white and amber glass (Fig 4.19).[90] One result of these works, from the passengers' point of view, was to dispel the sense of Paddington having distinct departure and arrival sides, though the terminology survived in use among the station's staff into the 1980s.

At the same time, Carpmael and Culverhouse gave the Great Western Royal Hotel a general overhaul, the first since its construction in the 1850s. Victorian architecture was at its critical nadir and Hardwick's grand interiors, including his magnificent two-storey coffee room, were destroyed. A series of low-key art deco interiors were created instead, with an American bar and a number of function rooms, lined with polished flush panelling throughout. On the station side, a new lounge was added above the new buildings and

Figure 4.17 (above) The 1928 masterplan for rebuilding Paddington, with immensely long classical façades by Sir Henry Tanner and a giant new hotel facing Westbourne Terrace. This was overcome by the Depression and Culverhouse's more modest plans were carried out instead.

Figure 4.18 (above) The new arrival side offices by P A Culverhouse (from the *GWR Magazine*, March 1933).

Figure 4.19 (right) The Lawn roof newly rebuilt, 1933.

overlooking the Lawn. Measuring 87ft (27m) by 34ft (10.5m), it was decorated in orange and cream colours with bronze light fittings. Hardwick's hotel façade was subjected to a similar process of simplification. The cast-iron porch was removed and the two lower storeys refaced in Patent Victoria stone in a much plainer style, with simple banding and plain window-surrounds.[91]

The waiting rooms on platform 1 were redecorated, panelled in oak with ebony inlay. Platform 1 also received a 'Quick-Lunch and Snack Bar', which sounds rather like a sign of the times, with its horse-shoe shaped bar surrounded by modish 'green-topped chromium-plated stools'.[92] At the north-west corner of the station, huge ground-works were carried out to widen the tracks, involving a partial rebuilding of the Bishop's Road Bridge.[93] The old Bishop's Road Station was demolished, the tracks widened, the name dropped, and the area redesignated as platforms 13 to 16 of Paddington Station proper.[94] A new booking-office was built on the bridge-link to the main station.[95] The permanent way was remodelled for three-quarters of a mile (1.2km) out from the station.[96] Culverhouse and Carpmael also designed a large new building for the stationery department, with hostel accommodation for the hotel and refreshment department, on a quarter acre (0.1 hectare) site between Westbourne Terrace and the railway tracks.

Unknown to Culverhouse and Carpmael as they were modernising Paddington in 1935, the station acquired a place in architectural history in a quite different way. Two American architects and brothers-in-law, Nathaniel Alexander Owings and Louis Skidmore, met in London and over refreshments at Paddington made a 'formal partnership' deal 'to offer a multidisciplinary service competent to design and build the multiplicity of shelters needed for man's habitat'. Thus Skidmore Owings Merrill, ultimately one of the largest and most influential architectural practices in the world, was born.[97]

By the time the modernisation of Paddington was complete, the company's business had recovered slightly from the depth of the Depression of 1929–31. The company had developed a fleet of lorries to supplement its horse-drawn van services; it had also set up bus services, though in 1928 it had sold a half-share in them.[98] These would have gone some way to offset the fall in railway revenues, but the long-term future was looking bleaker. The company's centenary in 1935 was celebrated on a grand scale, with re-enactments of the first company meeting and the departure of the first train from Paddington, and with distinctive new coaches for the Cornish Riviera Express.

In 1938 the 'big four' launched a 'square deal' campaign to appeal for government support against the rising road transport lobby.[99] If there was a bright spot anywhere in view, it was the continued prosperity of the company's holiday services, including its boat-trains to the Atlantic liners at Plymouth (Fig 4.20), its 'works specials' (Fig 4.21) and the Cornish Riviera

Express. Paddington was the pre-eminent 'holiday' station and the GWR had never been more popular, its image carefully polished by its skilful marketing department. The popular nostalgic image of the GWR, of gleaming green locomotives with burnished copper funnels pulling chocolate-and-cream carriages, of beautiful posters advertising West Country resorts, jigsaw puzzles of GWR engines and immaculately uniformed inspectors, is largely a recollection of the company in the 1920s and 1930s, its silver age. This image was warmly evoked by the comic novelist P G Wodehouse in his novel *Uncle Fred in the Springtime*, published in 1939. Lord Ickenham, on his way to Blandings Castle (by the 2.45 express – Paddington to Market Blandings, first stop Oxford), reflects on the station's dignified character:

…there is something very soothing in the note of refined calm which Paddington strikes. At Waterloo, all is hustle and bustle, and the society tends to be mixed. Here a leisured peace prevails, and you get only the best people

Figure 4.20 The arrival of the Boston boat-train, 1 May 1911: steamer trunks and horse-drawn cabs. The supports of a temporary roof on the site of the fourth span can be seen in the background.

Figure 4.21 (above)
Employees of Crosse &
Blackwell, off on an
outing to Porthcawl,
1939.

Figure 4.22 (right)
Women waving farewell to
soldiers departing from
Paddington, 1942.

**Figure 4.23 (below,
right)** Police and VAD
nurses shepherd a crowd
of young evacuees,
Paddington, 18 June
1940.

– cultured men accustomed to basset hounds, and
women in tailored suits who look like horses. Note the
chap next door. No doubt some son of the ruling classes,
returning after a quiet jaunt in London to his huntin',
shootin', and fishin'.[100]

One may imagine that the ghosts of the first GWR directors
would have been suitably gratified.

The GWR went to war with the nation in 1939 (Figs 4.22
and 4.23). This time, total mobilisation meant that its
resources were all at the state's disposal. Of the 15,000 of
the company's servants who served in the forces, over 600
were killed or reported missing in action. Another 68 were
killed by enemy action while in the company's service at
home.[101] The head office left for Beenham Grange in

Berkshire, which was probably just as well, for Paddington was badly scarred by bombing during the war; the passenger station being hit seven times and the goods station four times. Two bombs caused especially serious damage: on 17 April 1941 a parachute mine hit the Eastbourne Terrace buildings, demolishing a large part of the range just to the right of the platform 1 entrance together with the canopy over the cab road. On 22 March 1944 a pair of 500lb (227kg) bombs came through the train shed roof, blowing a great crater in the middle of the tracks (Fig 4.24).

Bombing and the demands of war placed great strains on the station and its staff. The writer Sir Osbert Sitwell left an evocation of this, having been summoned by Queen Mary to keep her company at Badminton House, Gloucestershire, for Christmas 1944:

The station-master's real office had been bombed, so the staff were using temporarily the royal waiting-room, a pretty octagonal room, crowned with a shallow dome, and having on one wall a rather pretty plaster medallion of Queen Victoria as a young woman. There were three men and two girls working, and the sound of feet outside was accompanied within by the tapping and click of typewriters, and the continual ringing of a telephone bell. The station-master himself often rang up a mysterious higher authority, active elsewhere. This power he approached rather as a mortal might attempt to speak to those who dwell on Olympus. 'Is Mr Williams there ? … I want to speak to Mr Williams Himself. It's the Station-Master. Yes, I said HIMSELF … Is that you Mr Williams? The lawns are dangerously crowded, sir. I thought you might care to inspect them, and pass your opinion. You may think the gates should be shut.' (It was the first time I had heard platforms referred to as *lawns*, and this interested me. It must be, I think, a relic of days when platforms were open strips of grass).

At this moment, attention was diverted, for from his olympian retreat the great Mr Williams gave the order to shut the gates of the station, and this was done, so that now two crowds roared and raved, one inside, the other outside and besieging the yellow bulk of Paddington … From the office, the noise they made sounded like a rough sea …[102]

The Great Western Railway coped well throughout the war, despite the demands of total mobilisation, bomb damage and the shortage of investment. After victory in 1945, though, the economic and political climate

Figure 4.24 A direct hit. On 22 March 1944, two 500lb bombs fell through Brunel's roof and exploded on the tracks.

looked bleak. Even before the war the 'big four' had been suffering from the sharp rise in motor transport and their revenues were falling.[103] State control and the demands of wartime service had sapped their independence and profitability. The deciding factor, though, was the Labour Party's landslide victory in the 1945 election. The Attlee government came to power on a manifesto of sweeping nationalisation that included the railway network. The GWR would have faced a difficult future whatever happened. Its achievements had been tremendous, and the company might well have faced its problems with all the vigour it had displayed in previous crises, but it was not allowed to: its fate was determined by politics, not economics. The British Railways Act received royal assent on 6 August 1947, and the vesting date was set as 1 January 1948.[104] The GWR ended its days as a going concern, returning a final dividend on its ordinary shares of 7.25 per cent. On New Years' Eve the company handed over 100,000 employees, 3,856 steam locomotives and over 3,800 route miles (6,100km) of track to the new British Railways Board. The last official act, the final shareholders' meeting, took place on 5 March 1948 in the hotel at Paddington and with that the Great Western Railway Company ceased to exist.[105]

5 THE STATION AT WORK, 1855–1947

In the Victorian age, the great railway companies were almost uniquely complex organisations. The only other bodies that could remotely be compared to them in their combination of human, financial and technological organisation were the Army, the East India Company and the Royal Navy with its dockyards, communications and victualling branches. For the whole of its history until nationalisation in 1947 Paddington was the hub of an industrial empire and was in itself a community the size of a small town. The artist William Powell Frith intuitively grasped that Paddington, like the Great Western Railway, could be seen as a microcosm of Victorian society (see Fig 4.2). Few historians have tried to set the railways in their social and economic context and no one has yet written a social history of the GWR.[1] A work of this kind, taking in the company's staff, its services and their impact on the communities they served, could be a lifetime's study: it is not possible in a book of this scope to accomplish very much in this direction. The aim is merely to set out some of the main themes and give a general idea of how the station operated.

Brunel designed the whole Great Western Railway as an operating system, and in the same kind of way he designed Paddington Station around the movement of trains and passengers. The three pages of his sketchbook, on which the plan of the station took shape in the last week of 1850, are essentially track diagrams, with the outlines of buildings sketched in around them (see Figs 3.7 and 3.8).

It is usual in planning a station to provide platforms on either side of the tracks, one platform for each direction. In planning a terminus, this translates into departure and arrival platforms, or in railwaymen's parlance 'down' and 'up'. In the 19th century it was unusual for a train to come in to a terminus, drop off passengers, pick up others and set out again (what are termed 'in and out' services): trains did not run frequently enough for this to be manageable. Instead, all trains arriving at a terminus would be disassembled, cleaned and serviced, and new trains put together to be shunted into the departure platforms.

Brunel's first thoughts for Paddington, as committed to his sketchbook, were for a grand central concourse with platforms and tracks on either side: one may presume that one side would have been for departures, the other for arrivals. As we have seen, the directors forced a change of plan. Instead, the middle of the train shed was occupied by a broad trackbed, running through to a group of turntables behind the hotel. The departure side was to the south, the arrival side to the north (Fig 5.1). It was normal for these to be clearly differentiated, but nevertheless unusual for them

to be so completely separate as Brunel made them at Paddington: departing and arriving passengers were to be kept apart, as in a modern airport. The two sides were linked by a covered footbridge at the east or town end, which also connected them to the hotel. There was a subway across the middle of the station, intended only for staff. In the middle, beneath the central trackbed, was a sizeable underground room. Its original purpose is not clear: it may have been a 'lamp room' for supplying oil lamps for the trains, but Brunel could have intended it to house hydraulic gear for operating machinery in the station, as discussed below.

Indeed, reconstructing how Brunel intended the new station to work is not easy as he left no general description of this, and there are no surviving drawings on which all the functions are marked. A certain amount can be inferred from various plans. There is also a useful series of articles on 'The Development of Paddington Passenger Station' in the *GWR Mazagine* for 1916 by E C Matthews, a company employee with an encyclopaedic knowledge of the station who had learnt much from old GWR hands. Even he did not fully understand Brunel's design.[2]

Passengers arriving at Paddington by carriage or cab or on foot would go down the ramp from Eastbourne Terrace to the main entrance loggia, leading onto the departure platform. Just to the right was the main booking hall. In 1845 the GWR adopted the 'Edmondson ticket' system, named for its inventor Thomas Edmondson, in which cardboard tickets were pre-printed and franked with the date on the day of travel (Fig 5.2). The tickets were printed by the million in the GWR's own presses at Paddington: they had monetary value and so had to be kept securely. It was a complex system, as colour-coded first-, second- and third-class tickets had to be printed for all destinations: in the 1860s the GWR was issuing twelve different kinds of ticket to every station on its network.[3] To the right of the booking hall there was the first-class waiting room, with its separate ladies' room and cloakrooms. Left of the loggia was the second-class waiting room and beyond that the royal waiting room and a refreshment room. There was, of course, no third-class waiting room.

The new station was provided with ten broad-gauge tracks, as shown on the plan in Figure 3.9. There was the departure platform, then tracks 1 and 2, then an island platform, and then tracks 3 to 9 under the central span. Track 9 faced another island platform, then came track 10 and the main arrival platform. The island platforms would have allowed two trains to be prepared and loaded (or unloaded)

simultaneously. Matthews thought they were also used as 'lamp platforms' being linked via the subway to the lamp room, beneath the central trackbed. In the days when trains were lit by oil lamps, servicing these was a 'heavy and important' business.[4] To provide access to these island platforms, Brunel and Armstrong designed hydraulically powered moving bridges, stored under the departure platform, to be rolled out across the tracks when needed (Fig 5.3). Rather oddly, the plans do not seem to show any such bridges for the island platform on the arrival side.[5]

Brunel was becoming fascinated by the hydraulic machinery being developed by the celebrated inventor and industrialist Sir William Armstrong in his works at Elswick on the Tyne. He collaborated with Armstrong in developing a whole series of machines for Paddington, as if testing how far the station's operations could be mechanised. The bridges and traversers were all to be hydraulically powered, as were the many turntables, sector tables, cranes and lifts around the station (Fig 5.4). All were designed and manufactured by Sir William Armstrong & Company at Elswick.[6] Brunel's office diaries for 1851 record frequent meetings with Sir William Armstrong, and in 1854 Armstrong wrote:

I have also applied it (hydraulic power) extensively to railway purposes, chiefly under the direction of Mr Brunel … Most of these applications are well exemplified at the new station of the Great Western Railway Company in London, where the loading and unloading of trucks, the hoisting into warehouses, the lifting of loaded trucks from one level to another, the moving of turntables and the hauling of trucks and traversing machines, are all performed, or about to be so, by means of hydraulic pressure supplied by one central steam engine with connected accumulators.[7]

None of this machinery now exists. There is enough documentary evidence to show that Brunel and Armstrong were attempting something very ambitious here, but it is difficult to reconstruct in detail. One aspect above all,

Figure 5.1 (left) Paddington Station, looking north from the departure side through Brunel's transepts to the arrival side.

Figure 5.2 (right) In the 19th century the GWR issued pre-printed Edmondson tickets for all its scheduled and special services.

Figure 5.3 Platform 1, December 1912, showing one of the moveable passenger bridges, providing access to the island platform, pulled halfway out.

concerning the station's plan and the role of 'traversing frames' in it, remains very puzzling indeed.

Brunel had incorporated at least one large, probably manually operated traverser, in the temporary station at Paddington (*see* Chapter 2). There has been a persistent story that Brunel designed the transepts of Paddington Station so as to house traversers, or at any rate to allow for them being installed, across its whole width. The origin of this seems to be his son's *Life of Isambard Kingdom Brunel*, which refers to it being crossed by 'two transepts 50ft [15m] wide, which gave space for large traversing frames'. On the face of it, this would offer a plausible rationale for the transepts: the regular column spacings in the train shed are around 30ft (9m) and in 1852 the GWR introduced new 38ft (11.6m) carriages known as 'long charlies'.

There is no other evidence for this, however, and various documents in Network Rail's archives paint a quite different picture, although it is rather a puzzling one. First, a foundation drawing, undated but probably from early 1851, does indeed show masonry foundations for two traversers, but not in the transepts. They were in adjacent bays and were around 26ft (7.9m) wide (which was thus the maximum wheelbase-length of a vehicle that could be carried on them).[8] Furthermore, they only spanned or linked lines 1 and 2, so they did not need to cross a row of columns in any case.[9] Other layout drawings, datable to 1851, seem to confirm that traversers were only planned for these two positions on the departure side.[10] There are numerous drawings for the traversers and the hydraulic machinery to work them, all by Sir William Armstrong

Figure 5.4 (above) Design for an 18ft turntable, probably by Sir William Armstrong & Company, 1852.

Figure 5.5 (right) 'Machines for Working Traversing Frames', a design by Sir William Armstrong & Company, 1852.

Figure 5.6 Platforms 1 and 2, *c* 1920: the locomotive is sitting on one of Brunel's traversers.

& Company of various dates between 1852 and 1854 (Fig 5.5).[11] Finally, there is photographic proof that traversers were built in these positions, one of which remained *in situ* into the 20th century (Fig 5.6).

So far, this seems clear enough: Brunel only wanted traversers to communicate between the two departure lines, to take vehicles with a maximum wheel-base of 26ft (7.9m). There would be no need for the transepts on this account. What is odd is that the transepts were apparently designed to house machinery, but something called 'descending platforms' rather than traversers. Surviving drawings show how sections of the island platforms, measuring 44ft (13.4m) by 24ft (7.3m), were to be constructed so they could be hydraulically lowered on iron frames to about track level.[12] One other plan has what seem to be the descending platforms roughly sketched in, marked '46 feet', in all four places (that is, sections of both island platforms, in each transept). It is clear from the plan that features of this size and shape would not have fitted between the standard 30ft (9.1m) intercolumniations: they must have been in the transepts but what were they for? The drawings give no clue as to the purpose of these things. Their decks or surfaces were of plain boarding, with just one feature, a narrow groove or channel in the middle, about 2ft (0.6m) deep and running in the transverse direction (at 90 degrees to the train tracks). It seems impossible that rolling stock could have moved across them – that would have required a traverser, a quite different piece of equipment.

It is not clear if these strange devices were ever installed: nevertheless, this is the only piece of evidence to 'explain' Paddington's transepts, a vital feature of its design. If they were built, they were quickly taken out again and seem to have been completely forgotten. By the time Isambard Brunel Junior wrote his father's life, the story was that the transepts had been intended to house a glorified system of traversers. E C Matthews, a well-informed member of the GWR's staff, recorded this story in around 1913 but did not know whether such a system had ever been installed. He expressed doubts as to whether it had but noted that when new platforms were being constructed in the 1880s 'a mass of girder-work and piping was discovered for which there was no apparent use, and in the writer's opinion this was intended to have formed a part of the traversers, the girder-work for carrying them, and the pipes for operating'.[13] In fact, the girder-work and piping seems more likely to have been for the mysterious descending platforms, but whether they were installed, and what their role was in Brunel's plan for the station, we do not know.

In the 1850s a typical GWR express train would be composed of an engine and tender, a guard's van and six to eight carriages, divided between the first and second classes. The second-class carriages would usually come after the engine with the first-class carriages at the back, corresponding to the positions of their respective waiting rooms as they opened onto the departure platform. Frith's painting (see Fig 4.2) has a train with third-class carriages at the front, but the GWR continued into the 1860s to carry most of its third-class passengers on separate trains. Until 1875 luggage was commonly stowed in metal racks on the carriage roofs, covered with tarpaulins, again as shown in Frith's painting.

Wealthy families travelling between London and the West Country would often want to take their horses and carriage with them. In the GWR's early years many richer passengers preferred to travel in their own carriages strapped to flat carriage trucks, an early Victorian equivalent to the Channel Tunnel's 'Le Shuttle' service. For this, the company tended to charge about a shilling less per person than for standard first-class travel. It is not clear how long this particular service endured, but the handling of private carriages and horses long remained a lucrative part of the GWR's business: in 1849 the company owned no fewer than 224 carriage trucks and they were kept at all major stations (see Fig 3.1). The service only needed to be booked the day before travel: horses and carriage had to be at the station 15 minutes before the scheduled departure time. In 1841 the company charged 48s (£2.40) to take a two-wheeled vehicle, or 58s (£2.90) for a four-wheeled vehicle, from London to Bristol. They would take a horse from London to Bristol for 48s, a pair for 73s (£3.65). The GWR's care for its smarter 'county' passengers was also manifested in its 'hunting services': for example, in 1865 a huntsman could take himself, his groom and a pair of horses to Oxford, Woodstock or Banbury for the season and back, for £18.[14]

Brunel made generous provision for the horse-and-carriage business in the layout of the new station. A wealthy family on their way to the West Country could be driven to Paddington and dropped off at the entrance to the first-class waiting room, while (presumably) a servant collected their tickets. Their coachman would take their carriage to the 'horse arch', at the eastern ('town') end of the cab road. Here, Brunel had designed a loading bay where four tracks ran up to the platform edge, linked to the main tracks by a set of small turntables. This feature formed part of his first sketch for the station layout, so it was clearly regarded as very important. The horses would be led into horseboxes, the carriage run up a ramp and strapped to a carriage truck, and these together would be turned on the turntables, before being manhandled along the tracks and hitched to the back of a train on the departure platform for the journey west. A very similar loading bay, again with four 'docking' positions, was provided at the outer end of the arrival side, presumably for horses and carriages making the journey up to town.[15]

This reconstruction is rather tentative: these turntables had been taken out by 1867, so in the event they were soon obsolete.[16] E C Matthews thought the area may have been designed for passengers who intended to travel in their own carriages on the train and that the justification for it died out with this practice. The GWR would not allow horses and carriages on its express services and it may be that its richer passengers preferred to travel by express and send their horses and carriages on ahead by night trains.

A curious detail of the plan was a single track of a narrower, 4ft gauge, just beyond the horse arch turntables, running from the back of the hotel to the end of the departure platform. According to Matthews, this carried a special luggage trolley, presumably to take hotel visitors' baggage to be loaded onto departing trains.[17]

The horse arch could also have been used for mail-sacks or parcel deliveries (which were always handled by the passenger station, not the goods station). Brunel provided the departure side with another loading bay, however, this one at the 'country end' and actually outside the train shed. This too had a wide vehicle entrance leading onto the platform and four lines running up at right angles to the platform edge, in this instance linked to a separate, dedicated line of track. By 1876 this area was known as the milk platform, though it would seem to represent a lot of investment merely for handling milk churns.

The most important point, perhaps, is that the layout was

very flexible. The horse arch platform was designed to allow horses, vehicles, sacks or parcels to be loaded conveniently into vans or trucks and hitched to the back of a passenger train on the main departure platform. The milk platform, outside the shed, could have been used to get churns, horses, vehicles, sacks and parcels onto dedicated services, or shunted onto the backs of departing passenger trains.

The arrival side, on the north flank of the station, was more simply planned and had no really substantial buildings (Fig 5.7). The three spans of the main roof were flanked by a lower aisle covered with flat trusses and glazed Paxton roofing: a long, solid brick wall closed the station on its north side. There were two arrival lines, 9 and 10, on either side of the island platform, so the station could cope with two incoming trains at once. Three relatively small timber-framed

Figure 5.7 'Soldiers of the Queen': troops returning from the second Boer War marching out of the arrival side, Paddington, 1900.

buildings stood on the arrival platform: reading from the hotel end, they were the main waiting room, a cloakroom and left luggage office and the royal arrival side waiting room.[18] Beyond them, under the Paxton roof, was a broad roadway, allowing vehicles to come right down into the station.

At the outer end of the arrival side was a loading (or rather, unloading) bay, like the two on the departure side. Like them, it had four docking positions, so that wagons or trucks could be detached from the back of a train, turned on small turntables and run end-on up to the platform edge. This, too, figures in Brunel's very first sketch plans. It presumably served for the unloading of horses and carriages and may have been for milk deliveries as well. It seems unlikely that mail and parcels were dealt with here, as the main parcels office, a long framed building, was 200 yards (183m) away under the far end of the arrival platform.[19] If we assume that parcels were often carried in the guard's van and that in the early days this was usually right behind the locomotive, then an incoming train would almost deliver them to the door.

One may picture a train arriving from Bristol soon after the opening of the arrival side. The locomotive would be detached from the carriages and run forward into the V-shaped 'sector table', diverted onto line 9, and reversed out to the engine shed at Westbourne Park.[20] Meanwhile, horseboxes and carriage trucks would be detached from the back of the train and manhandled into the unloading bay. The train would have come to a standstill parallel with the waiting rooms, and cabs and carriages would be standing ready under the roadway to greet the arrivals. Wheeled ladders were placed against the carriages so that the luggage could be unloaded from the roof racks and put in labelled bins on the platform, as provided for in the GWR's rule book:

> All articles of London luggage not taken charge of by the passengers themselves are to have red labels pasted on showing the initial letter of the owner's surname, and the porters at Paddington are, on the arrival of the trains, to take care that the luggage thus labelled is placed in the proper bins or divisions of the barrier on the platforms, and delivered to the proper owners.

There was an old Paddington story of a porter who told the Reverend Mr L——, enquiring after his luggage, to go to 'L', and being reported for insolence. One hopes the porter was not sacked: he could quite easily have been.[21]

As we have seen, beneath the wide central span there was a broad trackbed with seven lines, only the outer of which (lines 3 and 9) faced onto platforms. This had formed a feature of Brunel's first sketches for the station and had parallels at most other Victorian termini: these platform-less tracks seem to have been used for marshalling new passenger trains, or for holding carriages and wagons in readiness. E C Matthews made the interesting observation that Brunel might have intended the central span to be

occupied by the locomotive department: this would represent something of a parallel to his original design for Bristol Temple Meads, but I have not found any other evidence for it.[22] The station certainly was not fitted out for this purpose: the lines ran through to turntables, probably 22ft (6.7m) in diameter. These could have coped with the GWR's old six-wheel coaches, which were relatively light and whose wheel-bases were only 18ft 4in. (5.6m) long. They could not have coped with the new 38ft (11.6m) eight-wheel carriages, the long charlies, which in 1852 were being introduced for the Birmingham service.[23] Nor would they have been big or heavy enough to handle locomotives. So the group of turntables was presumably for handling short carriages and mail vans, which could thus be moved from any one line to another, and regrouped to form new trains. As it turned out, the turntables seem to have been rendered obsolete and were taken out again around 1867.

The evidence for all this is incomplete and, in the case of the descending platforms, positively mysterious. What emerges is the impression that Brunel was thinking in terms of an 'ideal station', in which muscle power would be replaced by steam power and rolling stock could be moved around with the greatest freedom possible. It may be that this vision of a mechanised station, like some of his other projects, proved to be over-ambitious. In the long run, the real value of the central span and of the Lawn area to the GWR was simply as growth-room.

One passenger mattered above anyone else to the Great Western Railway, and that was Queen Victoria. By good fortune the journey between the queen's two principal residences, Buckingham Palace and Windsor Castle, fell within their territory. The queen was persuaded to make her first train journey, from Slough to Paddington, on 13 June 1842. She professed herself to be 'quite charmed' with rail travel, and thereafter her journeys between the two palaces were almost invariably by the Great Western.[24] Soon, the London & South Western were pushing their line from Staines towards Windsor, and the GWR had to fight back, opening their short branch to Windsor Central station in October 1849, just two months before the enemy opened Windsor and Eton Riverside. The GWR went to great lengths to maintain their royal patronage: their station at Windsor was disproportionately large and splendid for so small a town[25] and as we have seen, the new Paddington was provided with two royal waiting rooms, the only one of the London termini to be thus equipped (see Fig 7.20).

These royal journeys from Windsor to Paddington and back may not have been long but they required precise

Figure 5.8 Platform 1 decorated for a visit by the Shah of Persia in 1889.

organisation and elaborate protocols were worked out. Notification was sent from the palace to the general manager well in advance. The GWR would send out a printed notice to all the stationmasters on the route, who had to indicate receipt of it by telegraph, twice. The stationmasters had then to notify every signal box on the route in person. On the day of the journey, one of the lines would be cleared of all other traffic: flagmen covered the whole distance within sight and hailing distance of each other. A pilot engine ran in front of the royal train and either the general manager or the superintendent of the line would be travelling on it.[26] In addition Paddington became a major

Figure 5.9 Queen Victoria's funeral procession arrives at Paddington, January 1901. The new King Edward VII and Kaiser William II are just recognisable on horseback, behind. Note the crowds standing on top of the buildings, displaying a characteristically Victorian attitude to 'health and safety'.

venue for various ceremonial events – for example visits by foreign royalty and dignitaries (Fig 5.8) – and, being on the official route to Windsor, it was used as a staging-post on such great state occasions as the funerals of Queen Victoria, Edward VII, George V and George VI (Figs 5.9 and 5.10).

For the first forty years or more of its existence, the GWR was about the most class-conscious and exclusive of the major British railway companies. The directors saw little profit and no benefit in carrying working people for tiny fares and their first timetables only offered first- and second-class services (Fig 5.11). J C Bourne, in his celebratory account of the railway of 1846, remarked on the high proportion of first-class traffic and the number of passengers travelling with their private carriages. At Slough 'the greater part of the traffic was of a very high description'.[27]

In its first two years, the GWR formally offered no third-class service at all. They ran goods trains hiring out wagons to carriers, and from 1838–40 they allowed a number of carriers to convey 'goods passengers' in open wagons fitted with wooden seats, absolutely unprotected from the weather: the seats were 18 inches (0.45m) off the floor, the sides and ends only 2ft (0.6m) high. From 1841 the company officially carried third-class passengers, still in open trucks. However, the GWR would not have them slowing down

Figure 5.10 King George V's funeral: the king's coffin is about to be placed on a train pulled by Locomotive 4082 *Windsor Castle*, 28 January 1936.

Figure 5.11 The GWR's first timetable, 1838.

passengers of quality and the third-class services left Paddington at 4.30am or 9.30pm.[28]

To modern eyes this looks callous. It would have seemed less so to contemporaries, accustomed as they were to the rigours of long-distance journeys on horseback or on foot, or being jolted for mile after mile in (or worse, on the outside of) the mail coach. Brunel had astringent views on the subject, telling one of his assistants that he 'should travel outside (the coach) – inside is, by day – in England – only fit for women and invalids'.[29]

Early Victorian Britons did not expect travel to be comfortable. Nor was it cheap. In 1841 one would pay 30s (£1.50) to travel from London to Bristol in first class (in a comfortable, fully glazed carriage with padded seats), 21s (£1.05) in second class (in an unglazed carriage with seats 15 inches (0.38m) wide), or 12s 6d (£0.63p) in third class (in an open truck on a different, slower train). All this was in an age when an average industrial workman's weekly wages might be £1 or less.[30]

The GWR were not alone in this rather contemptuous approach, but they were widely regarded as the worst offenders. *The Times*, in a leader of December 1842, said: 'The manner in which the GWR Company treats this class of passengers is described as worse than any other.' The service was dangerous too, a point tragically demonstrated by the Sonning accident of Christmas Eve 1841. A 4.30am goods train, pulling two wagons of third-class passengers and 17 goods wagons ran into a landslip in the cutting in the dark. The passenger wagons were at the front behind the engine and as a result the laden goods wagons crushed them against the locomotive tender. Of the 38 passengers, 8 were killed outright and 17 seriously injured. In response, the company raised the sides of its passenger wagons.[31]

The railway companies aroused such public anger that in 1844 W E Gladstone, then President of the Board of Trade, passed the Railway Regulation Act which obliged all the passenger railways in Britain to provide at least one 'workmen's train' a day on every line, stopping at all stations and charging no more than a penny a mile. The Act also obliged the companies to protect their passengers from the weather: the GWR had to provide third-class carriages instead of open wagons, but to modern eyes these would resemble cattle trucks furnished with narrow wooden benches, and having no windows, only ventilator grilles high up. This was the golden age of liberal *laissez faire* economics, and it is a measure of the strength of public feeling that the government felt obliged to legislate. Gladstone, nevertheless, did not feel that he could dictate the hours of these 'parliamentary trains'. As a result, until 1860 the GWR's normal services still only carried first- and second-class passengers, and their third-class 'parliamentary' service left Paddington at 7am: the company's servants referred to it disdainfully as the 'Plymouth Cheap'. Alternatively, there was the 'Night Goods' passenger service which departed at 9.30pm. A third-class passenger leaving Paddington at 7am would get to Bristol in nine hours with an hour-and-a-half stop at Swindon: first- and second-class passengers would make the journey in a third to a half of that time.[32]

The GWR's class-conscious culture was gradually diluted by competition and social change. In 1875 the

Midland Railway astonished the industry (and the public) by abolishing the second class altogether, while upgrading third-class carriages with such second-class comforts as upholstery and heating. The GWR and the London & North Western, the old-guard of the industry, were offended by the Midland's vulgar competitiveness, and said so.[33] The GWR were nevertheless finding that their initial vision of the railway as a smart mode of transport for smart people was fundamentally flawed and that the future of their business lay in providing services for the masses. In 1872 the general manager reported that in the past year first- and second-class receipts had dipped, while third-class takings had risen by £268,000.[34] From 1882, third-class carriages were provided on all trains except for the two fastest express services, the *Flying Dutchman* and the *Zulu*. They, at last, took third-class passengers from 1890.[35]

By the 1890s the volume of third-class traffic had vastly outstripped the other two: in 1893 the GWR carried 1.5 million first-class, 4.5 million second-class, and 55.5 million third-class passengers.[36] From being a despised low-margin service which they almost had to be forced to provide at all, the third class had become the bulk of their passenger business. Like the Midland Railway, the GWR found that it was the second class which was losing its *raison d'être*. The company's general manager, interviewed in 1894, said 'the traffic is a diminishing one, and the day will come when it will extinguish itself'.[37] In the same year, the company abolished the differential between their full third-class and 'parliamentary' fares, at the lower 'penny-a-mile' rate. The second class was finally abolished in October 1910.[38]

The carriages very gradually became more comfortable. For the first generation even first-class carriages were unheated. In 1856, first-class passengers were supplied with metal footwarmers filled with hot water or acetate of soda: these were extended to the second class in 1870 and to the third class in 1873.[39] By 1870 carriages were, rather tellingly, divided into 'best express', 'second best', 'ordinary' and 'excursion': the excursion carriages were 'never to be used in regular trains except in case of absolute necessity'.[40] The company continued to build spacious 10ft ¾in. (3.07m)-wide wide-bodied coaches until 1882: after that point, they were built with bodies of 8ft ¾in. (2.47m), designed to be easily converted to the standard gauge. The GWR introduced the first true 'corridor train' in Britain in 1892, on its services to Birkenhead.[41] Although the company offered refreshments on its platforms (Fig 5.12), it was less quick to provide dining cars, only putting them on in 1896, fourteen years behind the Midland Railway.[42]

The company had been rather quicker to see the possibilities of the tourist business. The idea of certain places being holiday destinations, spa towns and seaside resorts was already well established and these places were greatly helped by the railways (Fig 5.13). The GWR's timetable for 1865 listed tourist services for the south-western coastal resorts in its own heartland, but also advertised services provided jointly with other companies to Yorkshire, Buxton, the Lake District, North Wales, Scotland, Ireland, Boulogne and Calais.

Figure 5.12 Platform catering: a GWR tea trolley at Paddington, early 20th century.

Figure 5.13 Off on holiday, Paddington, 1910.

This was not, at any rate not yet, the start of a boom in mass tourism. In 1865 a return ticket from London to Penzance cost 78s (£3.90) in first class and 56s (£5.80) in second class, while a tourist ticket to the Dublin International Exhibition via Holyhead was 60s (£3.00) or 47s 6d (£2.38).[43] Until the First World War, a sum of this order would have represented the weekly wages of one of the GWR's clerks: these services were effectively for the upper and upper-middle classes. A trend was nevertheless established and the services grew. In 1852 Measom's *Illustrated Guide to the Great Western Railway* was published, with a second edition coming out in 1861, followed by Cassell & Co's new *Official Guide* of 1884. Essentially tourist guides to the historic and natural beauties of the GWR and its allied companies' territory, they provide clues to the nature of this part of the GWR's business and clientele in the shape of numerous advertisements, for example for hotels in Ilfracombe and Torquay, various private schools, porcelain, gentlemen's outfitters and bathing costumes ('he won't spoil his things, Auntie, they are made of Spearman's Royal Devonshire Serge, like yours and mine!').

Holidays in the West Country may still have been the preserve of the rich, but the GWR was also developing a busy traffic in day trips up the Thames valley for the less well off. In January 1863 the Lord's Day Observance Society wrote to the directors, enclosing a memorial signed by the archbishops and bishops of England, 'urging the discontinuance of Sunday Excursion trains'. The directors robustly refused, maintaining that the trains referred to 'are conducive to the good conduct as well as the innocent enjoyment and recreation of the poorer classes for whom they are principally promoted, and without leading in any way to the desecration or improper observance of the Sabbath…'.[44]

The GWR, like other companies, was not averse to promoting prize fights in order to drum up business: in 1863, when they put on a special train for Mace versus Gove at Wootton Bassett, there was a serious riot at Paddington. Victorian respectability, however, was catching up with this kind of thing, and a Regulation Act of 1868 forbade the companies to put on 'specials' for prize fights.[45]

In 1877 the GWR was advertising return tickets to Windsor for 2s 6d (12.5p) or to Henley for 3s 6d (17.5p): these were affordable for almost anyone in employment.[46] In 1881, after an especially busy Bank Holiday weekend, the company decided to introduce an extra platform at Paddington specially for 'excursion traffic'.[47] The company's general manager, interviewed in 1894, talked about how heavy the tourist traffic had become: the GWR had joined forces with the boat operators Messrs Salter, to sell combined tickets for days out on the river at Goring and Henley. It had introduced 'Friday night specials' to the West Country, returning the following Monday, or Monday week. In 1880 the GWR had 2,147 miles (3,455km) of track and appears to have carried 44,500,000 passengers a total of 13,202,399 train miles. By 1893 the track mileage had risen to 2,494 (4,013km), but the company carried 61,250,000 passengers a total of 18,817,118 train miles.[48] Rail travel was becoming more accessible for the Pooters as well as the Forsytes.

Goods traffic had also come a long way since the 1840s, when the depot only managed two incoming and two outgoing trains most days. After the opening of the Chepstow bridge allowing through-trains to South Wales in 1852–3, a huge traffic in coal developed and Brunel laid out the 'high-level goods yard' alongside the canal basin expressly for this. The GWR had probably the most extensive trade in foodstuffs of any of the major companies and began to develop special facilities for handling it. In 1863 the company opened a great new depot below the newly built Smithfield Market in partnership with the Metropolitan Railway.[49]

In the 1850s and 1860s the GWR developed their goods, parcels and milk delivery services in London, depending on carriers, hired horses and rented stables for the purpose. By the 1870s this no longer seemed adequate. The other large companies were moving towards having their own establishments and in 1875 the company resolved to build its own stables at Paddington and at Smithfield and Crutched Friars in the City of London. The most important was always the Mint stables, just north of Paddington, named for the Mint tavern on London Street. The first stage, with room for 288 horses, was built between 1875 and 1877 at a cost of £25,300. In December 1877 the company decided to start buying its own horses.[50] By 1894 they had 1,839, against the Midland Railway's 4,346. The stables continued in use surprisingly late, until after the Second World War, and indeed, until after nationalisation (Fig 5.14; see also Fig 7.51).

It is very difficult to estimate the number of Great Western Railway staff at Paddington in the later 19th century. Certainly there were many hundreds, well up from the 269 counted there in 1843. A number of staff lists have been found for 1873. A 'room allocation' document lists 76 'head office' staff in the chairman's office, the accounts department, the general manager's and engineer's departments and other central functions.[51] Another 41 managers and clerks ran the station operations[52] and a further 51 ran the goods station, giving a total of 168 'white

Figure 5.14 A GWR wagon and four outside the Mint stables, probably 1920s.

collar' staff.[53] No lists have been found, however, for the great numbers of porters, general labourers, carters and ostlers who were employed in the station, parcels office, goods depot and stables. Nor are there any lists of the train and track staff, the enginemen, inspectors, signalmen and guards who were based there. The grand total in 1873 would have been unlikely to be less than 500, perhaps nearer 1,000.

In later years, the GWR had a well-deserved reputation as a benevolent employer, but for its first fifty years the company treated its staff as harshly as many Victorian enterprises. The harshness was tempered with incentives. The company was meritocratic, rewarding zealous service with promotion. It had pay scales with maximum salaries attached to each post to reward staff for long service.[54] Enginemen

who gave good service without accident or cause for complaint for a year were given a standard bonus of £10, while efficient switchmen would receive a bonus of £5.[55] The company, however, maintained ferocious standards of industrial discipline. Until the 1860s the board handled serious disciplinary matters themselves: the accused were summoned to Paddington to stand at one end of the directors' polished mahogany table, an ordeal known to the staff as 'going to see the Picture' (Fig 5.15; see Chapter 4). The board minutes record great numbers of cases dealt with at alternate (that is, fortnightly) meetings, usually with brutal swiftness. A few typical examples from the early months of 1855 should give the modern reader a hint of what Victorian staff management techniques were like:

Figure 5.15 The Great Western Railway's board room, *c* 1900, dominated by a great map of the network. A bust of Brunel is just recognisable on the mantelpiece. The full-length portrait of the great chairman Charles Russell, known as 'the Picture', must have been at the other end of the room.

11 January 1855

John Peckham and George Hobbs, switchmen at Chippenham, were called in, and examined on a charge of being in the Refreshment Room at the station instead of attending to their duty. They expressed much regret at the cause of complaint, and their previous conduct having been exemplary they were only fined 20 shillings each with a caution for the future.[56]

Mr Graham reported that Henry Griffiths, a Policeman at Bath, had been brought before the magistrates on a charge of stealing a lady's jacket, but sufficient proof of his guilt had not been given to convict him. As there is no doubt, however, of his having stolen the jacket, he was ordered to be dismissed the service.[57]

25 January 1855

Jones, a porter at the Gabowen Station, was reported for being intoxicated, and the charge being proved, he was dismissed.[58]

Huckle, a porter at Didcot, was called and examined on a charge of attempting to give a light to a passenger for the purpose of lighting a pipe, which being proved he was severely reprimanded and fined 20 shillings for not telling the truth when charged with the offence. He was informed that had it not been for his very long and good service during 16 years he would have been dismissed.[59]

8 March 1855

Received a letter from Mr Fryer intimating that Mr Cooper, a Station Clerk at Harbury, had died in consequence of a Locomotive Engine having passed over his foot while in the discharge of his duty, and had requested that the Directors would allow him a month's salary, to be given to his Mother and Sister, who were in very indigent circumstances, after his decease, when the sum of £10 was ordered to be given to them.[60]

These are five examples out of hundreds: the shadow of the workhouse seems to loom over these dismal proceedings.

In the 1860s the GWR was in a very difficult financial position, and this seems to have driven the company towards harsher policies. In 1863 the general manager commissioned a report on staff and working expenses at all of its stations. The document is a monument of absolute utilitarianism: no considerations of loyalty to long-serving staff were to be allowed to stand in the way of economy. The big idea was to replace experienced employees with children. The second-class booking office at Paddington could handle the third-class business as well, so three clerks at £70 per annum each could be replaced by three boys at £20 per annum. Four porters could be replaced by six young men on trial at 12 shillings a week. Several clerks at Paddington Goods had been 'many years in the Company's service' and thus advanced to high salary levels: nine of them in the 'abstract office', receiving a total of £694, could be sacked and replaced with junior clerks, saving £150, and so on. One could imagine Dickens having a field day with this depressing document.[61] It is not clear whether the ideas were implemented, though it seems very likely that they were.[62]

The GWR's staff were not, however, without cultural resources. In 1843 a Mechanics Institute with a library was founded for them at Swindon 'for the purpose of disseminating useful knowledge and encouraging rational amusement among all classes of people' employed by the company.[63] This does not, however, seem to have been replicated at Paddington. By 1849, though, the company had established a station library at Paddington, with over 1,000 volumes, principally novels, for the use of the travelling public, who had free access to the books while waiting for trains for 1d, or could hire a volume and turn it in at their destination, for slightly more.[64] The GWR Literary Society, established there in 1852, seemed in its early years to embody the class divisions within the workforce, being reserved for the management and the salaried, office-based employees. It started with a library of 730 volumes and a generous budget provided by the company, and it charged subscriptions of 2s 6d (12.5p) a quarter.[65] The directors supported the new society and the chairman, the Earl of Shelburne, became its first president.

This does much to explain a remarkable event, a 'Conversazione of the Great Western Railway Literary Society', held at Paddington on 7 to 9 December 1859 and described by *The Illustrated London News* (Fig 5.16). The company's large meeting rooms were decorated with 'beautiful and rare specimens of pictures, sculpture, bronzes, books and other works of art' lent by the chairman,

directors and officers. The centrepiece was an elaborate bedstead presented to Queen Victoria by the Maharajah of Kashmir. Autograph letters of Charles I and ancient jars and vases excavated by Robert Stephenson in Alexandria were on display. The rooms were hung with works by eminent contemporary painters including Samuel Reynolds, David Wilkie and Clarkson Stanfield. Several companies lent pieces of decorative artwork: ceramics from the Copeland company, bronzes from the Coalbrookdale company, decorative papier-mâché, and gold and silver ware. A central window was 'arranged as a memorial to the genius of Brunel and Stephenson', both of whom had recently died. In this elaborate setting the society held concerts and poetry readings for three successive evenings, at which 'several amateur friends gave their services, including a reading from the "Ingoldsby Legends" by the honorary secretary of the Society, Mr Kinnaird'.[66]

The conversazione seems to have been a one-off, but the society prospered. There were lectures, a dining club was founded in 1860, and an 'essay class' in 1861 (members read

Figure 5.16 The 'Conversazione of the Great Western Railway Literary Society', Paddington (from *The Illustrated London News*, 17 December 1859).

essays to each other on subjects like 'Tennyson', 'The Qualities necessary to Success in Life' and 'The General Outlines of the Science of Ethnology'). In 1862–3 the *Great Western Railway Magazine and Temperance Union Record* was established for the first time. It recorded the Literary Society's growth: membership up from 403 to 416, the library collection up to 4,253 books. A member of the society, writing anonymously to the magazine, urged that its membership and reading room be opened to the 'second class' of staff – to inspectors, guards, drivers, mechanics and the like.[67]

The *GWR Magazine* was re-established in 1889, soon dropping the 'Temperance Union' from its title. It seems to have been formally adopted by the company and from then on appeared monthly, right up till the end of the GWR in 1947. The magazine exudes an intense corporate pride. Much space is devoted to engineering projects and rolling stock, but there are also substantial articles about the company's history, its stations and its art collection. There are regular profiles of staff in the various departments.

Every issue carries accounts of staff dinners: the 'down loading section' of the goods department, for example (dinner followed by toasts, harmony, recitations and the national anthem). Regular reports appear for any number of societies: the Pelican or Swimming Club, the ambulance classes, the Boating Club (annual regatta at Staines), the Football Club (founded in 1898, with a ground at Acton), the Paddington Madrigal Society and the Chess Club among others. In February 1898 the magazine reported the second concert of the forty-strong GWR Orchestra at the Ladbroke Hall: a programme of Gounod, Sullivan and Suppé, with numerous encores. Regular events were held in aid of the Widows and Orphans Fund, whose famous collecting dog, Tim, became a familiar sight at late-Victorian Paddington, greeting arriving trains on behalf of the fund for more than twenty years. GWR employees made up a whole company of the 2nd South Middlesex Volunteer Rifles: space was found in the goods station for a rifle range. In 1896 Messrs Elkington, the silversmiths, presented a shield for their annual shooting competition: it had pride of place in the 'general meeting room' at Paddington.[68] In the pages of the magazine, the company seems a kinder place to work, with a rich social and cultural life for all its employees (Fig 5.17).

In its golden age the Great Western Railway had as rich a corporate culture as has ever existed in this country, which endured right up to the Second World War and nationalisation. If one were to take a single episode to typify it, it might be an 'Exhibition of Art at Paddington Station',

Figure 5.17 Members of the Swindon GWR band, practising at Paddington for a competition at the Crystal Palace, 29 September 1934.

described by the *GWR Magazine* in 1925, in which 232 paintings, woodcarvings and embroideries, all by the Paddington porters, were exhibited in the 'seat registration office'. Various directors and senior managers showed willing and purchased items at the opening, in aid of the Widows and Orphans Fund. Cheerful events such as this never, of course, give one the whole picture: in the following year the GWR, like its rivals, was seriously affected by the General Strike.

By 1930 the Great Western Railway may have been in difficulties, but it had reached its greatest extent and its highest pitch of sophistication and complexity. In 1929 it had 8,900 miles (14,300km) of permanent way, representing 3,800 miles (6,100km) of route mileage, serving over 1,500 stations. It had over 110,000 employees, 86,000 freight vehicles, 10,000 passenger-train vehicles and 4,000 locomotives. It carried 131,000,000 passengers a year, not including season ticket holders and over 75,000,000 tons of merchandise and mineral traffic. The company had 2,650 horses, 212 miles of canal, 16 steamships and owned a larger area of docks than any other organisation in Britain.[69]

Paddington, the hub of this great industrial empire, was a world in itself. In January 1937 Mr F W Green, the assistant divisional superintendent of the line, gave a remarkable lecture on 'The Working of Paddington Passenger Station' to the GWR Lecture and Debating Society. Subsequently printed in the Society's magazine, it provides an unequalled insight into the life of the station in the GWR's silver age.[70]

The station then had 18 platforms: 15 for passengers, 3 for parcels and milk. Of the 15, 11 were around 1,000ft

Figure 5.18 The Paddington ticket office, with pre-printed Edmondson tickets, 1920. The system required the production of printed tickets to and from every destination in the GWR network.

(300m) long for long-distance services: 4 on the departure or down side, 5 on the arrival or up side, 2 for in and out services. The other 4 were the suburban and underground platforms on the north side of the station, about 600ft (180m) long. Four signal boxes (departure side, arrival side, suburban and Westbourne Bridge) regulated the traffic. Every day, 21 well-loaded long-distance trains reached Paddington by 10.30am. Engines were stabled out at Old Oak Common or at a subsidiary depot by Ranelagh Bridge: on the previous August Bank Holiday 165 of them left the shed. Trains were formed out at the carriage sheds, also at Old Oak Common.[71]

Over 2,000,000 passengers bought tickets in a year, at four booking offices (two on the departure side, one on the footbridge leading to the suburban platforms, and one 'passimeter office' containing automatic ticket machines at the Bishop's Road entrance) (Fig 5.18). For special events like Newbury races, portable offices could be put up on the Lawn. On 21 July and 1 August 1936, the peak days of the year, 14,646 and 16,238 passengers were booked. They could reserve seats at a separate reservation office on the Lawn: up to 25,000 seats could have been booked in a day, helped by the company's telephone system (Fig 5.19). Diagrams for the next day's trains were put together in the late afternoon and sent to the superintendent at Old Oak Common. The handling of taxis and cars was already a problem: over 6,000 road vehicles could pass through the station in a day, peaking on the departure side between 10am and 11am.

Figure 5.19 The GWR's telephone exchange, Paddington, *c* 1900.

It is startling to find that the passenger station handled far more than just passengers. Most of the GWR's market traffic, for example, passed through it. Anything from 50 to 200 tons of flowers, fish, fruit, meat and vegetables came into the arrival side early each morning: 38 men were needed to handle it and 28 horse vans were on hand to take it away, as well as 15 to 20 lorries. Then there was the milk traffic. At one time vast numbers of churns (2,000,000 per annum in 1929) were delivered to the arrival side every day to be manhandled onto vans, with the accompanying 'difficulty and noise' of returning the empties from the down side. This had caused so many complaints from neighbours that the handling of the empty churns had been transferred to the

cattle platform at the goods station. The GWR was replacing the 'churn service' with tanks and a new milk depot at Wood Lane.

The newspaper traffic was on a similar scale: 203 tons (206 tonnes) of newspapers were forwarded onto night trains in the passenger station every night, rising to 394 tons (400 tonnes) on a Saturday. This business employed 106 men on weeknights, 160 on Saturday nights, with 7 tractors for the platform trolleys.

The GWR had long encouraged the growth of special services. More than 2,000 cases of pastries from Messrs Lyons the bakers, for example, were handled each day, while hundreds of tons of poultry passed through the station in

Figure 5.20 Christmas turkeys being transferred from a train to waiting vans under the fourth span, December 1933.

the few days before Christmas (Fig 5.20). The ice-cream traffic was an important departure side business in hot weather: in August 1936 over 350 tons (356 tonnes) of it was sent outwards, in 6,000 containers. Bullion was also sent by rail – more than 20 tons had been sent in one recent month, presumably late in 1936.

These services were dwarfed by the parcels and mail departments. The parcels depot, just beyond the Bishop's Road Bridge on the departure side, had its own platform 1,000ft (300m) long, a through line on one side, a 600ft (180m) siding on the other. A tunnel connected it to the parcels subway, to platforms 1 to 8. On average, 22,000 parcels were forwarded a day, and 1,400 received for delivery in London or transfer to other companies. Over 95 motor vans were kept in the parcels depot, in addition to the legion of horses in the Mint stables. Seven four-wheel tractors were kept on the down side, four on the up side, with one spare.

In addition to all this there were the Royal Mail services coming through the Paddington sorting office on London Street. In an ordinary day it processed 4,500 mailbags and 2,400 bags of parcel post. Down mail went from the Post Office via a conveyor in a tunnel to the south-east corner of the Lawn, onto 'brutes' (wire-sided buggies) and then to waiting trains. Up mail bags, usually arriving on platform 11, were dropped down chutes onto another conveyor that took them to the London Street office for sorting, from where they were sometimes transferred on to Liverpool Street on the Post Office's underground railway.[72] During the Christmas rush the goods department had to help out, setting up a temporary depot on Alfred Road: over Christmas 1936, 79,389 parcel-post bags were sent in 28 special trains.

All of this teeming activity was handled by 723 station staff and 711 parcels depot staff, not including the extra hands taken on to cope with seasonal business. These, of course, were quite distinct from the 1,000 or so head office staff based at Paddington and the hundreds more employed in the goods station. Since nationalisation much of this activity has gone, but Paddington remains one of busiest passenger stations in Britain and has continued to evolve.

6 DECLINE AND REVIVAL, 1947–2001

With the GWR abolished, Paddington became the
headquarters of the British Railways Board's Western Region.
In 1949, a rededication of the war memorial, to
commemorate the GWR employees who had fallen in the
Second World War, represented a final farewell to the old
days. As with the whole of the railway industry, there was no
immediate prospect of new investment: the Attlee
government was chronically short of money. It was not until
1952–3 that the main war damage to Paddington was made
good: the shed roof was restored, though it seems that the
ridge-and-furrow Paxton glazing was removed from 'span
one' in the process, and the gap in the Eastbourne Terrace
buildings was filled with a simple contemporary structure
housing a new booking hall and ticket office in the place of
the old one. There was no money for frills and no attempt
was made to make them match the style of the original
buildings.

The centenary of the station in 1954 was celebrated with
the unveiling of a commemorative plaque. One further
alteration represented a welcome introduction of 1950s
style: a new ticket barrier screen in a 'Festival of Britain'

Figure 6.1 The new screen in 'Festival of Britain' style
across the platform heads, with the arms of the
counties served by British Rail's Western Region,
1950s.

Figure 6.2 Over a thousand West Indian immigrants
arrive at Paddington, 1956.

manner was installed in 1958, with panels representing the arms of the counties served by the Western Region (Fig 6.1). Much of the station remained grimy and cluttered, however, even though Paddington was now welcoming a host of new passengers (Fig 6.2) and still loomed large in public awareness. In 1957 Agatha Christie gave the station a walk-on part in her novel *4.50 from Paddington*, and the author Michael Bond gave the famous name a whole new layer of meaning for generations of children with his Paddington Bear books, the first of which appeared in 1958 (Fig 6.3).

In retrospect, it may have been fortunate that there was not more money available for Paddington (Fig 6.4). The 1960s saw the complete demolition and rebuilding of the two principal stations of the old London & North Western Railway, Euston (1960–68) and Birmingham New Street (1964–7). Many other fine Victorian stations were demolished in the 1960s and 1970s, but the demolition of Euston turned out to be a turning-point, galvanising public opinion and giving the conservation movement a national cause and national standing for the first time. In the 1970s,

Figure 6.3 (above) 'Please look after this Bear'. The publication of Michael Bond's first 'Paddington' book in 1958 gave a new meaning to the famous name. A sculpture on the Lawn provides a permanent reminder of this literary connection.

Figure 6.4 (right) 'High Paddington', a scheme for a nightmarish 'dream city' over the tracks and goods station (excerpt from the illustration published in *Picture Post*, March 1955).

94

KEY TO NUMBERS

1 Church
2 Apartments
3 Offices
4 Existing Offices
5 Vehicle Ramps
6 Shops
7 Self-Service Supermarket
8 Cinema and Swimming Baths
9 Flower Gardens
10 Green Roof Gardens
11 Central Court : Exhibitions etc.
12 Car Park beneath (1000 Vehicles)
13 Nurseries, Clubrooms etc.
14 Town Hall
15 Children's Playground
16 Primary School
17 Classrooms with Open Terraces
18 Administration
19 Playgrounds
20 Clinic and Isolation Hospital
21 Observation Bar
22 Restaurant and Dancing
23 Meteorological Station
24 Hotel
25 Commercial Television Studios
26 Roof Gardens
27 School recreational grounds
28 Parks

Figure 6.5 The redecorated restaurant, March 1974: a spirited exercise in seventies taste.

under the chairmanship of Sir Peter Parker, British Rail began to re-evaluate its architectural heritage. A wider revival of interest in Victorian architecture was under way and Paddington's outstanding quality and interest was being recognised: as long ago as 1951 it had been the subject of a ground-breaking article by Henry-Russell Hitchcock in the *Architectural Review*[1] and in 1961 it was listed. In contrast to this, at the end of 1965, steam power ceased to be used on British Rail's Western Region: this was effectively the end of the engineering tradition of Gooch, Churchward and Collett.

In 1968–9 British Rail spent large sums on alterations to Paddington, by their own Western Region architects and engineers together with Seymour Harris & Partners. More of the main shed roof was repaired and reglazed, involving the removal of the original Paxton roofing in favour of a simpler system. New electrical systems and lighting followed, along with a new ticket office, travel centre and platform barriers, and the tracks were curtailed by 40ft (12m) to make a more generous circulating area.[2] The revival of the station may be said to have begun. After this point, an increasing awareness of the station's architectural and historical importance began to have a direct influence on works to it, although some refurbishments continued to reflect contemporary style

rather than historical precedents (Fig 6.5).

Another bout of works in 1982–5, handled by the Western Region's architect's and civil engineer's departments, added a new 'tin-shed' depot on the north-eastern side of the station for Red Star parcel services and newspaper handling, together with some refurbishment of the offices.[3]

In 1985 British Rail moved its Western Region headquarters to new buildings in Swindon, ending Paddington's long history as the hub of a great network, and the GWR's old offices were refurbished for commercial letting. The station received a form of compensation for this loss of status: British Rail's architects produced the first 'masterplan' for managing the station better. This led, fairly quickly, to a shortening of the platforms to create a more spacious passenger concourse at the track heads, a new ticket office and the first works to restore some of Paddington's historic character. The royal waiting room was refurbished for business-class passengers and the clock arch on platform 1 reopened (all in c 1985).[4] This was a prelude to the major restoration of the three Brunel spans between 1985 and 1993, again by British Rail's Western Region Civil Engineer's Department, under George Connell

Figure 6.6 The Lawn area remodelled as part of the 1998–9 refurbishment of the station.

as project engineer. This was the fullest and most thorough repair of the roof ever to have been undertaken. The ironwork was cleaned right back, with up to twenty layers of paint removed. Serious corrosion was found, especially where the decorative cast-iron plates had been bolted to the arched ribs, which required the fixing of new steel plates to strengthen the original wrought iron. The cast-iron column capitals were repaired or replaced. The external coverings of the roof were replaced with profiled steel sheeting and a polycarbonate glazing; for reasons of weight and economy the ridge-and-furrow glazing was not restored. The roofs were redecorated in a scheme of white, grey and red, taking a cue from historic schemes without attempting exactly to replicate any one of them.[5]

Meanwhile, British Rail had been thinking about Paddington's long-term future. Brunel designed a magnificent station but he left a difficult legacy: the station is sunk in a cutting, hemmed in by the canal and the Westway, and surrounded by what were built as residential streets. The tracks into Paddington have a notably narrow 'throat' which represents a serious capacity constraint, compounded by the limited platform lengths within the station. British Rail commissioned a masterplan from the architects Michael Hopkins & Partners, while Westminster City Council commissioned a study of the area and its planning issues from the engineering practice, Alan Baxter & Associates (1990).

These deliberations were galvanised by the prospect of major new demands on the station. The Crossrail project, an idea of Brunel-like grandeur to make an east–west route for main-line trains below central London, had been actively canvassed and planned since the mid-1980s. It was envisaged from the outset that this would link Paddington to Liverpool Street, but this was clearly going to involve truly formidable engineering and architectural questions. Early Crossrail proposals envisaged taking the new bored tunnels right under Brunel's train shed and the hotel, but serious doubts arose about the feasibility of all this. It turned out that the effect of such a scheme on Brunel's great sheds could not be calculated and that the tunnel would interfere with the piled foundations of the 1930s extension behind the hotel. The scheme was revised to take the Crossrail line beneath Eastbourne Terrace and the architects Alsop & Störmer produced spectacular designs for a new underground concourse on this side of the station. At the time of writing, detailed design studies for Crossrail are under way: the scheme will be immensely expensive and complex to build and it is not yet clear when this will happen.

Following privatisation of the railway system in 1996 British Rail was split up. Railtrack plc, the new owners, had already taken on responsibility for Paddington in 1994. Railtrack wished to develop masterplans for all fourteen of its major stations and in 1995 they commissioned one for Paddington from Nicholas Grimshaw & Partners. The first phase of work was to be a remodelling of the Lawn area. The impending closure of the Post Office's sorting premises there represented an opportunity, while plans for a new Heathrow Express, an equivalent to the very successful Gatwick Express service from Victoria Station, represented a catalyst. The work involved realigning platforms 6, 7 and 8, building new platform canopies outside the 'country end' and bringing overhead 25kV power lines into the station. The footbridge was remodelled and a new tunnel formed beneath the platforms. A new taxi canopy and an elegant new glazed link to the Metropolitan Line platforms by John McAslan & Partners were among the associated works. Overhead electrification was introduced into the train shed for the first time.[6]

The next phase of work was a remodelling of the Lawn and the general concourse area at the platform heads to designs by Nicholas Grimshaw & Partners, carried out between 1989 and 1999. The entrance to the Underground station was moved forward to allow the Lawn to be paved uniformly and a lot of unsightly clutter to be cleared away. Culverhouse's simple elevations of Patent Victoria stone were cleaned and reglazed and airline baggage check-in facilities for the Heathrow Express created behind them (see Fig 7.26). The Lawn was repaved and provided with shops and amenities for travellers (Fig 6.6). The new mezzanine structures are in fair-faced precast concrete, while the fine new roof, its form reminiscent of the ridge-and-furrow Paxton glazing, has glazing fins, mullions and fixing pieces of sand-cast steel. Grimshaw & Partners had recently built the long and sinuous Eurostar terminal at Waterloo and their experience there was developed at Paddington, the carefully considered details and the emphasis on self-finished materials deriving from their close involvement in the manufacturing processes, an interest reminiscent of the engineering culture of Fox, Henderson & Co. Outside the Lawn, the row of train indicators which blocked the long views down Brunel's shed was removed, sharply-detailed new shop units built, and sleek new indicators built at right-angles, so as not to obstruct the view. A very welcome gain from the development was the reinstatement of the original end-glazing pattern to the three Brunel spans. These works restored much dignity to the station and enabled its splendid spatial and architectural qualities to be fully appreciated for the first time in a generation.[7]

Since railway privatisation, passenger numbers have risen steadily: recent predictions are that the numbers passing through the station will rise from c 60,000 a day to nearer 90,000. Once again Paddington is full to capacity and the problems of its position, below street level and hemmed in on most sides, arise again. The station needs more and longer platforms, better links to the underground, better links to the surrounding streets and more room for taxis. Railtrack commissioned designs from Nicholas Grimshaw & Partners for the replacement of the fourth span: these envisage a revised layout for the platforms and taxi approaches and above this a massive concrete transfer structure with a new façade towards Paddington Basin, supporting a major office development. The proposals were objected to on the grounds of the loss of the Edwardian fourth span and the scale of the proposed new buildings. Revised designs have been produced and at the time of writing these remain under discussion.

Paddington is one of the world's great railway stations and one of London's finest Victorian monuments, but it is not a museum. It remains one of the busiest stations in Britain, used by millions, as essential to the nation's economy as it was in the 1850s.

There used to be a widespread view of Victorian architecture which regarded buildings like the Crystal Palace as the harbingers of a bright modernist future and argued that reactionary Victorian society had ducked this challenge, preferring instead to hide the 'truth' of their industrial culture behind a veneer of historicist decoration. Applying this kind of thinking, one might well assume that an engineer like Brunel would have had little time for ornament on his buildings, this being added only to humour the taste of the board or the first-class passengers. In fact, as we have seen, Brunel arranged the involvement of Matthew Digby Wyatt and Owen Jones without telling the board and the whole of Paddington's rich decoration was smuggled in by them under the directors' noses and against their explicit opposition. For Brunel and Wyatt their station was a work of art as well as of engineering: its cathedral-like spatial qualities were appropriate to its status, as was the peculiarly original ornament which they devised for it. Paddington is a unified masterpiece, but perhaps the most original things about it were its ground plan and its ornament. It was a sad loss that Owen Jones' colour scheme was never carried out to complete the design. At Paddington one senses the Victorians' justifiable pride in their technology, coupled with a

feeling that colour and ornament still had important roles to play, and that without them, industrialisation and mass production might make the world sterile and uniform.

Brunel's achievements were on a heroic scale, but as Angus Buchanan has noted, as engineers have tamed the natural world, so their achievements have gone from seeming heroic to appearing merely workaday.[8] The 'heroic age of engineering' has passed into history: no engineer today would have the opportunity to do what Brunel did. He had plenty of vested interests to contend with, including parliamentary committees, avaricious landowners and a board of directors with a ferocious attachment to economy, but he did not have to operate within our overcrowded modern landscape with its inflated property values. Nor was he trapped inside the labyrinth of local plans, planning controls, amenity groups, multi-modal studies, public inquiries, health and safety regulations, environmental impact assessments, conservation legislation and political control over budgets, that contemporary architects and engineers inevitably have to contend with. Some observers have liked to remark on the 'modern' qualities of the great Victorian engineers, but in truth the men who built the railways needed quite different qualities to the primarily political and bureaucratic skills that are the key to success in contemporary engineering projects. Today, managing the politics, the finance and the paperwork is the really difficult part: the technical problems of building the railway or bridge tend (with distinguished exceptions like the Channel Tunnel and the Jubilee Line) to be straightforward by comparison.

No one could be more Victorian, or in many respects less modern, than Brunel. Paddington was the product of a very different culture, harsher and less democratic but more elevated and serious-minded, in which railways were too new and represented too much effort to be taken for granted and were instinctively seen as objects of corporate and national pride. Brunel and Stephenson were popular heroes; the GWR was nicknamed God's Wonderful Railway: would anyone invent such a nickname today?

Our culture has celebrities, not heroes, and very few of the celebrities engage in anything as useful as engineering. It is hard to see how our overcrowded society could allow any one architect or engineer the opportunity to display the synoptic boldness of the early railway builders. But one may at least hope that it is not too late to value our railways as they deserve, for their history and their immense and continuing contribution to society, and to rekindle some of the pride that once found such superb expression in Paddington Station.

7 THE ARCHITECTURE OF THE STATION

Paddington Station is a masterpiece, but it has flaws and is not the masterpiece Brunel intended to build (Figs 7.1 and 7.2). His original vision of 1850, dimly glimpsed in his sketchbooks, with its central entrance from Praed Street, would have expressed its layout and structure much more clearly to the outside, in the way that Lewis Cubitt's contemporary King's Cross does. As it is, the station is eminently conceived as an interior, at that time the largest single roofed space in London after the Crystal Palace, 'in a cutting, and admitting of no exterior, all interior and all roofed in …' With the rejection of his original central concourse scheme Brunel was driven back to a simpler plan, a two-sided station with a broad central trackbed separating the departure side and the arrival side. The shape of the train shed reflected these functional divisions: the narrower flanking sheds housed the arrival and departure platforms

Figure 7.1 Paddington Station in 2003.

1 Brunel's train sheds, 1851–5
2 Platform 1, the original departure platform
3 The clock arch
4 The Eastbourne Terrace buildings, 1851–5
5 Remaining part of the 1880 extension

6 The horse arch
7 Departure side office extension, *c* 1933
8 Departure side approach and the cab roof
9 Surviving area of Paxton roofing
10 Infill building, 1878–80
11 The Lawn

12 The Great Western Royal Hotel
13 Arrival side office, *c* 1933
14 Arrival side roadway
15 The fourth span, 1913–14
16 Lines and platforms beneath London Street
17 The basement of the former Mint stables

18 The Mint stables (at street level)
19 Platform footbridge
20 Metropolitan and Hammersmith & City Line platforms, formerly the Bishop's Road Station

Fig 7.2 Paddington and its environs in 2003.

Former British Rail Road Vehicle Maintenance Depot, now offices

Westway

Grand Junction Canal

Site of Paddington goods station

Cast-iron canal bridge

Suburban, Metropolitan and Hammersmith & City Line platforms, formerly the Bishops Road Station

Westbourne Bridge

Bishop's Road Bridge

Paddington Basin

Former GWR staff hostel

Former GWR parcels offices

The Mint Wing, St Mary's Hospital, formerly the GWR Mint stables

Bishop's Road

Eastbourne Terrace buildings

Paddington Station train sheds

Eastbourne Terrace

Westbourne Terrace

Arrival side offices

Praed Street

Departure side cab roof

Great Western Royal Hotel

Departure side offices

London Street

0 200 400 600 feet

0 100 200 metres

London Underground Circle Line platform, formerly Praed Street Station

and island platforms, while the central span, over 102ft (31m) wide, was given over to a broad trackbed, containing seven lines running right through to the turntables grouped behind the hotel. The original layout and its operation are discussed in Chapter 5.

The train shed

Brunel's great roof remains largely as built (Fig 7.3). When it was new this was the largest train shed in existence, the main roof measuring about 700ft (213m) by 240ft (73m). There are three spans or naves: the central one 102ft 6in. (31.2m) wide, that to the south 68ft (20.7m) wide and that

to the north 70ft (21.3m) wide. To the south it is enclosed by the immensely long façade of the departure platform (platform 1). To the north the shed originally opened into a lower aisle covered with ridge-and-furrow Paxton roofing: the site is now occupied by the fourth span of 1909–14 (Fig 7.4).

The train shed's immense length is modulated by the two transverse axes of transepts. Visually they were probably inspired by Paxton's transept at the Crystal Palace. There has been a persistent story, originating in Isambard Brunel Junior's biography of his father, that the transepts were designed to allow for the installation of traversers across the width of the station. The evidence, as discussed in Chapter 5, is rather more complex, though it seems clear that no

Figure 7.3 Brunel's triple-span train shed looking west from the main passenger concourse.

foundations for traversers were ever built in these positions. There is, however, some evidence that the transepts were designed to allow for the installation of descending platforms, sections of platform measuring 40ft (12.2m) by 25ft (7.6m) designed to be lowered on hydraulic arms. However, it is not at all clear whether these fittings were ever installed or what their purpose would have been. Certainly, the transepts made the design and manufacture of the roof more complicated and added to the cost, so there must have been very positive reasons for making them. They are a vital element in the superb architectural quality of the station, giving it a richness of spatial composition, which, as Henry-Russell Hitchcock remarked, is 'almost unique in Victorian railway stations'.[1]

The rows of columns divide the shed into bays. Counting from the outer end of the station, the rhythm is: 'country' end – 7 bays – transept – 6 bays – transept – 7 bays – 'town' end. Each bay is spanned by three of the arched roof trusses – 63 to each of the three spans, making a total of 189. Every third truss sits directly over a column. The others are carried by deep X-braced girders of wrought and cast iron, about 30ft (9m) long, which run longitudinally from column to column.

The most immediate precedent for the design of Paddington's roof was Newcastle Central Station, designed by the architect John Dobson with input from Robert Stephenson and built in 1847–50, the ironwork by the founders Hawks Crawshay (see Fig 3.4).[2] Newcastle has

Figure 7.4 (left) The fourth span, photographed by Eric de Maré *c* 1960.

Figure 7.5 (above) A view along the arches, showing Matthew Digby Wyatt's applied cast-iron ornament.

three parallel sheds, each about 60ft (18m) wide, with curved roofs sitting on arched trusses, the difference being that they have a segmental arched profile. Here too, every third roof truss sits over a column, the intermediate trusses being carried on the girders. At Newcastle, a difficult site was turned to advantage with the enhanced beauty of its curved plan.

In his sketches for Paddington, Brunel envisaged his roof as having a segmental profile too: such a roof would almost certainly have required tie-rods to restrain the outward thrust exerted by the segmental shape, as at Newcastle. Paddington, however, was built to a revised design whose five-centred arches direct the thrust vertically down onto the columns, and thus did not require ties. The result is more beautiful than Brunel's segmental arches would have been, having more visual 'lift' and not having the interruption of tie-rods. This crucial change to the design probably came from Fox, Henderson & Co, though it is unlike anything they had previously executed.

The arched trusses are of wrought iron, 16in. (406mm) to 18in. (457mm) deep. Most of Fox, Henderson's previous iron

Figure 7.6 Fox, Henderson & Co's design for the main roof, 1851.

roofs were based on triangular trusses, whose individual members were mainly light wrought-iron T-sections, angles and rods. These could be made in rolling mills and then easily transported and assembled on site – the kind of design typified by Charles Fox's platform roofs at Euston (1837–8). The Crystal Palace depended on flat wrought-iron trusses on a standard module of 24ft (7.3m), increased to 72ft (21.9m) for the main nave; it was possible for Fox, Henderson to build it in five months because of the limited number of component types and the modular simplicity of the design.

An arched roof required more elaborate preparation. One possibility was to do it in wood: Paxton's 'great stove' glasshouse at Chatsworth was based on laminated timber arches, as was the transept of the Crystal Palace. Brunel's

largest station roofs, at Bath and Bristol Temple Meads, both had rather unconventional timber trusses and Lewis Cubitt was simultaneously designing King's Cross with laminated timber arches. But a 100ft (30m) span would probably have been impossible in timber.

For whatever reason, Brunel does not seem to have entertained the idea. For an iron-arched roof, the available models were Richard Turner's palm house at Kew (1845–7), Newcastle Central Station (1847–50) and Liverpool Lime Street Station by Turner and Fairbairn (1849–50). At Kew, Turner had started with 12ft (3.7m) rolled I-section ships' beams of wrought iron, forged them together, and worked out how to bend them to the right curvature to make 50ft (15m) arches. Turner developed this technique for his even bolder 153ft (46.6m) roof at Liverpool Lime Street, where he fitted ships' beams, just 9in. (229mm) deep, together to form great segmental arches, trussed with cast-iron struts and wrought-iron rods – Turner had invented the crescent or sickle truss. Joseph Locke and William Fairbairn rightly insisted on tests, for in the first trials the design failed: Turner was pushing at the limits of the material.[3] At Newcastle, Hawks Crawshay had to span 60ft (18.3m) but found it impossible to bend I-section beams at this scale. Instead they built up their arches from riveted lengths of wrought-iron plate, together with L-sections attached to make the top and bottom flanges. They realised that cutting the sections of the web (the upstroke of the 'I') in the correct curved shape from wrought-iron sheets would have been prohibitively expensive: the really ingenious thing was to develop a bevelled rolling mill which could roll the sheet iron out in the right shape.[4]

This seems to be more or less what Fox, Henderson did at Paddington, though it is not clear whether they knew about Hawks Crawshay's work, nor do we know whether they used the same means of rolling the web sections to the correct shape. The contract drawings are very detailed and show exactly how the arches were made: sections of $1/4$in. (6.4mm) wrought-iron sheet were riveted together to make the webs, with L-shaped sections added to make the top and bottom flanges for stiffening.[5] A subtle point is that the flange pieces diminish in thickness, from $3/4$in. (19mm) to $1/2$in. (12.7 mm) to $3/8$in. (9.5mm) as the arches rise. The individual sections were doubtless assembled on site, though it is not exactly clear how: the arches may have been assembled on the ground and hoisted up in one piece, as Fox, Henderson had done at the Crystal Palace.

All the arches have round and star-shaped perforations in their webs – 'stars and planets' – presumably punched out with steam presses. These are certainly decorative, perhaps relating to the Victorian interest in astronomy, but may really have been made to reduce the weight. The arches also carry decorative panels of cast-iron tracery, their design based on gothic tracery, bolted to either side of the webs. These were designed by Matthew Digby Wyatt and do not appear on Brunel's sketches or on Fox, Henderson's contract drawings (Figs 7.5 and 7.6).[6] In 1988 they were found to be causing a serious problem because moisture trapped against the ribs was mixing with sulphur dioxide and other pollutants and eroding the ironwork. The solution adopted in 1988–91 was to fix steel reinforcing plates to the webs and to bolt the decorative cast-iron elements over these. The central nave, from the level of the tracks to the underside of the ribs at their apex, is 54ft 7in. (16.6m) high; the arches, from the springing point of the ribs to their apex, are 33ft (10m) high.[7]

The roof was originally supported on 69 identical cylindrical cast-iron columns, given flared bases and bolted to blocks of York Stone set in heavy concrete foundations. Their appearance is known in detail from drawings from Brunel's office and also from Frith's famous painting. Matthew Digby Wyatt probably designed their curious and very original ornament: the capitals branch out with tall lugs or 'handles'. In 1914 the row of columns on modern platforms 9 and 10 was replaced in riveted steel to support the weight of the new fourth span; the rest of Brunel's columns were replaced in like manner in 1922–3.[8] The new columns are octagonal and have a very different effect. Three original cast-iron columns survive at the 'country' end of the shed: a decorative lobed column on platform 1 and cylindrical columns between platforms 2 and 3, and 6 and 7. The former, a unique survival, was one of those designed to carry the roof over the Lawn area and has certainly been moved.

The columns carry the longitudinal girders, formed mostly of simple L- and X-shaped sections. The intermediate arches come down onto 'skewback' sections, which sit back to back and form the uprights of the girders. The original designs show an oak packing between the skewbacks and the bracket supporting the arch, presumably to allow for movement in the structure, especially during construction. The girders transmit the load of the intermediate arches sideways: as the architect Nicholas Grimshaw has observed, they must be the most heavily stressed elements in the building.[9] The weight of the intermediate arches is expressed visually by simple timber bosses suspended below the girders: they have no real structural purpose.

Paddington's roof is notable in not having purlins – that is, beams which run longitudinally to carry rafters (and thus the roof covering) and provide lateral support to the trusses. This is partly because the arches are so closely spaced. In place of purlins, there are lines of X-shaped braces made of flat wrought-iron straps, at three different levels on either side. These certainly help provide lateral stability but seem to be designed to flex with movements in the structure. The lower part of each roof was covered in corrugated galvanised iron sheeting, a popular new material for industrial buildings. Brunel seems to have had some involvement in the choice of this.[10] The use of a profiled cladding was probably intended to provide stiffening, giving lateral stability in conjunction with the X-shaped braces. Paddington is thus to some extent an early example of a 'stressed skin' design: the cladding material makes a positive contribution to the overall strength of the structure, it does not just sit there.

Figure 7.7 Fox, Henderson & Co, a large-scale detail of the glazed Paxton roofing for Paddington, 1851.

Figure 7.8 The Paxton roofing being cleaned, 27 October 1934.

The upper part of the roofs was covered with Paxton roofing (Figs 7.7 and 7.8), a system of ridge-and-furrow glazing made of plate glass and wood, which Joseph Paxton had devised for the Duke of Devonshire's greenhouses at Chatsworth and subsequently applied on an immense scale to the Crystal Palace. Twenty-six ounce (737gm) plate glass was used, probably from Chance Brothers of Smethwick, the firm who had provided the glass for the Crystal Palace.[11] The roofing has been renewed on many occasions: the board minutes for c 1905–15 contain numerous references to the overhaul of the main roof. It was removed entirely in 1968–9 and replaced with a simpler glazing system. In 1988–92 a major renovation of the roof was completed, involving the complete replacement of all the corrugated and glazed coverings in polycarbonate.

Figure 7.9 One of Brunel's sketch designs for Paddington, showing his first idea for the oriel windows overlooking the transepts, early 1851.

Each span is closed in and glazed at either end. These gable-ends all have elliptical shapes and were given a tracery of bars forming a decorative anthemion pattern on a huge scale, presumably designed by Matthew Digby Wyatt. Most of this had been destroyed in the 20th century but was restored on the basis of the original drawings in the course of works of 1988–95.[12] From the outset Brunel wanted his

shed to have ornament and commissioned Wyatt to supply this, as is shown above. At the time, Wyatt was also working with Henry Cole on the Architectural Courts of the Crystal Palace. Henry-Russell Hitchcock has considered his and Brunel's collaboration, writing that 'there seems to be so coherent an integration between the general handling of the interior space and the detailing of the structural elements that a true collaboration between Brunel and Wyatt on the over-all design must, I think, be assumed'.[13]

The ornament is determinedly eclectic and in marked contrast to the simple 'engineers' classical' of most early railway buildings. The columns have a vaguely Moorish quality, but Professor Hitchcock also related them to the 'overlappings and penetrations one finds in the detail of E B Lamb'. The tracery on the end-glazing, might again be considered Moorish but it might equally be thought of as based on classical 'anthemion' patterns. The panels of cast-iron tracery applied to the main roof trusses are gothic in character, with a certain quality of *art nouveau avant la lettre* about them.

The façade to platform 1 is a symmetrical composition, though it is so long that this can hardly be appreciated. In the centre is the five-bay entrance loggia, marked out by its square-headed openings and by the huge clock projecting above. To the east and west there are impressive set-piece compositions overlooking the two transepts of the train shed, which were illustrated by *The Builder* on 17 June 1854 (Figs 7.9 and 7.10). These have fine oriel windows in cast iron at the upper level, lighting the very long corridor serving the GWR offices. Below these were doorways – that to the east leading to the first-class waiting room, that to the west leading to the royal waiting room. The façade's decoration is more or less unclassifiable. Hitchcock wrote of it: 'if it is not iron but cement, Wyatt must have consciously assimilated the modelling to the character of ironwork'.[14]

In fact, the fat roll-mouldings and the faceted bosses, here and on the façade to Eastbourne Terrace, are all of cast iron: on some of them the scratched foundry numbers in Roman numerals can be made out. Wyatt may simply have halved sections of iron pipe and applied them to the façade as a decoration. The filigree spandrel panels about the arches and the strapwork panels at girder-height are of cast iron too: they look at first as if they might serve some practical ventilation purpose, but they do not.

This strange and original detailing reaches its height in the two fantastic oriel windows looking over the transepts and the lace-like ornament around the edge of the roof here. Hitchcock, discussing Wyatt's work, emphasised its qualities of character and reality and its slight ungainliness, without

Figure 7.10 'Entrance to Offices, Paddington Station'. Matthew Digby Wyatt worked up Brunel's sketch into this design, as built (from *The Builder*, 17 June 1854).

realising that Wyatt's designs were directly based on Brunel's sketches. Their work at Paddington may be seen as a step in the invention of an architectural vocabulary for dealing with structural ironwork. It was also a stage in the development of the most energetic, brutal phase of high Victorianism, with parallels in the work of S S and W M Teulon, E B Lamb, or R L Roumieu and A D Gough.

Owen Jones' bright colour-scheme, commissioned by Brunel and Wyatt, was vetoed by the GWR board. *The Builder*, describing the completed train shed, said 'colour is sparingly introduced – red and grey'.[15] This has been broadly confirmed by paint-scrapes made by the London Region of

English Heritage, which found several 19th-century paint layers but with shades of white, grey, ox-blood red and a kind of salmon-pink predominating. It is possible that what *The Builder* saw in 1854 was incomplete, for an engineer's report of 15 February 1855 said that the painting had 'been designedly postponed until next summer'.[16]

The royal waiting room entrance was redesigned in 1919 by Thomas Tait of Burnet, Tait & Lorne to accommodate the GWR's very fine war memorial. Its centrepiece is the magnificent bronze figure of an infantryman by Charles Sargeant Jagger (Fig 7.11).[17] The doors to either side are 20th century and presumably contemporary with it.

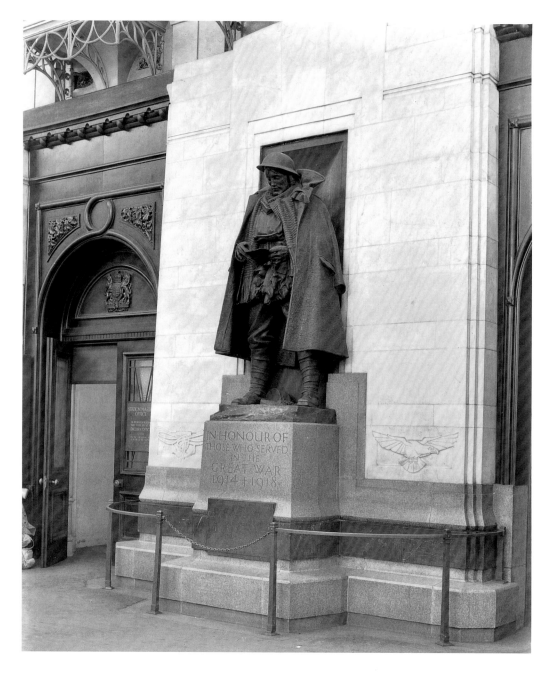

Figure 7.11 The GWR's war memorial, unveiled on Armistice Day 1922.

By 1900, the broad trackbed which originally filled the middle of the shed had been filled in with alternating tracks and platforms. These have been remodelled on several occasions to suit the company's (and later British Rail's) changing requirements. The original platforms had timber surfaces and very probably rested on timber structures. These have been replaced in masonry and concrete, at unknown dates and probably in several campaigns.

Figure 7.12 Paddington Station and Eastbourne Terrace *c* 1910, showing the houses opposite, many of them occupied by the GWR.

Figure 7.13 A design for the railings to Eastbourne Terrace.

Eastbourne Terrace

When Brunel wrote to his friend Matthew Digby Wyatt in January 1851, he described the station as 'in a cutting, and admitting of no exterior, all interior'. There is, of course, some exaggeration here and Brunel was evidently not counting P C Hardwick's intended hotel as part of the station. One sees his point, however: Paddington had no demonstrative façade and entrance to compare with the London & North Western's at Euston or the Great Northern Railway's at King's Cross. The building's one major external façade was that to Eastbourne Terrace (Fig 7.12). When built, this was only two storeys high, immensely long and low, and set about 15ft (4.6m) below street level: it was never very conspicuous. It seems clear that Brunel was basically responsible for its design, not Wyatt. In January 1851 he wrote to Saunders, the company secretary, 'at least you shan't say I don't try to adopt others' suggestions. I have been for some time past trying to see if I could not adopt your plan of putting the offices over the range of buildings of the booking office, and the two new features – an inclined plane parallel with Eastbourne Terrace and a glazed roof covering thereto …'[18]

All of these ideas feature prominently in the buildings as they developed and as they are today. The 'inclined plane' that Brunel referred to has not changed appreciably since its construction in 1851–2. It was originally paved in small granite blocks.[19] Towards Eastbourne Terrace there is a retaining wall that carries heavy cast-iron railings. These are mostly original except for the section beneath the cab roof, which is a rather thin modern replica. Several original designs for the railings survive, including a number of full-size drawings (Fig 7.13).[20]

Brunel, possibly with Wyatt's help, made an attempt to articulate this very long and plain façade in the manner of a terrace. The main building was 32 bays long, with a 20-bay centre and the 6 bays at either end standing very slightly forward. The ground floor was given a decorative arcaded treatment, with round-headed sash windows surrounded by rounded mouldings similar to those inside the station. The upper floors were (and are) plain and stuccoed, with tall sash windows. Network Rail's archives have a large undated elevation for the middle of the Eastbourne Terrace façade, showing a more elaborate decorative scheme with arches, window aedicules on the first floor and a bracketed cornice.[21] This was probably designed by Wyatt but was never executed, doubtless because of the need for haste and economy.

In the centre of this main 32-bay section is the loggia or vestibule which forms the main entrance through to platform 1 – the original departure platform. As built, this had 5 bays to the platform but 7 bays to the outside: the difference was accounted for by quadrant-shaped bays, which were filled in early in the 20th century, one of many ways in which the original design has been eroded. The loggia's ceiling originally had decoration in a late 16th-century 'strapwork' style, with pendants of wood and plaster, but this has been covered over with modern tiling: the original decoration does not seem to survive.[22] Intrusive light fittings and a crude modern statue of Brunel do little to adorn this space: Paddington and Brunel deserve better.

At ground-floor level only, the outer 7 bays at either end of this section are stressed with ornament. Each of these sections is centred on a large doorway, that to the west originally leading to the royal waiting room, that to the east, originally to the first-class waiting room. The royal waiting room survives but the first-class waiting room was destroyed in the Blitz.

When the buildings were new, the range jumped back by about 20ft (6m) to the west of the 32-bay centre and stretched westwards for another 20 very plain bays, with simple arcading framing round-headed windows on the ground floor. This took the building to just beyond the west ('country') end of the train shed. There was a break in the buildings, with a vehicle entrance to the departure platform and milk platform covered by a long run of Paxton roofing. Beyond lay another detached block, 15 bays long, of stock brick with stucco window-surrounds. In 1876 the gap was filled with another 14 bays of plain stock-brick building.[23] There are 6 bays of original Paxton roofing over the roadway here: neatly repaired in 1990, they are the only example of this style of roofing to remain at the station, which used to be largely covered with it (Fig 7.14).[24]

At the east end of the 32-bay centre, as built, there was a short spur of 4 bays and then a long gap to the south end of the hotel, where a high, blank screen wall concealed the train shed roofs: there was another vehicle entrance to the platforms. This gap was filled in stages, as the GWR needed ever more office space. In 1880 the 4-bay spur was doubled to 8 bays and a higher and more ornate 9-bay block added to the east to house a big new shareholders' meeting room and the engineer's department. This 9-bay block was considerably more ornate, being faced in Greenmoor stone with blind arcading at platform level, window aedicules to the first floor and a bracketed cornice interrupted by attic windows.[25] This building was damaged in 1941 by a parachute mine and part of it taken down afterwards.

In the 1930s the offices were extended further to the east as part of the great bout of alterations carried out by the GWR's own architect P A Culverhouse. He built a steel-framed extension, 115ft (35m) long and six storeys high, faced in granite lower down and with Patent Victoria stone above. It is the most explicitly classical of Culverhouse's additions but is quietly detailed, with pedimented window-surrounds on the first floor and a bracketed cornice.[26] This filled about half of the space between the 1880 building and the hotel and Culverhouse built a one-storey building spanning this gap.

Figure 7.14 A design for the canopy over the milk platform approach, Eastbourne Terrace.

A few years later, this one-storey extension was raised to six storeys in a matching style, producing a continuous row of six-storey buildings to Eastbourne Terrace.[27]

In 1879–81 the whole range of buildings was given a second floor of offices, along with a top floor, though much of this seems initially to have been left as empty loft space for future expansion.[28] This huge operation was handled in the same contract as the south-eastwards extension, by Kirk & Randall of Woolwich. It involved major strengthening works to the original 1850s building. Numerous drawings show the steel columns and beams that were inserted for this purpose.[29]

There has always been a glazed roof over the central section of the approach road. Brunel was more explicit in a further letter of January 1851, referring to the long retaining wall between the cab road and Eastbourne Terrace, which '… would carry a glass roof over the centre of the road approach in front of the Booking Offices – it would be anything but ugly towards Eastbourne Terrace, and I should think could not be objected to, it is only 12ft [3.7m] high as on the footpath and all open… by this means we could light the lower storey without skylights…' (Fig 7.15).[30]

Drawings for the original roof are extant.[31] Like the present roof, it rested on piers standing on the retaining wall (Fig 7.16). These were of brick covered in stucco or Roman cement, with banded rustication and simple capitals supporting bold dentilled cornice-blocks. The gaps between the piers were filled with heavily moulded railings and

Figure 7.15 (above) Brunel sketches the design for the cab roof on the Eastbourne Terrace in a letter to Charles Saunders, 23 January 1851.

Figure 7.16 (right) The façade beneath the cab roof, 2001.

full-size drawings also survive for these.[32] The original railings seem to survive to the north-west of the cab roof: the rest look like modern replacements. The original roof had Paxton glazing concealed at the 'town' end by a gable with a clock and the GWR arms. In 1881, when major alterations to the offices were carried out, the roof was extended by a further 8 bays to the east.[33] It was partly destroyed by the 1941 parachute mine, though some of the original ironwork may survive in the present structure. Beneath the cab roof, the entrance to the royal waiting room remains as built: a doorway flanked with Doric pilasters, with a crown supported by the lion and unicorn above, forms the centre of a 7-bay composition.

When the buildings were new, the ground floor was occupied (starting at the east end) by a vehicle entrance to the departure platform, a few small offices, the first-class ladies' waiting room, the first-class waiting room, the main booking office, the central loggia, the second-class waiting room, the royal waiting room, smaller offices and then another vehicle entrance. This was fairly close to Brunel's initial sketch plans made in 1851 (Fig 7.17). Drawings of the general office interiors and waiting rooms are dated August

1851 and on 4 December Brunel laid plans of the board and committee rooms before the directors.[34] Fitting out the interiors apparently took rather longer, for some of the surviving full-size detail drawings are dated 1855.[35] The booking office was the most important and impressive space: it was 9 bays long, with windows to the departure platform and to the approach road, but given the station's low situation these may not have admitted that much light. Perhaps for this reason, the centre of the ceiling rose as a high roof light through the first-floor level, with a glazed gallery looking down into the hall.[36] This handsome feature was lost in 1880 when the extra storeys were added to the building (Fig 7.18). The whole of this side of the range was gutted after bomb damage in 1941.

The western half of the range escaped bomb damage and a little more of the interior survives. Going westwards from the main entrance vestibule, there was a room for train guards and a large cantilevered staircase to the upper floors which survives largely in its original condition. Beyond was the second-class waiting room, later converted into a refreshment room, which was handsomely modernised by P A Culverhouse in 1923 with marble columns with brass

Figure 7.17 'Booking office buildings according to Plan No. 3, 5 January 1851'.

Figure 7.18 The booking office, *c* 1905.

Figure 7.19 The refreshment room as remodelled in 1923.

capitals and mahogany panelling (Fig 7.19). This has been subdivided but it is possible that some of the original decor survives.[37]

From the outset, Brunel intended that the new station should have a separate royal waiting room. A separate entrance under the cab roof leads to a lobby, into a main domed octagonal room, with an oblong room opening off it. Originally, another door led straight through onto platform 1 on an axis with the entrance door, but this was blocked by the GWR's war memorial in 1919 and another entrance made using an archway to one side instead. It would seem that, in 1851 or 1852, M D Wyatt asked the sculptor Alfred Stevens to produce designs for the waiting room, though the board seem to have been completely unaware of this. Stevens produced some sketches for a splendid Italianate design, but in the climate of economic difficulties and with the directors determined not to spend money on frills, this never stood any real chance of being executed (see Fig 3.20). Instead, Messrs Holland, who were decorating the hotel, tendered to decorate and furnish the room for £1,900 and were instructed to proceed on 10 November 1853. They gave the room stencilled decoration in a vaguely

Figure 7.20 The royal waiting room in the late 19th century.

Figure 7.21 The directors' smoking room, *c* 1905.

Florentine manner, part of which has been uncovered. Early in the 20th century, the room was redecorated in a simpler French manner and this scheme largely survives (Fig 7.20). After the Second World War, the waiting room was closed and declined into office use. In 1985 it was refurbished for use by business-class passengers. West of the royal waiting room in the late 19th century there was a bookstall, a servery and then a dining room, modernised by Culverhouse in 1923, now also converted to office space.

On the first and second floors were the GWR's principal offices. Long corridors ran along the train shed side. The first-floor corridor windows were for the most part above the line of the shed roof, but where the two transepts rose up, the oriel windows provided dramatic views over the train shed. As the company grew, more and more office space was needed. The building was extended at either end and in

1878–80 a whole upper storey was added. After 1880, two corridors 850ft (259m) long ran the whole length of the building at first- and second-floor levels.

From the 1850s, the first floor of the centre of the building housed the GWR's senior officers. Over the central vestibule there was the chairman and the secretary; to the west a waiting room and the deputy chairman; to the east, clerks, the committee room, board room and luncheon room. There were offices purposely designed for the solicitor, the general manager, the accountant, the 'superintendent of the line' and for Mr Bertram, Brunel's resident engineer. Numerous drawings survive for fitting out offices with bookshelves and plan-chests as well as standard interior joinery.[38] The work was of good quality but fairly plain: the board room and directors' luncheon room were given a slightly more decorative treatment with dado-height panelling and fine double doors. An inventory of works of art of 1926 gives an idea of the rooms' sober, conservative decoration. The board room was hung with portraits of the great founding figures of the company, including 'the Picture' of Charles Russell and a bust of Brunel, and a great map of the GWR network on the long wall. The adjacent directors' room had a copy of Frith's *Railway Station*, engravings of towns in the GWR's empire and the seals of the 160 or so companies which had been incorporated into it (Fig 7.21).[39] The immensely long corridors were also lined with paintings, watercolours, engineering drawings and models. Sadly, most of the collections seem to have been dispersed after nationalisation in 1947.[40]

The buildings were extended eastwards in 1880 and a new committee room and meeting room with a separate

Figure 7.23 The milk platform at the far end of platform 1, with the outer end of the Eastbourne Terrace buildings. Behind the barred windows was the GWR's printing department, where all their tickets, timetables, regulations and posters were produced.

Figure 7.22 The GWR's plan store. This great collection, including most of the designs for the station reproduced in this book, was housed next to the chief engineer's department in the Eastbourne Terrace buildings. It has since been moved to Swindon.

entrance were provided in the first floor of the 9-bay mansard-roofed block. The general meeting room was a place of corporate pride and commemoration, hung with photographs of the GWR's senior staff: successive general managers, chief goods managers, superintendents of the line, chief engineers, solicitors and the like were commemorated here. The Elkington Shield, the prize awarded for the company's Rifle Corps' annual shooting competition was here, as was the memorial to those of the company's servants who had died in the Boer War.[41] The room was damaged and truncated after the 1941 bombing but some of its decoration survives. The upper floors of this block were given over to the engineer's department: in the loft, beneath the mansard roof, was their plan store (Fig 7.22). This housed the great archive which subsequently moved to Swindon and now forms the greater part of Network Rail's

Western Region drawings collection: it has provided much of the primary information for this book.

After the 1880 expansion, the second floor of the central range was occupied by the committee's secretariat, the general manager's office, the library and the accountants. The top floor was also occupied by the engineers, who had their main 'parliamentary drawing office' here. The western end of the buildings, as we have seen, was originally a detached block, the gap being filled in the 1878–80 bout of works. The ground floor of the far wing housed the deeds office and the GWR's printing press, where timetables, posters, leaflets and tickets were produced by the thousands. Above were the finance and audit departments. The 'infill' building had the milk platform entrance at ground level (Fig 7.23) and above that the registration, telegraph and estates departments. When this immense range of buildings was full, the GWR started letting or buying houses on the other side of the street: by the early 20th century it occupied 21 of them.[42]

Almost the whole range must have been gutted and refitted during the drastic works required to add two extra storeys in 1880. Then a large section including the board room was completely destroyed by the 1941 parachute mine. Since 1947, repeated bouts of renovation have removed almost the last traces of GWR fittings from these buildings. The only interiors which are known to retain historic fittings or a degree of historic character, other than the royal waiting room, are the cantilevered staircase, the shareholders' meeting room on the first floor of the 1880 extension and, possibly, Culverhouse's 1923 refreshment room, opening off platform 1.

The arrival side and the fourth span

When Brunel built Paddington, the northern side of the train shed was formed by an aisle with a flat-span roof covered with Paxton glazing, sheltering the arrival platform. An entrance ramp ran down from Conduit (now Praed) Street in more or less the same position as it does now. North of the station ran London Street: this divided, one branch leading down a ramp and beneath the Bishop's Road Bridge into the goods station, the other leading onto the bridge itself. On the other (north) side of London Street was the GWR's coal depot, with tracks leading from the goods station. Immediately to the north of this was the Grand Junction Canal and Paddington Basin. All of this is clear from early plans of the station but few early views of the area have been found. In 1863 the Bishop's Road Station was built for the Metropolitan Railway, involving a change to the line of London Street, and in 1878–82 there were relatively minor alterations: the addition of more waiting rooms and a new milk platform abutting the north-western corner of the station.

The whole of the arrival side was reconstructed in the first major alteration to Brunel's station, between 1908 and 1914. The work was complex but the station had to remain fully operational, so it was undertaken in several phases, starting with the reconstruction of several of the bridges over the main lines. In 1908–9 London Street and the old high-level coal yard were closed and excavated right down to platform level and a massive new concrete retaining wall towards the Hammersmith & City Line tunnel built, 10ft (3m) thick, 15ft (4.5m) high and 550ft (168m) long. The company had long felt the shortage of storage space and between lines 10 and 11 the excavation was taken down deeper and a large basement created, spanned with rolled-steel joists and brick jack-arches. This provided storerooms for lost property, the newspaper business, and linen and clothing for the station staff. It probably also housed the stores for the hotels, refreshment rooms, restaurant cars and steamboat catering department, distributing everything from

groceries to linen and crockery around the company's empire. This long sequence of basement rooms and corridors, lined with glazed tiles, still exists.

Two trackbeds housing four lines (numbers 9–12) were built. The northernmost one (12) was planned for deliveries of milk, fresh fish and the like, with a ramp descending from London Street for the milk floats surfaced with a heavy textured 'hit and miss' paving to provide a good grip for the horses. The outer part of platform 12 was 3ft (0.9m) high and could be used for passengers, while the inner part was made 3ft 9in. (1.1m) high so the milk cans could be rolled out on trucks. Provision of the new platforms entailed moving the steel-framed bridge that brought the taxi approach into the station. At the same time, the south end of the Mint stables was demolished, its site dug out to platform level and a great new basement created. This opened off platform 12 as the new up parcels office and was constructed in Hennebique ferroconcrete, with the board-marking and chamfered beams characteristic of that technique.[43] A massive steel structure, 400ft (122m) long and up to 80ft (24m) wide, rose over the new platforms 11 and 12, to carry the re-routed London Street: the platforms beneath are dark and cavernous. This structure forms the northern flank of the fourth span itself, above platforms 9 and 10. Here, the riveted steel columns and the longitudinal girders have to carry the weight of the fourth span as well as London Street, so the engineering is on a massive scale: the columns, some of them weighing 18 tons (18.3 tonnes), sit on steel mesh 'grillage' foundations 16ft (4.9m) square to spread the load. The girders have X-bracing mirroring that on the Brunel shed but greatly thickened up.

The new roof went up in 1913–14, designed by the GWR's engineer W Armstrong, the steelwork made by the Horseley Bridge & Engineering Company, and constructed by Messrs Holliday & Greenwood (see Fig 7.4).[44] The site tapered at the east end, so the new span could not be quite uniform in shape (Fig 7.24). The roof has 62 ribs, which line up with those of the Brunel roof but are made of steel plate girder instead of wrought iron, the webs of which taper from 2ft (610mm) depth at the springing point to 1ft 10in. (559mm) at the crown of the arches. Armstrong gave them the same decorative perforations of 'stars and planets' and applied cast-iron tracery as the Brunel spans. Wrought iron rings, 3in. (76mm) in diameter, were fixed to the bottom flange of each rib, from which to hang scaffolding for painting and maintenance. The roof was covered in the same style as the Brunel roofs, the lower parts covered with corrugated sheeting, while the upper part was glazed with 'Rendle's

Figure 7.24 The design for the tapering south-east end of the fourth span, 1914.

patent glazing', not far in appearance from the glazing of the 1850s. The north flank of the new span to London Street is faced with panels of sheet steel, the riveting of which makes a rhythmic pattern, capped by a dramatically projecting cast-iron cornice and gutter.

At the time of writing, the fourth span is largely concealed by internal scaffolding and proposals have been brought forward for its demolition and replacement with a concrete structure supporting a major commercial office development, designed by Nicholas Grimshaw & Partners. Finally, two features at the 'town' end of platforms 11 and 12 deserve notice: two splendid sets of Edwardian hydraulic buffers made by Ransomes & Rapier of Ipswich, dated 1912, remain *in situ*. The guard railing around them is formed of reused pieces of bull-nose rail and broad-gauge rail.[45] Both buffers and railings are precious survivals.

The Lawn

This part of Paddington is said to derive its name from having been the stationmaster's garden in the period of the temporary station at the Bishop's Road Bridge between 1837 and 1850. This area was lost when Brunel built the present terminus between his great train shed and the back of the Great Western Royal Hotel. Brunel excavated it out and laid tracks up to the back of the hotel. A simple ridge-and-furrow Paxton roof was built above and iron galleries led from the back of the hotel to the departure and arrival platforms to north and south.

By 1900 the tracks had been curtailed. The area was levelled up and paved as a vehicle entrance (Fig 7.25). It remained in this state until 1930–34, when it was entirely reconstructed by P A Culverhouse. He lined the area with

Figure 7.25 The Lawn in 1923 with its original Paxton roofing, but with the tracks curtailed as a vehicle delivery area.

Figure 7.26 The Lawn, showing P A Culverhouse's simple classical architecture, adapted to house the Heathrow Express check-in facilities.

the simple classical façades of Patent Victoria stone which survive today. A new steel and glass roof was built, with three main spans carried on eight columns. Around the perimeter of the area, was a lower ceiling, with flat decorative rooflights originally glazed in white and amber diffusing glass.[46] The interiors behind Culverhouse's simple façades have been stripped out and renewed on several occasions.

The whole of the Lawn area was rebuilt between 1995 and 1998, to designs by Nicholas Grimshaw & Partners. In the process a new steel and glass roof was installed at a much higher level, Culverhouse's simple patent stone façades were cleaned and several later accretions removed. This has re-emphasised the Lawn's quality and function as a concourse or entrance to the station. Several new facilities have been provided, including a separate ticket sales area for the Heathrow Express service (Fig 7.26).

Arrival side offices

This handsome block in P A Culverhouse's own art deco style, of five storeys over a platform-level ground floor, was built in 1932–3 on the site of the 1851–4 parcels office. The building has a steel frame and concrete floors, and is distinguished by the tiers of very shallow oriel windows, a motif which Culverhouse used elsewhere on the GWR

Figure 7.27 The Great Western Royal Hotel, a late 19th-century view.

estate.[47] The words 'G.W.R. PADDINGTON' high up on the attic storey, were originally lit by shell-shaped uplighters. At platform level the block housed the station buffet, at mezzanine level there was the GWR's advertising and publicity department, on the first and second floors the superintendent of the London Division, and on the upper floors the chief goods manager's department (see Fig 4.18).[48]

The Great Western Royal Hotel

The Great Western Royal Hotel at Paddington has considerable claims to historic importance in its own right. It was the first hotel in London to be a major and deliberate architectural statement and at its opening was hailed as the 'largest and most sumptuous hotel in England'. It marked a

Figure 7.28 The pediment sculpture, *Commerce Attended by Plenty and the Four Continents*, John Thomas, 1852.

Figure 7.29 Philip Charles Hardwick's design for the hotel's coffee room, 1851, showing it largely as built.

crucial development in scale and opulence for hotel architecture.[49] It was also the first major example in Britain of what would become known as the 'Second Empire' style (Fig 7.27; see *also* Fig 3.10).

Hardwick's design is a notably early exercise in the kind of French-influenced building which became popular in the 1860s and 1870s. Its determining features, the tall pilaster-bands cum quoins, the bracketed cornices, heavy window aedicules, tall mansard roofs, corner towers with prominent pavilion roofs and chimneys, are part of the vocabulary of the Second Empire style. Henry-Russell Hitchcock pointed out that Hardwick was actually anticipating Second Empire here.[50] This kind of commercial architecture became so widespread that the building's impact is today rather blunted.

Hardwick's watercolour views of the main elevation and the grand coffee room were exhibited at the Royal Academy in 1851.[51] Despite the GWR's generally very cheese-paring approach to ornament and furnishings, Hardwick was given a degree of leeway. The sculptor John Thomas, who had previously produced relief sculptures for Hardwick's 'great hall' at Euston, made the fine pediment sculpture with its allegorical figures of Commerce attended by Plenty and the Four Continents, in a rather more chaste style than the rest of the façade would suggest (Fig 7.28).[52] The façade was originally a good deal more ornate, with caryatids and atlantes and stucco garlands, also by Thomas, decorating the centre and four copies of the Warwick vase on the cornice above.

The Illustrated London News published a long description of the new establishment on 18 December 1852.[53] It had 112 suites of bedroom and dressing room and 15 private sitting rooms, most of them part of suites. At one end of the ground floor was a suite of club-rooms with a separate entrance. The largest and grandest interior was the coffee room, which set a new standard in hotel and restaurant design. It rose through two storeys, measuring 59ft (18m) by 30ft (9.1m), and 27ft (8.2m) high, and was decorated in a lavish Louis XIV style with marbled columns and caryatids supporting the ceiling (Fig 7.29).[54] Most of the hotel's decorations and furniture were provided by Messrs Holland but several suites were decorated by one Herr Remon.

The Great Western Royal Hotel was the first really grand, monumental hotel in Britain. It set a new standard in size, amenities and comfort; it was also influential in introducing a new kind of commercial opulence into Victorian architecture. Second Empire fast became the most popular style for hotel buildings in Britain, the high mansard and pavilion roofs making for a distinctive skyline while housing the servants' accommodation. The Grosvenor Hotel at Victoria Station by James Knowles (1860), the Queen's Hotel at Birmingham New Street Station by Livock (1864, demolished), the Grand Hotel at Scarborough by Cuthbert Brodrick (1863–7) and the Hotel Cecil in London by Perry & Reed (1885–97, demolished) will serve as examples.

In 1931 the hotel was much remodelled by P A Culverhouse, the GWR's architect. The exterior was greatly simplified, with the atlantes and caryatids and much of the ornament removed from the middle, as well as the fine iron and glass canopy. The lower storeys were refaced with a granite plinth and the Patent Victoria stone which Culverhouse used elsewhere in the station. At the back, towards the station, a new entrance to the Lawn area was made and a major extension to the hotel built. The whole of the ground floor was remodelled and, sadly, Hardwick's great coffee room was subdivided. In 2001 the hotel was fully refurbished and reopened as the Hilton Paddington Hotel.

Related buildings and structures

As the Great Western Railway grew and became increasingly complex, the station needed more and more space for its many supporting operations. Several of these related buildings survive but many, particularly those of the goods and locomotive departments, do not. The passenger station never operated in isolation and to leave these other buildings out of the account would give a very lopsided picture of it. The summary account of them given below is not exhaustive and the subject would bear a good deal more research.

Metropolitan and Hammersmith & City Line platforms – the former Bishop's Road Station

The original Bishop's Road Station was built in 1863 as the western terminus of the Metropolitan Railway.[55] It was approached from London Street and the Bishop's Road, with modest iron and timber buildings at platform level. The station was modified to allow the great replanning of the terminus to go ahead in 1906–14 (Fig 7.30). It was remodelled more fully in c 1936, when it lost its separate entrance and was absorbed into the terminus as the suburban platforms. It is today platforms 13–16 of the main station, including the Metropolitan and Hammersmith & City Line platforms.

Figure 7.30 The entrance building of the old Bishop's Road Station, with the arrival side signal box and the Bishop's Road Bridge to the left and the goods depot offices in the background, c 1927.

Circle Line platforms – the former Praed Street Station

Praed Street Station (Fig 7.31; see also Fig 4.6), just over the road from the Great Western Royal Hotel, was built c 1865 as part of the extension of the Metropolitan Railway southwards from Paddington to Kensington. Designed by Sir John Fowler or his office in a similar style to other Metropolitan Railway stations (for example the Metropolitan Line platforms at Farringdon and Baker Street), it was made in a cutting with massive heavily buttressed retaining walls of yellow brick, using very simple classical ornament. The station

retains its original roof, or at any rate the original frame, carried on handsome wrought-iron arches with an elliptical profile, not dissimilar to those in the main Paddington train shed. The façade to Praed Street is of c 1925, probably by C W Clark, architect to the Metropolitan Railway from 1921. It is neoclassical, faced in white faience, and very similar to his station façades at Farringdon (1921) and Great Portland Street (1930). The station no longer has a clear separate identity, being simply the Circle Line platforms at Paddington.

Figure 7.31 A late 19th-century view of Praed Street Station on the Metropolitan Railway, now the Circle Line platforms.

The Bakerloo Line platforms

The Bakerloo Line platforms, Paddington's only true underground station, were opened with the Bakerloo extension line from Edgware Road to Queen's Park on 1 December 1913. They were built as part of the fourth span works, the concourse and the escalators being directly beneath the train tracks. The most striking feature of the addition was the absence of lifts and the use instead of 'moving staircases or "escalators", the largest that have yet been constructed'. The original escalators have, of course, been replaced with new ones of similar dimensions, but the

bold classical ornament on the archway above, and the doorways to the platforms, remain.[56]

Signal boxes

Information on the station's signal boxes has been very hard to come by: no drawings for them have been found, nor have any references to their construction. The first edition Ordnance Survey 25in. map of 1869, however, does mark them. A substantial signal box is marked on the south (departure) side of the tracks, just west of the Westbourne Bridge, opposite the carriage department's workshops. A much smaller signal box is marked just west of the Bishop's Road Bridge towards the north side of the tracks: from its position, this may have regulated Metropolitan Railway traffic into the Bishop's Road Station, rather than main-line traffic. By the third edition of the map (1914–16), a larger signal box had been established on the north side of the tracks, between the Bishop's Road Bridge and the Bishop's Road Station, probably as part of the 1906–14 redevelopment, and a couple of photographs show this (see Fig 7.30). The 1930–35 works seem to have provided two new boxes, both in solid brick, which still survive. The departure side box seems to have been a one-storey wing of the parcels depot building on Bishop's Road of 1932–3. The arrival side box was presumably the free-standing structure which remains on the north side of the tracks, just west of the Bishop's Road Bridge.

Paddington goods station

The history of Paddington's goods station and the host of related industrial buildings which once opened off the tracks is at least as complex as that of the passenger station. Hardly a trace now remains of this great group of buildings and only a short account of them is given here. When Brunel started planning for Paddington in 1836, his first 'concourse' design included a goods depot on more or less its eventual site, with a new basin opening off the Grand Junction Canal (see Fig 2.6).[57] The prospects for trans-shipping goods from railway to canal and vice versa were presumably a significant inducement for the GWR to choose Paddington as a site. In the event, as we have seen, these early plans were shelved and for the first twenty years the GWR made do with a timber-framed and timber-clad goods depot on the site of the present passenger station: it was 330ft (100m) long by

120ft (36m) wide, with three parallel roofs.[58]

This was not an ambitious start, but the GWR seems to have been oddly slow to develop its goods and parcels business. In the early years the service was run by carriers, who paid the company 15s (75p) per ton for general goods and 10s (50p) per head for cattle and horses. When the line opened to Bristol, the company put on just two goods trains each way per day: in 1842, the £26,845 in goods receipts represented just 3 per cent of the company's revenue. The company was, however, already beginning to think in terms of the trade in coal and building materials: to develop the former, they encouraged their engineer Daniel Gooch to form a partnership with a Welsh coal company.

By 1850 the GWR's goods service was carrying over 350,000 tons of merchandise a year, producing £202,978, or 24 per cent of turnover. More accommodation was needed and Brunel reserved a large area north-west of the Bishop's Road Bridge, between the main lines and the canal (Fig 7.32). It was important to link the railway with the canal, but the change in level (the canal side is 6m above the line of the tracks) presented a difficulty. Brunel planned a 'high-level

yard' alongside the canal: a viaduct led up to this from the tracks. This was primarily used for the company's coal trade, the idea being to get this heavy bulk material up to street level, for easy loading onto wagons. After the GWR's lines reached Wales their coal business grew steadily and by 1846 they were transporting 4,350 tons (4,420 tonnes) a month to London. In 1856, shortly after the new high-level yard was fitted out, the GWR signed an agreement with the Ruabon Coal Company whose takeover of the South Wales Railway in 1861 increased the trade further (Fig 7.33). By 1900 the company was transporting over 1,000,000 tons of coal a year to London. The coal yard was complicated to manage. A difficult junction between the viaduct and the high-level yard tracks was too sharp to be turned by a train, which meant that every wagon had to be uncoupled and turned individually on a turntable, a rather labour-intensive process.

The viaduct to the high-level yard divided the goods depot site in two and Brunel built the larger, northern part of it first. A sketch of January 1851 represents his first thoughts for this area: a north–south section through the buildings, it shows how he planned to cope with the change

Figure 7.32 General plan of the goods station, *c* 1856.

Figure 7.33 An office *c* 1870, probably sited in the high-level goods yard for the Ruabon Coal Company. It is a measure of the high standards of Victorian draughtsmanship that so much attention could be lavished on this tiny building, hardly larger than a garden shed.

Figure 7.34 A drawing for the first phase of the goods station, showing the granary in section and elevation.

Figure 7.35 The goods depot, *c* 1910.

in level.[59] Brunel told the GWR board that the plans for the goods depot were complete on 12 June 1851 and in July a tender of £23,432 was accepted from Messrs Sherwood.[60]

The higher, northern side of this complex was formed by a very large granary (Fig 7.34), a warehouse four storeys high and 30 bays long. Its lower floor opened directly onto the goods shed at track level. The next floor up opened northwards onto a large yard, entered from the Harrow Road. Detailed drawings in Network Rail's archives show the steel columns and roof trusses for this building. To the south of this a broad area of track and platforms was covered with two 32ft (9.8m) spans of iron and glass roofing, carried on cross-braced trusses with a segmental profile. To the south this was flanked by a narrower roof over a roadway, and beyond that another broad segmental-profile roof.[61] Then came the viaduct rising to the high-level yard, which was carried on cast-iron columns: in 1906, for reasons which are

not apparent, it was given a segmental-profiled roof[62] and then partly rebuilt in 1909 (Fig 7.35).[63]

This first stage of the goods station was complete by the end of 1852, allowing the old timber shed site to be demolished, clearing the way for the second phase of the new passenger station. In March 1853 Brunel presented the board with outline plans for the rest of the goods station south of the viaduct, at an estimated cost of £50,000.[64] This was fitted into a confined area between the viaduct and the main tracks. At the east end Brunel planned a warehouse, five storeys high with an irregular four-sided shape. Running westwards from this were four trackbeds under a long three-span roof, the central span 76ft (23.2m) wide with segmental tied trusses covered in galvanised iron, flanked by flat spans 41ft (12.5m) wide covered in Paxton roofing. Flanking this to the south was an approach road covered with a 36ft (11m) lean-to roof with raked bowstring trusses,

Figure 7.36 The goods depot, *c* 1926. The viaduct to the high-level yard has just been demolished, but its columns are still in place.

again covered in galvanised iron. Detailed drawings for these buildings are dated June 1854 and August 1855.[65] The new goods buildings were equipped with hydraulic equipment made by Sir William Armstrong & Company at Elswick on the Tyne.[66]

The first goods offices were housed partly in a simple two-storey building at the 'town' (east) end of the goods yard and partly within the northern goods shed, over the tracks.[67] In the great Edwardian rebuilding a huge new range of goods offices was built facing directly onto the Bishop's Road Bridge. Four storeys high and 22 bays long, these were completed in 1906 (*see* Fig 7.30).[68] The goods department had filled the whole available site at Paddington, but the GWR's goods services continued to develop. They expanded eastwards over the Metropolitan Railway (now the northern part of the Circle Line) and involved the opening of new depots at Smithfield Market (1869), Poplar Dock (1878),

the Victoria and Albert Docks (1900) and in South Lambeth (1913). To the west, a large new depot was constructed at Westbourne Park (1908). By the 1920s the Paddington depot was, nevertheless, still handling 500,000 tons of general merchandise a year and had 900 road vehicles passing through it every working day.[69] Significant alterations and renovation had been carried out at the time of the 1908–14 works, but in 1925 the company decided to rebuild the goods station completely.[70]

The Victorian buildings were cleared in stages (Fig 7.36; *see also* Fig 4.13), a process recorded by the GWR's photographers: only the long warehouse on the north side remained. The old high-level yard was closed and cleared, the cast-iron viaduct leading to it demolished (Fig 7.37). Huge reinforced concrete cellars were built beneath the eastern part of the site by the Indented Bar & Concrete Engineering Company, then six double-rail bays were laid out, served by

Figure 7.37 The former high-level goods yard with its tracks taken up and the goods offices in the distance.

Figure 7.38 The new goods depot in use, 1927.

six platforms varying in width from 21ft (6.4m) to 39ft (11.9m). An immense, uniform roof of seven steel-framed spans was built by the Cleveland Bridge & Engineering Company, with enough clearance to allow for the installation of overhead electric lines in the future.[71] The new shed was designed to house up to 330 wagons (Fig 7.38). The old hydraulic equipment was replaced by new electric plant, a fleet of electric trucks was bought and, in an echo of Brunel's ideas, movable bridges were installed to span the rail-bays, allowing greater ease of movement across the width of the depot.[72]

The goods station remained busy into the 1950s. Thereafter, like all the other London goods stations, and like London Docks, it fell victim to changing patterns of trade. The use of coal fell dramatically with the Clean Air Acts, while deliveries of milk and foodstuffs had overwhelmingly been transferred to road traffic. The goods depot was closed, cleared and sold in fairly short order during the late 1970s. The last major section to go was the 1906 goods offices, demolished in 1986. The demolition contractors, Higgs & Hill, generously arranged for the main entrance doors and doorcase, the mosaic floor from the entrance hall and the giant wooden letters which spelt the words 'Great Western Railway Goods Station' and 'Great Western Railway Goods Office' on the sides of the building, to be given to the Great Western Trust at Didcot.[73] As for the site, the Westway flyover was built over part of it in c 1967. At the time of writing, the remainder has just been developed with large-scale apartment blocks.

The locomotive department

The GWR's first engine sheds tended to be makeshift timber affairs, but at Paddington Daniel Gooch designed an interesting roundhouse shed, probably the first of this pattern to be built, in 1837–8. The main octagonal structure was 130ft (39m) in diameter and straight-sided sheds projected from this to the east and west, making an overall composition 360ft (110m) long. Inside the roundhouse, a turntable gave access to eight radial roads. The whole was timber-framed and timber-clad and only one historic view of it is known (see Fig 2.11). As the traffic increased more space was needed and another engine house was built further to the west in 1848.

Brunel needed the site of Gooch's roundhouse for the new goods station and as part of the great redevelopment of 1851–5 he moved the whole locomotive department

about a mile to the west, to Westbourne Park (Fig 7.39). An immense brick engine shed was built there, 71ft (21.6m) wide and 663ft (202m) long (for comparison, Winchester Cathedral, the longest medieval church in Europe, is 556ft (169m) long). It housed four engine tracks spanned with a simple roof of tied wrought-iron trusses and was built by Messrs Locke & Nesham for what seems the comparatively small sum of £14,130: the contract was signed in July 1852.[74] Parallel to this, just to the north, Brunel planned another range to house offices and workshops. A one-storey range, eleven bays long, housed shops for the smiths, fitters, coppersmiths and a carpenter. At either end were two-storey wings, one with a storeroom below and sleeping quarters for the enginemen above, the other with an office below and a room for Daniel Gooch above (Fig 7.40).[75]

In 1861 a new shed was needed for narrow-gauge engines. This was just to the west of the big broad-gauge shed, measuring about 135ft (41.1m) by 45ft (13.7m) and housing three tracks. It was doubled in size to 135ft (41.1m) by 90ft (27.4m) to accommodate another three tracks in 1873.[76] As the broad gauge lost ground, so the bigger shed was gradually converted to the mixed gauge. Nevertheless, the two buildings continued to be known as the broad-gauge and narrow-gauge sheds up to their demolition c 1906.

On the opposite, south side, of the main line a broad area was laid out as a mileage yard, with another group of workshops entered from Westbourne Park Road. A coal stage with cranes surmounted by a clock tower straddled the Green Lane bridge, a site later given over to relief lines for Westbourne Park Station. Finally, a 42ft (12.8m) turntable

Figure 7.39 The locomotive department at Westbourne Park in the late 19th century.

133

Figure 7.40 Offices and workshops for the engine department, *c* 1853: workshops for smiths and carpenters in the middle; a dormitory and dayroom for the enginemen to the left; and an office for Daniel Gooch to the right, first floor.

stood to the west of the broad-gauge shed, believed to be the only one on the GWR at the time that was worked by steam: a small boiler house adjoining it provided the power.[77]

More or less the whole of this complex seems to have been cleared in *c* 1906, when an even larger new group of buildings was completed further out at Old Oak Common. The immense new engine shed, designed by the locomotive superintendent G J Churchward, was built by the Walkerdine Company of Derby. Measuring 444ft (135.3m) by 360ft (109.7m) and built of steel framing faced in red brick, this was the largest engine shed on the GWR network, its interior an awesome sight. It was divided in four, each

quarter containing a 65ft (19.8m) turntable giving access to 28 radial roads, and there was room for 56 tender and 56 tank engines (Fig 7.41). Close by was the lifting and repair shop, 195ft (59.4m) by 101ft (30.8m), with twelve 59ft (18m)-long inspection pits along one side. An overhead crane, with a span of 49ft (14.9m) and a capacity of 30 tons (30.5 tonnes), could run the length of the shop. The subsidiary buildings were on a comparably grand scale: the stores and offices 117ft (35.7m) by 42ft (12.8m), the smiths' shop 74ft (22.6m) by 47ft (14.3m), the carpenters' and coppersmiths' shops both 61ft (18.6m) by 23ft (7m). Around these main buildings were disposed offices, the coal stage,

Figure 7.41 A photograph of the engine house at Old Oak Common, probably taken soon after its completion in 1906.

coal tips and the water tank.[78] Old Oak Common remains in use and parts of the GWR buildings are still standing and plainly visible from passing trains.

Carriage sheds, wagon sheds and stores

From an early stage, the GWR ran into difficulties caused by shortage of space and by the narrow 'throat' of their trackbed as it ran into the terminus. For the carriage department, Brunel planned a long series of buildings running along the south side of the tracks. Like the goods

Figure 7.42 An end elevation for the new carriage sheds, *c* 1855.

station and the locomotive department, their appearance could be reconstructed in detail from the sets of contract drawings in Network Rail's archives. From the Bishop's Road Bridge to the Westbourne Bridge was a continuous series of buildings, a short range of offices and stores followed (going west) by sets of carriage sheds one and two storeys high and with an overall length of around 250ft (76m) (Fig 7.42).[79] Just beyond the Westbourne Bridge was an irregularly shaped building housing the department's stores and offices.[80] Beyond this was a large group of workshops, including an L-shaped group of smiths' shops, one wing of which was 107ft (32.6m) long and the other about 120ft (36.6m).[81] Further west was a huge wagon shop, 275ft (83.8m) long and 94ft (28.7m) wide, for which another set of contract drawings survive.[82] All of these buildings seem to have been swept away after 1900 to make room for an extended milk platform between the Bishop's Road Bridge and the Westbourne Bridge; the area was again redeveloped in the 1930s as the main down parcels depot.

Staff hostel

From the outset, the GWR found that in order to run daily train services, they had to be able to accommodate their train crews overnight at their principal stations. In c 1852 a staff hostel was built just outside the 'country' end of the new Paddington train shed. Fitted in between the tracks, it was a long rectangular building in a simple 'engineers classical' style, ten bays long and two storeys high.[83] A couple of plans and historic photographs record its appearance and it is just visible in the background of Frith's painting *The Railway Station*. It was demolished in c 1906 to make way for the major redevelopment of the station.

Bridges over the main line

When the GWR widened and replanned their main lines between 1903 and 1911, they were obliged to rebuild ten bridges. Originally built as brick viaducts, these were all

replaced with long-span steel girders, designed by the GWR's own engineering department. The first four of these, counting from the station, are briefly considered here.

Bishop's Road Bridge (Figs 7.43 and 7.44)

When the GWR obtained the Act of Parliament for its extension to Paddington in July 1837, one of the major conditions attached to it related to the construction of a number of bridges. The easternmost of these carried a new road, the Bishop's Road, from Westbourne Place to join the Harrow Road. This involved spanning the shallow valley in which Brunel was putting the tracks and station with a long brick viaduct and the contract for this was let in 1837 to Messrs B and N Sherwood. The new road also had to cross the arm of the Grand Junction Canal which led to Paddington Basin. This represented both a problem and an opportunity for the GWR. The benefits of having their terminus next to the canal were clear enough and for Brunel it provided a ready means of bringing materials to this end of the line. At the same time it presented him with a problem of levels. The new bridge had to clear the canal, giving the Grand Junction Canal Company a minimum clearance above the water and towpath, before dropping down sharply to meet the Harrow Road. Brunel's letter-books show how he tackled the problem. On 18 May 1838 he wrote to R C Sale at the canal company's office, as follows (displaying his characteristic economy with punctuation):

My dear Sir,

I forward you an elevation of the Bridge we propose to erect over the basin at Paddington in lieu of the present foot bridge by the provision of our Act it is to be a carriage road bridge – 40 feet [12.2m] wide and to communicate with the Harrow road which limits out height. The bridge will therefore be of Cast Iron.

I have made the principal opening as large as I possibly could consistent with safety and have provided a second Arch which is also large enough for barges to pass freely. And the whole is as wide as the present basin.

I propose to get in the foundations during the stoppage of your canal next month and shall therefore feel obliged by an early reply. If Mr Holland wishes to see me on the subject, I shall be happy to meet him, but I must ask him to call on me, as I am still somewhat of an invalid. I am dear Sir,

Yours very truly, I. K. Brunel[84]

Figure 7.43 Brunel designed this cast-iron bridge, probably the first he had built, in 1838 to carry the Bishop's Road over the Grand Junction Canal. Only recently discovered, it has been dismantled to make way for a new bridge and its reconstruction is planned.

Sale clearly discussed the design with Mr Holland, who seems to have been the canal company's engineer, and who objected. Their reply has not been found, but on 25 May Brunel wrote to Sale again:

My Dear Sir,

I think Mr Holland does not bear in mind that the basin and Towing path at the point of crossing is upwards of 60ft [18.3m] with the head way we have it would be impossible to build such in one opening, perhaps a larger opening than the one I have proposed might be made although really I should not like to try it, but there would not be room to navigate the small arch – by the present proportion.

The large opening is very ample probably the largest on your Canal while the side arch is still quite large enough for all barges – moving about without a tow rope.

With respect to the loss of water, that difficulty also may be removed as it is proposed to drive a stank or dam across the basin and thus save the water south of it, and to drain only that part of it between the stank and the present bridge.

I trust these explanations will be quite satisfactory and that so far as the sanction of your company is necessary we may proceed. A plan shall be sent.
I am my dear Sir,
Yours very truly, I.K. Brunel[85]

On 30 May the directors of the Grand Junction Canal Company considered the design. They do not seem to have viewed it with much enthusiasm:

Mr Bouverie reported that Mr Holland had had an interview with the Engineer of the Great Western Railway, for the purpose of considering whether they could devise any less objectionable plan for making a Bridge over the canal at Paddington in lieu of the wooden footbridge than that of which he had sent a plan, but they agreeing that it would not be safe to carry one flat arch over the whole space,

Resolved – that the plan as proposed be sanctioned.[86]

For all the difficulties of the job, Brunel had produced a handsome tripartite design, with brick piers, a Portland stone cornice and a fine cast-iron railing. The middle and northern spans had very shallow segmental arches, formed of cast-iron beams or girders carrying cast-iron plates, while the

Figure 7.44 The Bishop's Road Bridge.

southern span could be a simple brick arch, but with a facing to match the northern span.

It is not clear if Brunel got the foundations in during the summer of 1838, as he wished, but the main contract for the canal bridge was let to Messrs Sherwood on 27 October 1838. The total price has not been found, but Brunel recorded the tender prices in one of his notebooks and it shows that the Sherwoods offered to provide the cast iron for 'ribs, bedplates, bridging pieces, covering plates, railings...' at £15 12s 6d (£15.63) per ton.[87]

Brunel had clearly been obliged to use cast iron here by the tight headroom involved: a brick arch would have added too much height to his bridge, making for a steeper gradient down to the Harrow Road. However, he was cautious about using cast iron, for we have very interesting evidence of how he load-tested the beams from one of his volumes of 'Facts', a series of notebooks in which he entered an amazing miscellany of research notes and information of all kinds.[88]

Four pages record the results of load-tests, dated December 1838 and carried out by one J Colthurst (Fig 7.45).[89] The Sherwoods had subcontracted the manufacture of the beams to Messrs Gordon of Deptford. Two sets of eleven arched beams were tested. The first set were 35ft (10.7m) long, for the main span. These were tested to 20, 25 and 30 tons, and the deflection measured in each case. At 30 tons, his beams deflected by ⁵⁄₈ in. (16mm) to ⁸⁄₈ in. (25mm), but beam number nine broke at 28 tons. Brunel drew it in cross-section, noting that 'the parts marked with dots composed of nothing but Slag, refuse cinder & Sand'. The smaller girders, for the 16ft (4.9m) arch, were also tested to

30 tons: these deflected by around ³⁄₄ in. (18mm). For both arches, Brunel had arranged that the outermost beams, which would have to carry the parapets, should 'be of a stronger section', and these tended to deflect by less.

Brunel provided sketches of the beams, together with a sketch of 'the manner in which the girders for the Canal Bridge at the GWR Terminus were tested', but this is quite hard to understand. It appears to show a shallow frame of wrought iron bars, within which two of the girders are shown in section, held between what look like cylindrical blocks, with a pipe or cord attached to one of them. The cylindrical blocks seem to represent some kind of hydraulic press, though the information given here is incomplete.

These tests, although clearly intended to provide a specific design for a specific location, form part of a series of experiments on materials which Brunel recorded in his books of 'Facts'. The same volume, for example, records a series of tests of iron castings from 49 different named foundries, to examine their elasticity, deflection, breaking weight, specific gravity and power to resist impact.

Brunel's caution was further borne out by the degree to which he over-designed the bridge, with its closely spaced beams. His caution was well justified, as was shown seven years later, when in 1845 his friend Robert Stephenson's railway bridge over the Dee at Chester, built of massive cast-iron beams trussed with wrought-iron straps, collapsed while a train was crossing it, with serious loss of life. Brunel gave evidence in support of his friend at the subsequent enquiry.

The canal bridge was such an inconspicuous thing that it entirely sank from notice as a work by Brunel. It probably had a narrow escape in 1906–7 when the major part of the Bishop's Road Bridge was replaced by a single steel truss and the remaining part of the brick viaduct was widened by the GWR's engineers, Grierson and Armstrong. The board approved a vote of £24,000 for the purpose on 14 June 1906 and the principal contract (for £17,843) was let to Messrs Jackaman on 19 July 1906.[90] The new bridge has one clear span of 200ft (61m) with a 'hog's-back' girder, the steelwork made by Westwood's of Millwall.[91]

It is reasonable to suppose that Grierson and Armstrong must have examined the cast-iron canal bridge and given it a clean bill of health, but at the same time they partly refaced it and removed its handsome railings, replacing them with higher brick parapets. The parapets effectively shut the canal off from the road and helped to obscure the canal bridge's separate identity. Nevertheless, it is remarkable that a documented iron bridge by Brunel could remain completely unnoticed in the heart of London until the research for

Figure 7.45 Brunel's design for load-testing the cast-iron beams for the Paddington canal bridge, December 1838.

this book. The fact that we have a cast-iron bridge by Brunel, complete with the records of his load tests for it, appears to make it unique.

At the time of writing, the entire Bishop's Road Bridge is due to be demolished and replaced with a wider bridge that will meet modern vehicle-weight standards, a major infrastructure project that has been in preparation since 1999. The discovery of Brunel's cast-iron bridge has come just in time to save it and to allow provision to be made for it to be surveyed and carefully dismantled. It is hoped that this unique bridge will be re-erected as a footbridge on an appropriate site and plans for this are in hand at the time of writing.

Westbourne Bridge

The original viaduct, for which Grissell & Peto signed a contract on 26 June 1837, had ten brick arches.[92] At an unknown date, nine of the ten spans were replaced with flat iron girders. The bridge was rebuilt in c 1907–10, the contract for £37,562 being let to Messrs A Handyside on 6 August 1907 and the bridge opened in 1910.[93] It crosses the line at a skewed angle and is thus much longer than the other bridges. The two spans rest on impressive granite piers and are carried by exceptionally long bowstring trusses: the southern span has two trusses each of 232ft (70.7m), the northern span has trusses of 215ft (65.5m) and 244ft (74.4m), of differing lengths because of the skewed plan. The steelwork, made by Messrs Handyside of Derby, weighed 2,150 tons (2,184 tonnes). The sides of the roadway are enclosed with solid iron panels and at either end there are big classical pedestals, also of iron. The bridge is listed at Grade II.[94]

Ranelagh Bridge

Grissell & Peto signed a contract to build the original nine-arch brick viaduct on 2 October 1837.[95] It was replaced with two spans of N-braced hog's-back girders, the southern one of 160ft (49m) across the main lines, the northern one of 140ft (43m) over sidings, completed in the summer of 1909 (Fig 7.46). Much care was taken with the detailing of the impressive granite piers and the decorative mouldings at street level.[96]

Figure 7.46 The Ranelagh Bridge, before and after rebuilding.

Lord Hill's Bridge

This, the fourth bridge out from the station, was named for General Sir Rowland Hill, 1st Viscount Hill, one of Wellington's most liked and trusted commanders. He was created Commander in Chief in 1828 and lived at Westbourne Place, a substantial villa just to the south of the GWR's main line. The original viaduct had five brick arches, two of them later replaced with cast-iron girders. The brief for rebuilding was complicated by requirements that the bridge should climb gently from south to north and carry gas and water mains. It also had a very tight clearance: to maintain a minimum height of 14ft 6in. (4.42m) over the tracks, the road deck of the south span could only be 3ft (0.9m) deep. The Horseley Bridge Company made the very heavy hog's-back girders for the two spans, 1,112 tons (1,130 tonnes) of steel being used in all.[97]

Former GWR stationery store, Porchester Road

Some way to the west of the station, on the south side of the tracks next to Lord Hill's Bridge, the stationery store is a square block of four storeys over a track-level basement. It was built in 1906–7 to rehouse the stationery department, previously in the arrival side of the terminus, and was thus one of the preparatory works for the remodelling of the station between 1907 and 1914. The stationery store was designed by W Armstrong, the GWR's new-works engineer, and its whole structure, including the floors, represent one of the company's earliest uses of the Hennebique reinforced concrete system. The building has handsome classical detailing, of hard red brick with dressings of Patent Victoria stone. It incorporated an electricity sub-station, supplying power from the GWR's new generating station at Park Royal both to Paddington and to the Metropolitan Railway.[98]

Former down parcels depot, 4–14, Bishop's Road

After the construction of the GWR's main line, a restricted triangular site was left over between the tracks to the north, the Bishop's Road to the south and Westbourne Terrace to the south-east. The company's long carriage sheds rose on the north side of this and the rest of the site was filled with tall terraced houses, and Bishop's Mews behind. The GWR bought up the leases and replaced most of the houses with two large concrete-framed buildings as part of its 1930s expansion.[99] The parcels depot, designed by P A Culverhouse and built between 1932 and 1933, occupies the eastern part of this site and looks south onto the Bishop's Road. It is of five storeys plus a mansard attic, with a simple classical façade of brick and patent stone.[100] A low wing of the building facing over the tracks housed the departure side signal box. The building has long since been sold, but behind the façade the depot yard and platforms remain under their plain steel-framed roof, in use as a National Car Park. From platform 1 a rewarding walk may be had, right through the depot and beyond as far as the Ranelagh Bridge. The long timber cover in the depot platform represents the duct which took electrical cables from the sub-station under the Porchester Road stationery store.

Figure 7.47 The stationery stores and staff hostel under construction, *c* 1934.

Figure 7.48 Workers from the station restaurant playing table-tennis on the roof of their staff hostel, 19 August 1935.

Former GWR stationery store and hostel for GWR employees, 167–9, Westbourne Terrace

This irregularly shaped building was designed by P A Culverhouse and constructed between 1932 and 1935 close to the former down parcels depot, just south of the tracks and hard by the Westbourne Bridge (Fig 7.47). It is concrete framed and of six storeys, with façades towards the road and the tracks in the same restrained art deco style that Culverhouse employed on the arrival side offices, with similar shallow oriel windows. The top two floors were a hostel for women staff, mostly employed in Paddington's refreshment rooms, and Culverhouse provided them with a spacious roof-top terrace (Fig 7.48).[101]

The former Mint stables, Winsland Street and South Wharf Road

The Mint stables, now the Mint Wing of St Mary's Hospital, Paddington, are a rare historical survival and a vivid reminder that the railways, so far from displacing horse-drawn transport, greatly increased the demand for it. The GWR, like all major railway companies, used horses for general road haulage, for parcel delivery services and for shunting wagons and locomotives. In the early days, railway horses tended to be given makeshift accommodation, under railway arches or in odd corners of their goods yards, and most of the companies relied to some degree on livery stables. As the goods traffic grew, these makeshift arrangements were

G.W.R
PADDINGTON STATION

SOUTH WHARF ROAD

PROPOSED STABLES
GROUND PLAN

MINT
PUBLIC HOUSE

SAINT MARYS
HOSPITAL

FRANCIS STREET

SCALE 10 FEET TO AN INCH

Figure 7.49 Lancaster Owen's ground-floor plan for the Mint stables, 1876.

superseded. By the 1850s, better quality purpose-built stables began to appear, such as the London & North Western Railway's at Chalk Farm, Camden, which also survive.[102]

In the mid-1870s, the GWR decided that it would be more economic to end their use of livery stables and build up their own fleet of horses. By 1890 they had about 1,110 horses working in London, out of a total of around 6,000 railway horses in the city. An irregular triangular site, north of the station, was available. The GWR already had makeshift timber stables at the south end of the site, the rest of which was occupied by the Mint public house (from which the stables took their name) facing South Wharf Road, cottages and an open yard. A lease was acquired in 1876 and the company's architect, Lancaster Owen, produced a design for the whole site (Fig 7.49). A contract was signed for a first phase, filling the open, northern part of the site. This provided stabling for about 220 horses. In a second phase of work in 1882–3 the southern part was added, leaving the pub surrounded by stable buildings on three sides.[103] This took the Mint stables' capacity to around 500; another 140 animals were kept in a stable adjoining the goods depot. The GWR had a number of out-stations, the largest at Goswell Road, on the boundary of the City of London, housing

another 200 horses. A 'horse hospital' was established at West Ealing for convalescent animals.[104]

As designed, the buildings were two storeys high, of stock brick (Fig 7.50). They looked inwards onto an irregularly shaped yard, in the middle of which were separate buildings housing the provender store, mess room and a farrier's shop. Ramps led up to a gallery running around the courtyard, to give access to the upper storey. Both floors were divided into rooms, housing ten to twelve stalls each. The floors were of granite setts below and asphalt above, the first floor being laid over brick jack-arches carried on cast-iron columns. The roof was carried on king-post trusses. The stalls had wooden dividers and the horses were provided with iron 'Swindon pattern' troughs. In the later part of the building, it seems that the stalls were separated with swinging bales to lessen the damage and injury to a horse caused by the kicking of its neighbour.

In 1910 a major remodelling of the stables was carried out, part of the general campaign of improvements to the station. First, the southern range (that towards the station) was demolished; the site was excavated out and a massive basement of Hennebique ferroconcrete created at platform level as the new up parcels depot. Lifts took the parcels up to a circulating area with six loading docks for the GWR's

SECTION ON LINE C.D

SECTION ON LINE A.B

Figure 7.50 The Mint stables – a cross-section and part-elevation, 1876.

Figure 7.51 The Mint stables, horses being led down the ramps, early 20th century.

horse wagons, opening onto London Street and Francis Street.[105]

As the south range had been given to the parcels depot, an extra storey was added to the whole Mint stables group to make up for the lost space. Extra columns were inserted into the existing buildings, some of them improvised by placing two lengths of rail back to back. The work was carried out one 60ft (18m) section at a time so the stables could be kept in use. The GWR, ingenious and economical as ever, literally raised the roof by removing the slates over a section, inserting screwjacks at 20ft (6m) centres and lifting the roof-frame as the walls were carried up. The original king-post trusses are still in place. Outside, the galleries and ramps were rebuilt to give access to the first and second floors: like the new basement, they were of Hennebique ferroconcrete (Fig 7.51).[106]

The remodelled stables housed 50 horses in the basement, 261 on the ground floor, 288 on the first floor and 66 on the top floor. The historian Robert Thorne has likened the remodelled courtyard to 'an open-air theatre, set to life twice a day when the horses were led to and from their duties'.[107] The working week started at 2am on Monday morning and the horses might be out for up to eighteen hours. A heavy railway van might weigh two tons, and carry another seven, requiring four horses to pull it, a total mass of thirteen tons moving at a slow walk. A light parcel cart would be drawn by a single horse, trotting at around 8 miles (12.9km) an hour.[108]

The stables housed horses into the 1950s. Thereafter, British Rail converted them for a variety of other uses: the upper floors became the chief engineer's drawing office for a while. It was probably about this time that the ramps and galleries were glazed in and the second-floor windows enlarged. Most of the stable fittings, of course, were lost. In 1965 the stables were acquired by St Mary's Hospital and further alterations carried out to fit them for new purposes. They are listed at Grade II.

Motor vehicle maintenance depot, now offices, Harrow Road (Fig 7.52)

It is satisfying to be able to conclude this account of Paddington's architecture with a modern building of outstanding quality, though it may seem somewhat paradoxical that this maintenance depot was built for road vehicles rather than railway rolling stock. In the 1960s, the construction of the Westway flyover transformed the setting

Figure 7.52 The former motor maintenance depot, now offices of Monsoon Ltd, seen at night.

of the station, vividly expressing the new dominance of road transport. British Rail, like the GWR, maintained a vast freight operation. Just as the GWR had needed hundreds of horses, so British Rail found that it needed large fleets of road vehicles: the depot was the mid-20th-century equivalent of the Mint stables.[109]

A cramped, interstitial site was available, hemmed in between the canal, the Harrow Road and the Westway, at the point where a slip road drops from the Westway to a roundabout. The site was blighted by the flyover, lacked a conventional street frontage and over 80,000 cubic yards (61,000 cubic metres) of earth had to be extracted before work could begin. These drawbacks were brilliantly exploited by Paul Hamilton, who designed the depot in 1967. The east block, within the well of the roundabout and housing the garage and the maintenance area, is a long oval, with a raked leaded roof with oval lights and central top-lighting.

The west block occupies a difficult triangular site hemmed in between roads. It is on five levels, rising to seven at its east end. At the bottom, at the level of the maintenance area, was plant and storage, and above this workshop space. On the third floor there was a machine shop and on the fourth and upper levels, mess rooms and offices. The upper floors are slightly jettied: this, the curved outline, and the continuous bands of glazing, give the building an elegant 'moderne' quality. The paired chimneys rising at the western 'prow' of the building enhance its rather nautical quality. Inside, the staircase, dramatically curved and top-lit, echoes the shape of the building. The maintenance depot reads to great advantage from the Westway, from where its curved, jettied forms seem to advance and recede as one approaches and moves past, a rare instance of architecture relating positively and successfully to modern highway engineering. The building was sold after British Rail's privatisation, but has been very successfully renovated as office space for the public relations company Monsoon Ltd. The journal *Official Architecture and Planning*, reviewing the newly completed building in February 1969, remarked that 'if British Rail continue to appoint talent of this quality, in AD 2068 a preservation society will nominate the Paddington Maintenance Depot one of the most significant railway buildings of its era and in its urban context'. It is satisfying to record that the depot's outstanding quality was recognised rather sooner than that and that it was listed at Grade II* in 2001.

NOTES

The following abbreviations have been used here and in the Bibliography:

BUL   Bristol University Library (The Brunel Collection is held in Special Collections, the Arts & Social Sciences Library, University of Bristol)

GWR   Great Western Railway

NRWRPR   Network Rail Western Region Plans Room

NA Rail   National Archives (formerly Public Record Office) British Rail Archive

Preface

1 The main elements of the proposed World Heritage Site would be Paddington Station, the Hanwell Viaduct, Maidenhead Bridge, Reading Station, the GWR's original village and workshops at Swindon, Twerton and Box Tunnels, the viaducts into Bath, Bath Station, and Bristol Temple Meads Station.

Chapter 1

1 Vaughan 1991, 56.

2 MacDermot 1964a, 1–2. MacDermot's official history, first published in 1927 and revised in 1964 by C R Clinker, has been followed by others, notably Nock 1962 and Booker 1977.

3 Booker 1977, 16.

4 MacDermot 1964a, 2–3.

5 Ibid, 2–3; Vaughan 1991, 44–5.

6 MacDermot 1964a 2

7 Vaughan 1991, 45.

8 The question of which was the first true railway is something of a conundrum, and depends on what is meant by the word 'railway'. Horse-drawn tramways had been in use at collieries for some decades, and in the early 1800s the first horse-drawn railways had been built independently of collieries: the Surrey Iron Railway (1803) and the Cromford & High Peak line. The Stockton to Darlington was the first railway designed for steam-hauled traffic but was primarily intended for goods. The Liverpool & Manchester was the first railway designed to operate regular passenger services.

9 Buchanan 2002, chapters 1 and 2.

10 Vaughan 1991, 1–41; Buchanan 2002, 22–7, 43–62.

11 Vaughan 1991, 47; Rolt 1957, 51–68.

12 Brunel 1870, 65.

13 Vaughan 1991, 48.

14 MacDermot 1964a, 4, says that the name was changed at the first joint meeting of the two committees. Vaughan (1991, 49) says that the meeting in question was on 22 Aug. Vaughan also draws attention to Marc Brunel's fondness for the word 'great', suggesting that Brunel may have been responsible for the new name.

15 Ibid, 49.

16 NA Rail 250/2, GWR board minutes 1835–41, 15 Sep 1835.

17 MacDermot 1964a, 5.

18 Ibid, 5–15.

19 The principal exceptions would appear to be the London & Southampton (1835) and the Eastern Counties Railway (1836), which were on a rather smaller scale. Reed (1996, 3 and 10–11), remarks that most of the money for the London & Birmingham Railway came from Liverpool, though its management passed to London, and that the Grand Junction Railway was both financed and run from Liverpool. A large part, perhaps as much as 40%, of the GWR's share capital came from Lancashire, too. The predominance of northern engineers and Lancashire money in the early years of the railway industry is an important but under-researched subject.

20 Conder 1983, 118–23. F R Conder, a railway engineer, remarked in his memoirs on the contrast between Brunel's way of doing things and everyone else's: 'one was the scientific knowledge of a pupil of the "Ecole Polytechnique", which contrasted rather sharply with the general and time-honoured English system of the "rule of thumb"'.

21 Buchanan 2002, 65.

22 MacDermot 1964a, 16–17. George Stephenson had been working at Killingworth Colliery, which had a tramway with a 4ft 8½in. (1.4m) gauge, not of his designing: this was where he built his first locomotive. The Stockton to Darlington Railway was based on this specific model.

23 Ibid, 26–8, 39.

24 NA Rail 1149/4, Brunel letter-book, 1836, 262. Brunel wrote to the engineer Nicholas Wood with calculations of the additional cost of making the line wider, arriving at a total of £151,840.

25 MacDermot 1964a, 26–9. Much has been written on the subject of the broad gauge: see Bryan 2000, 37–52.

26 MacDermot 1964a, 17, quotes Brunel's testimony to the Gauge Commission of 1844–5: 'I think the impression grew upon me gradually, so that it is difficult to fix the time when I first thought a wide gauge desirable, but I daresay there were stages between of wishing that it could be so and determining to try and do it.'

27 Brunel's letter is quoted in full in MacDermot 1964a, 17–19.

28 NA Rail 250/2, 18, GWR board minutes for 29 Oct 1835.

29 NA Rail 250/2, 91, GWR board minutes for 27 Dec 1835; MacDermot 1964a, 35–47; Vaughan 1991, 108–19.

30 NA Rail 250/2, 9, GWR board minutes for 15 Sep 1835.

31 Buchanan 2000, 15–24.

32 Vaughan 1991, 62–5, 128–33; Rolt 1970, 105–7.

33 Many of Brunel's sketchbooks survive in the possession of Bristol University Library. Several sketches from this source are referred to below.

34 Buchanan 2000, 16; Vaughan 1991, 62–3.

35 Conder 1983, 118, stresses Brunel's dictatorial style and control over every detail.

36 Vaughan 1991, 64–5, gives a number of examples.

37 Latimer 1887, quoted in Binding 2001, 11–12.

38 Conder 1983, 118–123. F R Conder was himself a railway engineer and contractor, and his detailed account of Brunel's dictatorial methods seems to have been written from first-hand testimony.

39 Ibid; Vaughan 1991, 68–70. Vaughan emphasises Brunel's tendency to use small and under-capitalised contractors, but this was not invariably so, as he also used Betts, and Grissell & Peto, amongst the best-organised builders of the age. Ranger was a case in point. He lost his claim against the GWR for compensation in 1843, died insolvent, and his creditors kept the case going in Chancery until 1859 (see Binding 2001, 23). Vaughan (1991, 134–9) gives a very interesting account of Brunel's arbitrary and scarcely legal treatment of the Scottish firm of Hugh and David McIntosh. Brunel withheld payments on a huge scale, the McIntoshes sued, and the case was only resolved in 1865, when the Lord Chancellor found for the McIntoshes, and ordered the GWR to pay them £100,000 with 20 years' accrued interest and costs. Vaughan certainly gives a truer and more rounded picture than is supplied by Rolt (1970) or MacDermot (1964a, 55): the former never mentions the McIntosh case, the latter brushes it aside with a quip about 'Jarndyce & Jarndyce'.

40 NA Rail 250/64, 14. At the first meeting of the GWR Proprietors in Oct 1835, it was argued that 'the moderate amount of excavations, not exceeding ten million cubic yards for the whole line' would tend to keep the costs down; it is not known how far this prediction was borne out.

41 NA Rail, 250/2, 43. It was named after Lord Wharncliffe, chairman of the committee, on the GWR's Act of Incorporation in the House of Lords.

His coat of arms was carved on the centre of the south face.

42 MacDermot 1964a, 48–9.

43 Ibid, 30–33.

44 Ibid, 48–4.

45 Binding 2001, 71.

46 Macdermot 1964a, 63–71, says that a hundred men lost their lives in the Box Tunnel, though it has been suggested (Rolt, 138–9) that this was the loss of life involved in the construction of the whole line.

47 Macdermot 1964a, 72.

48 Buchanan 2002, 76; Booker 1977, 39–40. There is some uncertainty about the Bristol and Exeter Railway board – John Binding (2001, 119) observes that, surprisingly, none of the original Bristol & Exeter directors were on the GWR board.

49 Simmons 1971, 6–8.

50 Buchanan 2002, 58–62.

51 Buchanan 2002, 52–62 gives a good account of the Bristol Dock Company's slothfulness and want of enterprise: both the *Great Western* and the *Great Britain* were too large to use Bristol's Floating Harbour, and could only be got out of it after their construction by, in the one case, the paddle wheels being taken off, and in the other, the entrance lock being widened. Clearly, the harbour was too small to handle such ships on any regular basis and Brunel's response was to urge the Dock Company to build deep-water facilities at Avonmouth. Their refusal to take any such action drove the Great Western Steamship Company to operate the *Great Britain* out of Liverpool and discouraged them from commissioning further ships. When the *Great Britain* ran aground in 1846, the cost of refloating her finished off the Great Western Steamship Company. By this point, the future had effectively been handed to Liverpool and to Edward Cunard.

52 MacDermot 1964a, 100–176.

53 Buchanan 2002, 78–9.

54 MacDermot 1964a, 196–207; Booker 1977, 103–7.

55 MacDermot 1964a, chapter 15; NA Rail 1149/4, Brunel's letter-book for Mar to Nov 1836, has a number of letters on the subject.

56 MacDermot 1964a, 372–97; Vaughan

1991, 103, 116.

57 MacDermot 1964a, 29, 397–401. *The North Star* was delivered in Nov 1837. A 'sister' engine, the *Morning Star*, also commissioned by the New Orleans Railway, was converted and delivered to the GWR in Dec 1838, by which time the railway had opened.

58 Ibid, 329.

59 Vaughan 1991, 119–125.

60 NA Rail 250/2, 97–8. The board authorised the commissioning of twenty new locomotives on 10 Jan 1839; MacDermot 1964a, 397–401.

61 Cattell and Falconer 1995.

62 MacDermot 1964a, 335; Booker 1977, 78.

Chapter 2

1 'Bristol and London Railway – At a numerous and respectable meeting of inhabitants of Bristol and its Neighbourhood, desirous of assisting in the Establishment of a Railway to London held (pursuant to public advertisement) at the Guildhall, Bristol, on Tuesday the 30th day of Jul 1833 – Report of the Provisional Committee,' copy in the Science Museum, London, quoted in Tutton 1999, 3, note 1. Mr Tutton's scholarly and thorough dissertation has been invaluable in the preparation of the present work.

2 NA Rail 1014/1, album of prospectuses for the GWR.

3 NA Rail 252/2.

4 Tutton 1999, 5–6, points out that Saunders revealed details of what had been private negotiations with Lord Cadogan under questioning during the Committee stage of the bill, and that Lord Cadogan, offended by this, opposed the bill in the Lords.

5 NA Rail 250/1, 45.

6 MacDermot 1964a, 9.

7 Ellaway 1994, 1–3.

8 The discussions are briefly recorded in the GWR's board minutes, NA Rail 250/2, 8, 16, 27; and in the report to the general meetings of the proprietors of 26 Feb 1836, NA Rail 250/64. More can be gleaned from an abstract of the minutes of the GWR London Committee for 1833–8, NA Rail 250/83: unfortunately, the minute books for these years are missing, lent to a firm of solicitors at some point

and never returned. *See also* Tutton
1999, 7–8. The London &
Birmingham's side of the negotiations
can be read in the minutes of their
London Committee for 1835, NA Rail
384/41, and 1835–6, NA Rail 384/42.

9   NA Rail, 250/82, I K Brunel's reports
to the board of directors, 19 Nov
1835; Tutton 1999, 13–14. The
London & Birmingham Railway
operated the stationary steam engine
system until 1845, when they began
to run locomotives into Euston in the
usual way.

10 NA Rail 250/64, reports of general
meetings of the proprietors, for 26
Feb 1836. The directors explained
that, their request to purchase or to
acquire a 21-year lease having been
refused, 'it had come to their notice
that a large and influential body of
distant proprietors were urging the
Directors of the London &
Birmingham Railway to retain in their
hands the power of breaking off any
arrangement that might be made with
the Great Western Railway Company
at the shortest possible notice, as well
as from a hope of afterwards
obtaining higher pecuniary terms, as
from a fear that there would not be
room for the traffic of both the lines
and of their respective branches at
the depot'.

11 The letter is quoted in full in
MacDermot 1964a, 17–19.

12 NA Rail 250/2, GWR board minutes,
29 Oct 1835.

13 NA Rail 250/83, abstract of minutes
of the GWR London Committee,
1833–8, meetings of 21 Nov 1835, 24
Nov 1835 and 26 Nov 1835.

14 NA Rail 250/82, 49, Brunel's report to
the board of 9 Feb 1836. This stage of
events is covered in detail in Simmons
1971, 18–23. Gibbs was one of the
GWR directors, Tutton 1999, 16–18.

15 NA Rail 250/64.

16 NA Rail 250/82, 16–18. Hardwick's
design seems to have represented
exactly what he had agreed with
Brunel on 19 Nov 1835.

17 Sir Nikolaus Pevsner (1976, 227), for
example, completely misunderstood
Hardwick's design: 'the functionalist is
bound to deny that Hardwick worked
on the purest principle of
functionalism. This display of solemn

monumentality is a screen: it is no
more. That is: the rails and the
necessary buildings alongside of them
were not even on axis with the
propylaea.'

18 NA Rail 384/43, 75ff, minutes of the
London Committee of the London &
Birmingham Railway, 14 Sep 1836.
Stephenson advised them that 'more
accommodation could be obtained
for passenger traffic by a double
station than by any possible
arrangement of a single station'.

19 NA Rail 384/43, 110, 12 Oct 1836:
Hardwick laid detailed plans before
the committee, which were approved,
and expressed his readiness to go to
Liverpool to explain the plans to the
'Lancashire Directors'. NA Rail
384/43, 175, 7 Dec 1836: Hardwick
reported that he had shown the
designs to 'non-resident Directors and
some of the principal proprietors' at
Liverpool on 5 Dec 1836, and had
received their 'unqualified
approbation'.

20 NA Rail 384/155, contract for the
portico, lodge and gates of Euston
Station, £39,850. NA Rail 384/156,
contract for arrival and departure
stages, iron slated roofs, drains, fence
walls, paving roads and laying
permanent way at Euston, £13,890,
both contracts with William and Lewis
Cubitt.

21 MacDermot 1964a, 32–47.

22 NA Rail 384/43, 75ff. The minutes for
the London & Birmingham Railway's
London Committee of 14 Sep 1836,
which decided to go ahead with the
'double station', do not mention the
GWR at all, but make it clear that the
London & Birmingham thought that
half of the planned station would
easily cope with their existing traffic,
with room for growth by lengthening
the platforms. So the idea that Euston
was built with a view to the London
& Birmingham taking control of the
GWR is suppositional, but not
unreasonable in the light of what
happened in 1836–8.

23 MacDermot 1964a, 22.

24 Shaun Richardson 1999, 'Paddington
Basin, London W2: an Archaeological
Addendum to the Archaeological
Impact Assessment'. Unpublished
report, AOC Archaeology.

25 G Gutch, plan of the parish of
Paddington, 1828, Westminster
Archives.

26 Tutton 1999, 19–20; Simmons 1971,
20.

27 NRWRPR 7494, includes plans of the
site, including the property plan
'attached to the agreement with Mr
Cockerell', undated. Tutton 1999,
Appendix i, 51–3, lists all of the
landowners and lessees from whom
the GWR bought property, quoted
from 'Great Western Railway Book of
Reference' (attached to their
Parliamentary Deposited Plan, Nov
1836), Metropolitan Record Centre,
London.

28 NA Rail 1008/64. Land at Paddington
– notes of a committee appointed by
the Paddington Vestry on the
application of the GWR Directors.

29 Paddington Vestry minutes, 4 Feb
1837, Westminster Archives, quoted in
Tutton 1999, 22, note 36: 'Brunel and
Saunders attended the meeting of
Paddington Vestry on 4 Feb 1837, the
main points of the agreement being
(1) that the GWR would built a 60
foot [18m] wide road – the present
Bishop's Bridge Road, including the
bridge over the railway and canal; (2)
that the railway would be below
street level; (3) the company would
pay compensation for wear and tear
to the roads about; (4) the GWR
would purchase some parish land, the
'Bread and Cheese Lands', for £1,200;
(5) the GWR would built all sewers
caused by changes in level of the
roads; (6) the new bridge over the
railway at the intersection of Black
Lion Lane (Lord Hill's Bridge) should
not be less than 40 feet [12m] wide;
(7) the new Bishop's Bridge Road and
bridge should be made within 18
months of the passage of the
Paddington Extension Act.'

30 NA Rail 250/83, 10, minutes of GWR
London Committee.

31 Tutton 1999, 26.

32 Ibid, Appendix iii, 60, estimated costs
of the extension to Paddington, from
a summary read at the half-year
shareholders' meeting on 15 Aug
1838.

33 Tutton 1999, 22, quoting Paddington
Vestry Minutes for 1836, Westminster
Archives.

34 BUL, Brunel Collection, sketchbook labelled 'GWR 1836', 47–9; NRWRPR 7494. Both the latter plans are unsigned and undated, but they relate fairly directly to Brunel's sketchbook.

35 NA Rail 1005/82, extract from minutes of the GWR General Committee, 6 Nov 1845.

36 NA Rail 250/64, half-yearly meeting, 31 Aug 1837.

37 Tutton 1999, Appendix ii, 54, quoting from NA Rail 272/38–42, London General Ledgers, and NA Rail 272/67–71, London General Journals, 1836–45.

38 NA Rail 1149/44, GWR Tenders, 35, tenders for 'London Terminus – various works': this gives the schedules of prices for the contracts, but not the main contract sums: 'retaining walls on Lord Hill's ground' (Sherwood, 23 May 1837); Black Lion Road Bridge (Sherwood, 19 Jun 1837); Westbourne Bridge (Grissell & Peto, 26 Jun 1837); Ranelagh Bridge (Grissell & Peto, 2 Oct 1837); Paddington Sewer (Grissell & Peto, 4 Mar 1837); Arrival and Departure Sides (Grissell & Peto, 17 Nov 1837); Paddington Canal Bridge (Sherwood, 27 Oct 1838). NA Rail 1149/8, one of Brunel's volumes of 'Facts', has Grissell & Peto's schedule of prices for the terminus buildings, dated 17 Nov 1837, listing the unit cost of all the materials: 24 shillings per cubic yard of brick set in mortar, as against 31 shillings per cubic yard set in cement, for example. NA Rail 250/82, board minutes for 6 Jul 1837: Brunel described both firms as 'highly respectable brick layers and excellent workmen'.

39 Tutton 1999, Appendix ii, 54.

40 MacDermot 1964a, 29–30.

41 Tutton 1999, Appendix iii, 60, quoting NA Rail 250/64, 6th Half Yearly General Meeting, 15 Aug 1838.

42 Tutton 1999, Appendix ii, 56–7.

43 NRWRPR roll 14891–8, has an unsigned, undated drawing for the gates and lodge, marked 'Great Western Railway – London Terminus'.

44 NRWRPR 14909–21, is a fine series of coloured drawings for the Paddington goods shed, showing a triple-roofed timber-framed shed. These look similar, but not identical, to contemporary views of the Paddington goods depot, but they are unsigned and undated, and it is possible that they relate to a reconstruction of c 1845–6. NRWRPR roll 14891 has two un-numbered and unlabelled drawings, which also appear to be for the first goods shed.

45 E C Matthews (1916b, 205) gives the dimensions of the departure platforms as, No. 1, 240ft (72m) long by 17ft 6in. (5.3m) wide, and No. 2, 235ft (71.6m) long by 17ft (5.2m) wide.

46 Ibid, gives the dimensions of the arrival platforms: No. 1, 255ft (77.7m) long by 25ft (7.6m) wide, No. 2, 340ft (103.6m) long by 34ft (10.4m) wide.

47 Tutton 1999, 55; NRWRPR roll 7494, includes an undated plan for the building.

48 NA Rail 1149/5, Brunel letter-book, 150, 233, letters to Philip Hardwick, architect of the Reading engine house. The first letter, dated 28 May 1839, says that the traverser in the engine house would not have to take a carriage but the one outside would. The second, dated 3 Oct 1839, directs Hardwick to make the foundations for the engine house traverser 25ft (7.6m) long. Binding 2001, 109–10, gives a good account of the Bristol traversers, quoting a description of them by one A J Dodson in the *Proceedings of the Institution of Civil Engineers*, iii, 1844. It is not clear whether the traversers formed part of the original design, or when exactly they were installed. A key feature of the design seems to have been that a part of the framework rose, actually lifting the carriage or wagon off the rails to keep it immobile while the traversers was shifted sideways.

49 One of the traversers at Reading, referred to above, was in the engine house: one would have thought that locomotives would be too heavy for this to be moved by hand, and it is not clear how this was supposed to work. Matthews (1916b, 203) thought that the Paddington traverser must have been manually operated, as the station does not seem to have had a steam engine to supply hydraulic power at this date.

50 Wilson 1972, 27–8.

51 Thompson's engine house at Derby was demolished in 1985, with what remained of his trijunct station: Pevsner 1978, 176. Gooch's first sketch design for the GWR's locomotive department at Swindon, which accompanied a letter to Brunel in Sep 1840, also included a round engine house, but this was never built: Cattell and Falconer 1995, 6–10.

52 NA Rail 1149/9, 201, sketch by T H Bertram dated 1 Sep 1840.

53 Westminster Archives, detached copy of steel engraving, dated 1843 and probably from the *Illustrated London News*.

54 NA Rail 1008/64. Letter from Paddington Vestry to Charles Saunders, 13 Mar 1841.

55 MacDermot 1964a, 52.

56 Ibid. First-class passengers had a choice between sitting in the 'posting carriage', with upholstered seats, and riding in their own carriage on a carriage truck, while second-class passengers had to choose between a coach with wooden seats and a roof but no glass in the windows, and an unroofed open truck.

57 MacDermot 1964a, 333.

58 Ibid, 331.

59 Ellis 1975, 4–9.

60 Tutton 1999, 43.

61 Ibid, 43–6; MacDermot 1964a, 325–6.

62 Quoted in MacDermot 1964a, 326.

63 Ibid, 326–8.

64 NA Rail 1005/82, typed transcript, extracts from the minutes of the General Committee, 6 Nov 1845.

65 NRWRPR 14909–21, is a set of fine large coloured drawings for a timber-framed shed with wrought-iron trusses. They are unsigned and undated but are labelled 'Paddington Goods Shed'. These may be the unexecuted Proposal of 1845–6.

66 NRWRPR 7494.

67 Michael Tutton (1999, 50) appears to be the only author who has noticed them: I am indebted to him for his sharp observation.

Chapter 3

1 NRWRPR 14891–2, drawings for new one-storey carriage shops adjoining the existing paint shop, signed Joseph

Griffiths, undated, but dated to 1847 in the catalogue; 14893–8, undated drawings of new timber-clad carriage sheds and engine house, with variant brick and timber clad elevations, seem likely to be of the 1840s, but this is not certain.

2   The original volume of half-yearly reports covering 1850 appears to be missing. I have used typed transcripts in NA Rail 1005/82, miscellaneous historical documents.

3   Vaughan 1997, chapters 12 and 13; Binding 2001, 51.

4   Jackson 1969, 39–42; Hobhouse 1976, 41.

5   NA Rail 1005/82, transcripts of GWR half-yearly reports.

6   Meeks 1957, 39.

7   Binding 2001, 53–4.

8   Meeks 1957, 61–2.

9   BUL, Brunel Collection, Small Sketchbook 22, fol 7.

10 BUL, Brunel Collection, Large Sketchbook 3, fols 1, 7.

11 Idem. The dimensions do not quite tally between the two sketches. For example, on fol 1 the central concourse is clearly marked as 450ft (137.2m) long, on fol 7, adding up a number of measurements it seems to come to 420ft (128m): this is perhaps only to be expected in rough initial sketches like this.

12 BUL, Brunel Collection, Large Sketchbook 3, fol 5, 10. These sketches relate closely to the tiny vignette on fol 1 of the same sketchbook.

13 Binding 2001, 78–102. Mr Binding (ibid, 153) says that no drawings for the Bath Station roof have ever been found. Early views suggest that it was a smaller version of the Bristol roof, which came first.

14 Ibid, 78–102. Mr Binding estimates that 80–9 % of the stiffness in the Bristol roof comes from the ironwork. Heavy horizontal timber cross-pieces were also added over the aisles, apparently to help hold the roof down and counteract the outward forces: it is clear, though, that the walls and columns have deflected over time.

15 Sutherland 1989, 107–26.

16 Addyman and Fawcett 1999, chapter 5; Meeks 1957, 59–60.

17 Ibid; Turner 1850, 204.

18 Brunel was also a member of the Machinery Section Committee, and the chairman and reporter of the judges for Class 7 exhibits, on civil engineering, architecture and building technology. Rolt 1970, 230.

19 McKean 1994, 4–9.

20 Buchanan 2002, 188, quotes Brunel writing in May 1850 that he was 'brim full of the details of dome and specification'. Unfortunately, no detailed drawings of the dome are known, so we cannot assess Brunel's approach to this novel problem.

21 McKean 1994, 10–13.

22 Ibid.

23 NA Rail 250/4, GWR board minutes, 248.

24 Hobhouse 1976, 40–2.

25 NA Rail 250/4, 259.

26 NA Rail 250/4, 274.

27 BUL, Brunel Collection, Large Sketchbook 3, fol 1.

28 BUL, Brunel Collection, office diaries for 1850, 1851.

29 NA Rail 250/4, 254, GWR board minutes. The board also discussed their need for additional capacity in view of the Great Exhibition, due to open on 1 May 1851. This might have encouraged them to go ahead but can hardly have been a determining factor as the new station could not have been ready in time for the exhibition.

30 Ibid.

31 BUL, Brunel Collection, Large Sketchbook 3, fols 11–13.

32 BUL, Brunel Collection, office diary for 1850.

33 NA Rail 250/4, 298.

34 Binding 2001, 53–77.

35 Hobhouse 1976, 40–42.

36 Ibid.

37 Ibid, 310.

38 BUL, Brunel Collection, office diaries for 1850, 1851.

39 Vaughan 1991, 62, 68–9, 81–2, 119–20, and the office diaries.

40 The whereabouts of the original MS is unknown. There is a typescript in NA Rail 1005/82, and it is quoted in full in Rolt, 231–2.

41 BUL, Brunel Collection, office diary for 1851.

42 Ibid. Brunel saw Fox and Henderson at 10.15am, Bertram at 11.45, Bertram again at 4.30pm, as well as having meetings about the West Cornwall, South Wales, Oxford & Worcester and Vale of Neath railways, the Clifton bridge, the Chepstow bridge, Sunderland Docks, the Eastern Steam Navigation Company, the Galvanised Iron Company and the Vulcanized Rubber Company.

43 NA Rail 250/4, 328; NRWRPR 13320, contract drawings for Fox Henderson's first contract.

44 *Dictionary of National Biography*, **7**, 533–4; Conder, 10–11.

45 Weiler 1987, 144. James Sutherland considers that it was the use of rolled wrought-iron angles and tees here, which was particularly significant: pers comm.

46 *Victoria County History* 1976, 110–11; Sutherland, 1989, 116.

47 Weiler 1987, i, 143–61; Sutherland 1989, 116.

48 Cattell and Falconer 1985 32–4.

49 *Victoria County History* 1976, 111.

50 Sutherland 1975, 69–72. It used to be thought that the Oxford building was built from 'spare parts' for the Crystal Palace: James Sutherland demonstrates that it was similar (built to the same 24ft (7.3m) module), but not identical. In particular, the wedged fixings of the Crystal Palace's beams and trusses were replaced by a more solid bolted fixing. The Oxford building has been dismantled and reconstructed at the Buckinghamshire Railway Centre, Quainton Road.

51 Weiler 1987, 143.

52 Cowper 1854.

53 NA Rail 1005/82, *The Josser*, 20 Mar 1889: this appears to have been an unofficial, privately circulated staff newsletter.

54 BUL, Brunel Collection, Large Sketchbook 1, fol 40, Large Sketchbook fols 3, 15, 35.

55 NA Rail 1005/82, typescript copy of the specification for Fox, Henderson's second contract for Paddington passenger station, dated 8 Nov 1852. 'Generally the curved roof is to be similar in its construction and character to that already executed at Paddington New Station which is referred to as an example of the work required and in all cases unless otherwise specified the details of construction and description of materials and workmanship are to be similar to those adopted in like positions in the work already executed.

Materials. Wrought Iron – ribs, girders, angle irons, etc. Cast Iron – columns, plinths and baseplates and ornamental castings. Paxton Glass roofing in part – patent rolled plate 26 oz [793gm]. Galvanized Corrugated Iron Roofing in part – No. 18 gauge. York Stone bases for columns. Timber – red pine or memel and deal battens for gallery. Arched spans – to be 102 feet 6 inches [31.2m] and 68 feet [20.2m] respectively. Height above rails – 54 feet 6 inches [16.6m] and 46 feet [14m] respectively. Estimated quantities – 300 cubic yards [223 cubic metres] of brick work, 100 cubic yards [76.5 cubic metres] of concrete, 50 tons [50.8 tonnes] of wrought iron girders, 20 tons [20.3 tonnes] of cast iron columns, brackets, etc. 8 tons [8.1 tonnes] of lead guttering, 4,582 cubic yards [3,503 cubic metres] of excavation. Maintenance of Works – twelve months after works constructed under the contract have been executed.' There is something of a mystery about the figures of 50 tons for the wrought iron and 20 tons for the cast iron, which look far too small.

56　BUL, Brunel Collection, Large Sketchbook 3, fols 22, 28, 37. Fol 22 shows the transept with a semicircular arched profile, as executed.

57　The southern span was given tie-rods early in the 20th century, which it retains.

58　Binding 2001, 86, illustrates the 'tie-rod' design, observing that the decision to omit the rods 'had a significant effect on the subsequent behaviour of the roof in service, by introducing horizontal forces at the walls'.

59　Hitchcock, 1951 and 1972; Dixon and Muthesius, 1978,105; Pevsner 1950.

60　This assumes that Brunel used his sketchbooks sequentially: on fol 11, there is the first sketch plan for the revised design, as built, which seems to confirm that fols 5 and 10 relate to the rejected central concourse scheme.

61　Journal of the Royal Institute of British Architects, 3rd series, 11, 19 Dec 1903, 116. I am grateful to Mr Robert Thorne for this information. Fowler signed some of the very fine drawings for railings and gates on Eastbourne Terrace, NRWRPR 13315A.

62　NRWRPR 10270.

63　Ruskin 1849, 36–7.

64　Review of the The Seven Lamps of Architecture in The Journal of Design, 2, 1849–50, 72 . The review is anonymous but attributed to Wyatt by Sir Nicholas Pevsner on the grounds that the opinions are close to those expressed in other articles by him.

65　Wyatt 1850.

66　NRWRPR, 420.

67　NA Rail 250/5, 24.

68　Ibid, 37.

69　BUL, Brunel Collection, Large Sketchbook, fols 4, 15, dated 29 Jan 1851.

70　NA Rail 250/5, 53. The drawings seem to be those in NRWRPR 13324. These relate to the area north of the viaduct leading up to the high level yard, about two-thirds of the site. The southern part of the goods depot was not designed until 1853: NRWRPR, rolls 16122, 13304, 17842.

71　NA Rail 250/5, 73.

72　Ibid, 96.

73　Ibid, 211.

74　Ibid, 243.

75　Ibid, 251.

76　BUL, Brunel Collection, office diary for 1851. Armstrong is misnamed as W J – he was W G – but there seems to be no doubt that it was indeed him. Brunel met him on 3 Feb and 14 Mar, then there was a hiatus, then meetings on 8, 10 and 11 Apr, 3 and 19 May, then one more meeting on 15 Jul. NRWRPR has numerous drawings of hydraulic machinery for Paddington by Sir William Armstrong & Company, for example 13309, 13310, 13312. Further rolls of drawings for machinery are listed at 18674–8 and 18679–82, but appear to be missing. See below, Chapter 5, for a fuller discussion of these documents.

77　NA Rail 250/5, 258.

78　Ibid, 377.

79　Ibid, 398.

80　NA Rail 1008/35, Brunel to Saunders, 17 Mar 1852.

81　NA Rail 250/5, 405.

82　Owen Jones was on the Executive Committee of the 1851 Exhibition, and was responsible for the much-acclaimed colour scheme for the Crystal Palace. This seems likely to be how Wyatt and Brunel knew him. There do not appear to be any references to Jones in the GWR records, presumably because the company was never responsible for employing him. References to his work at the station come from the Athenaeum magazine, in turn referring to William Powell Frith's famous painting The Railway Station.

83　NA Rail 1005/82, Saunders to Brunel, 15 Apr 1852.

84　Levien 1930, article about the painting. See NA Rail 1005/56, file relating to the painting.

85　M D Wyatt would have known Alfred Stevens, like Owen Jones, through his work on the Great Exhibition. It is thought that Stevens's designs for the royal waiting room probably date from 1854 (Beattie 1975, 32–3). Three letters on the subject from Stevens to Wyatt are preserved, Victoria and Albert Museum Library, E996–1914. Stevens produced a number of variations of his design, quoting a price of £15 for each of the eight sides of the ceiling. He asked for payment in 1856, noting that 'it seems unlikely that the scheme for decorating the Queen's waiting room at Paddington Station will ever be carried out'. Wyatt replied on 29 Mar 1856 enclosing a cheque for £10 and both drawings, regretting that they 'had not been able to succeed in getting the decoration carried into effect'.

86　NA Rail 250/6, 6, 24, 31, 196 and 274–5. The Great Western Royal Hotel Company, thus formed, took a 42-year lease and ran the hotel until 1986, MacDermot 1964a, 269.

87　NA Rail 1005/82, Directors' report to shareholders, 17 Feb 1853.

88　Ibid.

89　Brunel 1870, 86.

90　NA Rail 250/6, 41–2.

91　Ibid, 49, 71. A copy of the specification for Fox, Henderson's second contract, dated 8 Nov 1852, is in NA Rail 1005/82. The drawings for the second contract are in NRWRPR 13320.

92　NA Rail 250/6, 71, GWR board minutes for 22 Jul 1852.

93　NA Rail 250/6, 229. Two of Gainsford's reports to the board are extant, for Jul and Aug 1854, NA Rail 1014/33.

94　NA Rail 250/6, 354.

95　Ibid, 358.

96　Ibid, 381–2.

97 Ibid, 414.

98 NA Rail 1005/82, Saunders to Brunel, 4 Apr 1853.

99 Vaughan 1991, 153–6, 215–7.

100 NA Rail 1005/82. 'During the last fortnight, several of the Board having themselves visited and inspected the buildings and offices, in which scarcely any human being is at work, they have taken it upon themselves, in the absence of Mr Brunel from London, to give the orders they deem requisite for insuring early use and occupation of the building. They will be glad that your clerks shall vacate the rooms within two or three days, which they have been using in the upper floor, in order that they may be made fit for the clerks of the Company… I am also to say that the inaction in all that relates to the new roofs for the Carriage Sheds oblige the Board very shortly unless they perceive a manifest change, to take that work into their own hands to be finished – for there is not the least appearance of its being completed – according to the present state of it.'

101 NA Rail 1008/35, Brunel's reports to the GWR board.

102 NA Rail 250/7, GWR board minutes for 1853–4, 45, 11 Aug 1853, record a decision that the arrival platform be made wider, and the intermediate platform reduced by the same amount. Ibid, 141, 27 Aug 1853, note that the 'Rooms for the reception of Her Majesty' were incomplete: the sub-committee (it is not clear which) were to obtain designs for furnishing it from Messrs Holland.

103 NA Rail 250/7, 45, 151, 155, 189, 201, 233, 247.

104 The Builder, 12, 28 Jan 1854, 41.

105 The Builder, 12, 3 Jun 1854, 290–1.

106 The Builder, 12, 17 Jun 1854, 322–3.

107 NA Rail 250/7, 373, 387.

108 The Directors were obliged to seek support for any major capital project from the GWR's half-yearly shareholders' meetings, at which estimates were presented. Thus it is possible to plot the rising cost of the station at six-monthly intervals in the Reports to Shareholders. The station cost £250,037 to the end of 1853, £318,089 by 30 Jun 1854, £411,828 to the end of 1854, £480,661 to the end of 1855, £563,875 by the end of 1856, rising to £608,825 by the end of 1857, as work continued on fitting out the goods yard etc. This was in addition to the money spent on the hotel, which amounted to £49,134 by 30 Jun 1854 and £59,965 by 30 Jun 1855.

109 Birmingham New Street was damaged by bombing in the Second World War and partly dismantled. The entire station was destroyed and replaced with the present concrete bunker in the 1960s.

110 Buchanan 2002, 139–44, letter quoted on 141.

111 Victoria County History 1976, 111; Evans, 1859, Appendix, xciii–xciv. I am very grateful to Mr Robert Thorne for this information

112 Vaughan 1991, 215–17; Binding 2000, 86–99.

113 Brunel 1870, 461–73. I am very grateful to Andrew Saint for this information.

114 Buchanan 2002, chapter 8; Vaughan 1991, 230–5, 245–69; Griffiths 2000, 112–27.

115 Wilson 1972, 76.

Chapter 4

1 MacDermot 1964a, 163–4. MacDermot used the portrait as the frontispiece illustration to Vol I of his History. Later, the painting was loaned to Reading Town Hall, and was unfortunately cut down in size. It has recently been acquired by STEAM, Museum of the Great Western Railway, Swindon.

2 Ibid, 207–9.

3 Chapel 1982, No. 23, pp 87–92.

4 MacDermot 1964a, 223–6.

5 In 1854, interest payments represented about 32% of all the GWR's spending (£252,822 out of £783,769), as against c 24% for the London & North Western Railway (£398,781 out of £1,687,712) and 18.3% for the Midland (£158,051 out of £862,573). I have not found figures for the 1860s, but it seems unlikely that the GWR's position would have improved.

6 MacDermot 1964b, 19–22; Booker 1977, 84–6. The company weathered the storm by drastic economies, by raiding its (mercifully strong) cash flow, and by offering the shareholders preference shares instead of dividends.

7 Thorne 1978, chapter 4, especially 44–52.

8 The Times, 1 Sep 1935, letter from Mr Jasper Lambert, written in reference to a recent issue celebrating the centenary of the GWR. Mr Lambert recalled that he had known a Mr Woolaston, once a pupil of Brunel's. Woolaston once asked Brunel, 'I wish you would tell me, Sir, why you constructed Paddington Station at the level at which it stands today?' 'Well', replied Brunel, 'I will tell you. For one thing, by so doing, I was able to get a quantity of very good gravel, but I had another reason. I felt convinced that one day there would be an underground railway running around London at about that level.'

9 BUL, Brunel Collection, office diaries, 2 Nov 1852. Brunel was engaged with 'Messrs Barratt, Davis and another gentleman'.

10 MacDermot 1964a, 229–31.

11 Barker and Robbins 1975, 99–125. A long account of the opening of the Metropolitan Railway is given in The Builder, 21, 10 Jan 1863, 21–3. See also Menear 1984, 7–8; Trench and Hillman 1984, 130–38.

12 Barker and Robbins 1975, chapter 4.

13 Ibid, 126–7.

14 Ibid, 127, 145–6.

15 Barker and Robbins 1975, 104–26; Menear, 1984, 9.

16 Railway Magazine, Dec 1933, 419–27.

17 NA Rail 267/6, General Manager's report on suburban passenger traffic, 4 Feb 1869.

18 I am grateful to Mr John Lewis for information on these points.

19 NA Rail 267/230, report on a Proposed railway between High Wycombe and Paddington, 8 Oct 1896; White 1963, 121. The new route ran from Old Oak Common to High Wycombe, where it met the existing line from Maidenhead, via High Wycombe to Oxford. The line thus provided a new direct route to Birmingham, via Wycombe and Oxford, and was promoted as such. I am grateful to Mr John Lewis and Dr Gavin Stamp for information and advice on this point.

20 NA Rail 250/1661, special report on the working of traffic at Paddington by W Hart, 1 Aug 1881.

21 NRWRPR 7494, new departure platform under the central span, Jul 1873; 24581, new departure platform,

1883; 27903, additional platform, 1889.

22 NRWRPR 24562, dated 4 Jan 1878 shows the Proposed new works; 24575 is a drawing for a new canopy over the milk platform, signed J Olander, 1882.

23 NRWRPR GWR Drawing Catalogue, II, lists plan 14949 as being for this.

24 NRWRPR GWR Drawings Catalogue, I, No. 421. The drawing itself seems not to be extant.

25 NRWRPR roll 13316, unexecuted designs for a 20-bay range initialled ETA, 22 Apr 1872.

26 NA Rail 258/343, contains detailed specifications for the building dated 1873; NRWRPR roll 17021, has contract drawings dated 1876.

27 NRWRPR 17162, additional storey of offices, contract drawings signed by Kirk & Randall and dated 31 May 1879; 17840, 'additional offices', drawings for the eastwards extension, 1879–81; 17841, designs of 1880–1 for additional offices including part of the new top storey; contract drawings signed by Kirk & Randall, 23 Nov 1880.

28 NA Rail 258/343.

29 The Engineer 52, 16 Nov 1881.

30 The date at which the tracks were curtailed is not known. The 1867 Ordnance Survey map shows them going right up to the rear of the hotel; by the 3rd edition (1912), the track heads had been pulled back into the area of Brunel's main shed roofs.

31 NA Rail 258/343, various documents. NRWRPR MS catalogue, lists drawings 16149–51 as being for these alterations (not seen).

32 NA Rail 280/31, 383, GWR board minutes for 10 Nov 1880; 450, minutes for 5 Jan 1881.

33 Saint, Pettit and Irlam 1992, 33. Thomas Edison also invented the incandescent light bulb, quite independently of Swan but several months later, in the United States.

34 Engineering, 21 May 1886, copy in NA Rail 258/508; NA Rail 250/165, minutes of the GWR Electric Lighting Committee. These rather haphazard minutes mostly deal with the legal and contractual difficulties the company encountered over the installation of this system, 1884–6; Tweedie 1906, 282 gives a rather sanitised account.

35 The Electrician, May 1886. The rival for this title would seem to be the system

installed at the Grosvenor Gallery on New Bond Street in 1883.

36 MacDermot 1964b, 231. The Metropolitan Railway obtained an Act to run the Hammersmith & City Line by electricity in 1902, and in 1906 the GWR completed a power station at Park Royal to supply electricity for this, and also to supply Paddington, replacing the equipment at Westbourne Bridge.

37 Ellis 1959, 40.

38 White, 1987, 119.

39 MacDermot 1964b, chapters 9 and 10. I am grateful to Mr Peter Treloar and Mr John Lewis for advice and information about the end of the broad gauge. In some areas where there was mixed-gauge track the third rail was left in place to be taken up later.

40 Booker 1977, 10 and 103.

41 MacDermot 1964b, chapter 11.

42 I am grateful to Mr John Lewis for information about Churchward and his achievements.

43 Booker 1977, 101–15.

44 NA Rail 250/343, GWR Traffic Committee minutes, 1903–5, 7. This was done at an estimated cost of £19,000.

45 Ibid, 149; GWR Traffic Committee minutes, 8 Jun. The General Manager referred to the extended Up Relief line, but said that even so, 'additional platform accommodation should be provided forthwith. He submitted a plan which, while departing from the approved scheme of alterations, may be regarded as an improvement on it. The Proposal is, by utilising the space between No. 9 platform and the High Level Coal Yard, to provide two additional Main Line platforms with roadway between, and a short platform for suburban traffic. The plan also includes substituted provision for Cabs in South Wharf Road and the maintenance of the access between that Road and London Street, which will be the subject of an agreement with the Paddington Borough Council.' The estimate, of £93,000 for engineering works and £3,950 for signalling and telegraph works, was approved by the board on 9 Jun 1904, NA Rail 250/47, GWR board minutes 1903–5, 219.

46 NA Rail 250/344, Traffic Committee

minutes 1905–6, 257, 8 Aug 1906. Referring to GWR board minute 12 of 8 Jun 1904, the General Manager said that 'in working out Proposals for Paddington, it had been found desirable to make variations, and submitted an amended plan. In this scheme the accommodations on the platform level has been slightly rearranged and an access given from the end of the South Wharf Road, which will greatly facilitate the working of the Milk Traffic. The scheme also involves the removal of the buildings on the Down Platform at Bishops Road Station to enable an improvement to be effected in the line serving No. 12 platform and platforms Nos 10 and 11 extended. A new Waiting Room and Urinals will be provided at the West End of that Station, and a new footbridge and booking offices in lieu of the existing structure, while provision is also made for the erection of a length of covering in the Cab Yard.' The estimate had risen to £111,000 for engineering and £4,500 for signalling works. This was approved by the board the next day, 9 Aug 1906: NA Rail 250/48, board minutes 1905–8, 184.

47 MacDermot 1964b, 230; GWR Magazine, May 1906, 85, anonymous article, 'New locomotive depot at Old Oak Common'.

48 NA Rail 250/344, GWR Traffic Committee minutes 1905/6, 225, 13 Jun 1906, report to the committee to the effect that the original vote of £19,720 had lapsed due to the protracted negotiations with Paddington Borough Council, and a new vote of £24,000 was agreed to. NA Rail 250/48, GWR board minutes, 147, the board's agreement on 14 Jun 1906 to the new vote; 173, the board agrees on 19 Jul 1906 to the main contract for the reconstruction of the Bishops Road Bridge, for £17,843, let to Messrs Jackaman. NA Rail 250/49, the contract for the reconstruction of Westbourne Bridge was let to Messrs A Handyside on 6 Aug 1908 for £37,562.

49 The Railway Engineer, Mar and Apr 1906 has articles on the completion of the building; I am grateful to Mr Peter Rance of the Great Western Trust for this reference.

50 *GWR Magazine*, Mar 1907, 63–4; Nov 1907, 244.

51 Matthews 1917a, 28–31.

52 NA Rail 250/49, GWR board minutes for 30 Apr 1909. The minutes are very terse, and do not make any explicit reference to reinforced concrete. No detailed discussion of the design has been found in the GWR archives in the NA.

53 NRWRPR 50537, roll of 21 drawings for ferroconcrete by L G Mouchel & Co.

54 Cusack 1986, 183–95; Cusack 1987, 61–7.

55 Ibid.

56 *GWR Magazine*, Nov 1907, 243–5, anonymous article 'Reinforced concrete in railway structures' makes it clear that the GWR was using the Hennebique system.

57 Unpublished reports by Andrew Saint, English Heritage, Historic Analysis and Research Team, Historical research files, CITY 228, 28–31.

58 Matthews 1917a, 28–31; 1917b, 69–70.

59 NA Rail 250/49, 230.

60 NA Rail 250/50, 35. GWR board minutes for 16 Dec 1910, approved letting a contract for £6,750 to Messrs Jackaman, for excavation and removal of 45,000cu yds (34,407 cubic metres) of material beneath the superstructure for carrying the new goods and cab approaches.

61 NA Rail 250/50, 246. GWR board minutes for 7 Feb 1912, approved letting a contract for £18,285 to Messrs Holliday & Greenwood for the diversion of London Street and construction of new underground conveniences.

62 NA Rail 250/50, 282. GWR board minutes for 26 Apr 1912, approved letting a contract for £720 to Messrs Jackaman for building a retaining wall instead of the ordinary platform wall included in the contract. Contract No. 4.

63 NA Rail 250/50, 434. GWR board minutes for 10 Jan 1913, approved letting a contract for £820 to Messrs Jackaman, for cellarage accommodation and the cab ramp, including extra foundations and the facing of the cellars with glazed brick.

64 NA Rail 250/50, 488. GWR board minutes for 11 Apr 1913, contract for £945.

65 NA Rail 250/51, 127. GWR board minutes for 21 Nov 1913, approved letting a contract for £28,969 to Messrs Holliday & Greenwood, for construction of a roof over platforms 9, 10 and 11 at Paddington.

66 NA Rail 250/51, 145. Board minutes for 16 Jan 1914, approved letting a contract for £505 to Messrs Jackaman, for deepening the foundations of two concrete bases to main roof columns. NRWRPR 52134, 2 drawings, Contract 17, details of new steel columns to roof, Armstrong.

67 NRWRPR 51526, Contract 12, 12 drawings for roof over platforms 9, 10, 11, W Armstrong, Dec 1913; 52131, Contract 14, 20 drawings for roof extension, Gleadow & Armstrong; 52141, Contract 16, 4 drawings of details of end screen, Gleadow.

68 NRWRPR 52149, 3 drawings of tie-rods to the new span, Gleadow. These are dated 1913, well before the engineers' report, so tie-rods would seem to have been envisaged but not installed.

69 NA Rail 267/304, report on Paddington Station roof, 9 Jul 1915.

70 NRWRPR 52657, 6 drawings for new steel columns between platforms 2 and 3, Aug 1923; 52658, 5 drawings for new steel columns between platforms 7 and 8, May 1923, both sets of drawings by the Cleveland Bridge & Engineering Company.

71 Booker 1977, 118–9.

72 NA Rail 447.

73 They were: the Great Western Railway, the London, Midland & Scottish Railway, the London & North Eastern Railway, and the Southern Railway.

74 MacDermot 1964b, 242–2. The new group was composed of the GWR with 3,005 miles of line, two small English companies, and thirteen small Welsh lines ranging in size from the Cardiff Railway with less than 12 miles to the Cambrian Railway with 295 miles. *See also* Nock 1967, 1–2.

75 Booker 1977, 120–8.

76 Waters 1993 107–9.

77 Pole 1926, 23.

78 Booker 1977, chapter 6.

79 Simmons 1968, 43.

80 NRWRPR, T S Todd, 'The Future of Paddington Station', 1926, bound typescript volume.

81 A table of traffic numbers and revenue on the GWR shows total receipts at Paddington as £1,089,914 in 1903, £1,261,611 in 1913, £2,115,552 in 1923, peaking at £2,303,054 in 1928, and falling in each successive year to £1,886,281 in 1933. The figures for Paddington goods show a similar profile.

82 Nock 1967, 87–8, 95–6. This was part of a £4,500,000 programme of capital works affecting much of the GWR network, assisted by the government under the 1929 Act.

83 'Modernising Paddington Station', in *The Railway Gazette*, 8 Sep 1933, 345–6; Culverhouse 1934; The *Daily Telegraph*, 11 May 1933.

84 Binding 2001, 149. The work at Bristol was also funded under the 1929 Loans and Guarantee Act.

85 NRWRPR 63400, 33 drawings for new offices on the departure side, May 1931, Culverhouse; microfilm 13924–13938, formerly roll 63588, steelwork drawings for new offices and hotel extension on the departure side, 1930, E C & J Keay.

86 NRWRPR microfilm 14984, formerly roll 64611, 14 architectural drawings and 127 steelwork drawings for a new extension of the departure side office block, undated, Culverhouse.

87 NRWRPR 63653, 3 drawings for demolition of buildings for the arrival side roadway, Feb 1932, Culverhouse.

88 NRWRPR, microfilm 1344–61, formerly roll 63687, 17 drawings for new offices on the arrival side and over the Lawn, Sep 1932, Culverhouse; microfilm 4402–37, 28496–98, formerly roll 64029, 32 steelwork drawings for new arrival side offices and the hotel extension, Oct 1933, J S Nicholas and E C & J Keay.

89 NRWRPR microfilm 33382–98, 33401–11, formerly roll 63474, 27 drawings for additions and alterations to the GWR hotel, 1935, Culverhouse, E C & J Keay.

90 NRWRPR 63818, 9 drawings for the reconstruction of roofing over the circulation area, Jan 1933, J S Nicholas.

91 NRWRPR 63474; 64951, 19 steelwork drawings for alterations and additions in the old part of the hotel, undated, R G Sargent and A D Dawney & Co.

92 GWR Magazine, Aug 1935, 532–3:

information from Mr John Lewis.

93 NRWRPR 63266, 6 drawings for contracts 5 and 6, new spur tunnel and retaining walls at the Bishop's Road Station, Jun 1931, Carpmael; 63708, 14 drawings for the partial rebuilding of the Bishop's Road Bridge, Sep 1932, Carpmael; 63769, 8 drawings for the Bishop's Road Bridge, 1932, Carpmael, Cleveland Bridge & Engineering Company.

94 NRWRPR 63406, demolition of the Bishop's Road Station, undated, Carpmael; 63751, reconstruction of Bishop's Road Station, 1932, Carpmael; 63791, 26 drawings for excavation, demolition and reconstruction of west end of tunnel, Feb 1932, Carpmael.

95 Nock 1967, 97.

96 *The Railway Gazette*, 8 Sep 1933, 352.

97 Owings 1973. I am very grateful to Andrew Saint for this information.

98 The GWR set up its first bus services in 1903, but sold 50 % of the company in 1928: Nock 1967, 82. I am grateful to Mr Peter Rance for pointing this out.

99 Simmons 1968, 40–1.

100 Wodehouse 1954, 84–5.

101 Nock 1967, 216, gives figures of 444 GWR employees killed, 155 reported missing, and 271 prisoners of war, to Mar 1944. No figure for the whole war has been found. On page 222 he gives figures of 68 employees killed and 241 injured while on company service, with another 88 killed and 255 injured while off duty.

102 Sitwell 1974, 52–3. I am very grateful to Dr Michael Turner for providing me with this quotation.

103 Nock 1967, 148–52, describes the 'Square Deal Now' campaign launched by the 'big four' companies in 1938.

104 Ibid, 221–3, 233–7.

105 Booker 1977, 162.

Chapter 5

1 This point is made rather more trenchantly by Nicholas Faith (1990) in the preface to his *The World the Railways Made*. There are, of course, a number of eminent exceptions to this observation, such as Barker and Robbins 1975; Kellett 1969; Simmons 1968; and Faith himself, but there have not been enough of them. E T MacDermot's great *History of the Great Western Railway*, completed by C R

Clinker and O S Nock (MacDermott 1964 a and b), partakes in large measure of both the strengths and weaknesses of its genre. It is a superb piece of sustained research and an invaluable resource for all students of the GWR, including the present author, but it does little to relate the GWR to the culture that created it and is fairly demanding for the general reader.

2 E C Matthews' article, 'The development of Paddington passenger station', appeared in seven parts in the *Great Western Railway Magazine* (Matthews 1916a, b and c; 1917 a, b, c and d). The most valuable section for understanding Brunel's design is 1916c.

3 NA Rail 1005/11, 1st Class Express and Ordinary, 2nd Class Express and Ordinary, 3rd Class Ordinary and 3rd Class Parliamentary, single and return in each case.

4 Matthews 1916b, 251.

5 Ibid, NRWRPR 13309, has designs for a 'moveable bridge' at Paddington. Roll 18700 has a foundation plan for the departure side, undated but presumably of early 1851, which clearly shows the two open bays, 16ft (4.9m) wide, made beneath the platform for the bridges, and they are faintly indicated on the large general plan for the station, roll 6262, undated, also early 1851. One of the bridges survived into the 20th century.

6 All the drawings for machinery in NRWRPR roll 13309 are stamped as by Sir William Armstrong & Company.

7 *Journal of the British Association*, 1854, quoted in Matthews 1916c, 251.

8 Mr John Lewis points out that the length of the traverser would govern the maximum wheelbase-length of a vehicle that could be carried on it, not the overall length, and that this could have taken any of the GWR's 4- and 6-wheel coaches of the period, a 31ft (9.5m) coach having a wheelbase of just 19ft (5.8m).

9 NRWRPR 18700, now folder 138, 'Paddington Station, plan of foundations', unsigned and undated, but clearly the foundations for Fox, Henderson's first contract, so from early 1851.

10 NRWRPR 18700, an annotated outline plan, again undated but clearly from early 1851, has the positions of the

traversers marked in (and labelled 'traversers'); 6262, a large outline plan of the station, marks the zones with dotted lines and their breadth, 26ft (7.9m), without explicitly saying what this is.

11 NRWRPR roll 13309 has four drawings for traversing frames, and for hydraulic machinery to power them, which seem to fit with these locations, on the departure platform. None of them explicitly shows the width of the traversers (that is, the length of the vehicle that could be got on one); the dimension of 26ft (7.9m) comes from the foundation drawing, and from the outline plan, 6262.

12 NRWRPR roll 13309, two drawings for a 'dropping' or 'descending' platform, hydraulically powered.

13 Matthews 1916b, 253. Matthews added that 'the difficulty of the auxiliary intermediate platforms was to have been overcome by making a portion of them capable of being lowered to rail level, to permit the passage of the traverser arrangement, but so far as can be ascertained this was never effected. Probably the difficulties attendant on the installation and operation proved insurmountable.' In other words, Matthews knew about the 'descending platforms', and on the face of it, this would seem like a convincing explanation for them. However, he does not seem to have seen the drawings for them or he would have realised that their surfaces were of plain boarding and did not have rails for the traverser to run on. Equally importantly, traversers need solid foundations and, as is noted in note 9, the foundation plans for contract 1 clearly show footings for traversers but in different positions, not in the transepts and not spanning the whole width of the shed.

14 GWR 1971. Reprint of *Great Western Railway Timetable* for 1865.

15 Matthews 1916c, 251, said that the use of this area was 'not positively known', but interpreted it as being for owners of private carriages who were intending to travel in them. The area was long known to staff into relatively recent times as the horse arch: information from Mr Robert Thornton.

16 Ibid, 251.

17 Ibid, 253–4. Mr John Lewis has informed me that a similar narrow-gauge 'railway' was installed for moving baggage at Millbay Docks, Plymouth: pers comm.

18 Ibid, 251. This is the only reference I have found to there being a royal waiting room on the arrival side. It is not clear when it was removed. The three waiting rooms had substantial brick footings, a drawing for which is in NRWRPR roll 13314.

19 No drawing for the up parcels office has been found, but NRWRPR roll 13315 includes an undated drawing for adding an upper floor of offices to it.

20 NRWRPR roll 13309 has a drawing for hydraulic machinery for the sector table, dated 3 Jun 1854.

21 MacDermot 1964a, 370.

22 Ibid. 'Twelve months later it was decided to proceed with the passenger arrival sheds and platforms, and accommodation for the locomotive establishment, which might have meant the central span of the present day station roof…' As we know, Brunel envisaged the overall plan of the station from the outset, and there is no indication on the early sketches that he saw the central span as being for locomotives. As John Binding (2001, 53–4) demonstrates, in the original terminus at Bristol Temple Meads the engine shed was essentially the 'town' end of the main passenger shed, the equivalent to the Lawn area at Paddington.

23 MacDermot 1964a, chapter 16, 'Carriages and Wagons'. Some of the early carriages 18ft (5.5m) long, would have fitted on a 22ft (6.7m) turntable, but the 38ft (11.6m) 'Long Charlies' introduced in 1852 clearly would not.

24 MacDermot 1964a, 349–52, section on royal trains.

25 So much so that the greater part of it is today converted into a spacious shopping and eating place for tourists, with the trains confined to one mean platform at the back. Sic transit gloria mundi.

26 NA Rail, miscellaneous history file, 1005/66.

27 Quoted in Acworth 1889, 250.

28 MacDermot 1964a, 332–5.

29 Buchanan 2002, 164.

30 Macdermot 1964a, 339, reproduces a GWR timetable dated 30 Jul 1841.

31 Ibid, 334.

32 In 1845–6, the time of the fastest London to Bristol expresses came down to three hours or less.

33 Simmons 1968, 24–5.

34 NA Rail 267/16, General Manager's report on third-class fares, 18 Jan 1874. The company had raised third-class fares experimentally in South Wales to one and a quarter old pence a mile. First-class passenger numbers had fallen by 736, second-class by 37,144, third-class numbers had risen by 1,037,808.

35 Booker 1977, 102.

36 GWR Magazine, 7, Nov 1894, 3–4, anonymous article, 'An interview with the General Manager'.

37 Ibid.

38 GWR Magazine, Mar 1930.

39 Simmons 1968, 145.

40 Booker 1977, 80.

41 As John Lewis kindly told me, 'the first corridor train' should be expressed in the singular as the GWR had just the one set of corridor coaches for the first several months.

42 Simmons 1968, 146–7.

43 GWR 1971.

44 NA Rail 250/18, 448, GWR board meeting of 7 Jan 1863.

45 Simmons 1986, 89, quoting an article in The Globe, 3 Sep 1863.

46 Barker and Robbins 1975, 204.

47 NA Rail 267/166.

48 GWR Magazine, 7, Nov 1894, 3–4, anonymous article, 'An interview with the General Manager'. At first sight, these figures look anomalous – as if each journey was of only c 0.3 miles (0.5km)! I think that 'passenger miles' must be interpreted as meaning passenger miles run by every train-service, not by every passenger. If each train carried in the order of 50 to 300 passengers, this would seem to raise the mean journey-length to a more plausible range.

49 MacDermot 1964a, 230.

50 NA Rail 267/39, report on the London horse establishment, 6 Dec 1877. With the first stage of the stables nearing completion the company had to decide whether to let them or buy their own horses. The capital cost of buying 130 horses with equipment and a year's provender and running costs was estimated at £11,168.

51 NA Rail 258/243, estimate of space allocations needed, 29 Jul 1873. This document needs to be used with care, as it is not at all clear that it is complete. It lists the following staff: accountants, 17; finance, 9; Mr Friend, 1; Mr Tyrell, 2; Mr Grant, 5; general manager, 4; board and committees, 4; chairman, 1; deputy chairman, 1; secretary, 3; messengers, 5; solicitor, 8; rates and taxes, 2; Dr Cooper, 1; estate, 3; storeroom, 1; engineers, 9. The square footage occupied by each department or person is also listed. The document is very bald and it is just possible that the numbers refer to rooms, not people, but analysis of the list suggests that this is very unlikely, nor does it seem to square with plans of the building. This only refers to the upper floors of Eastbourne Terrace, as functions like the booking office, the waiting rooms, buffet and printing press, all on the ground floor, are not listed here.

52 NA Rail 267/145. This list is stamped 3 Apr 1873, but was compiled for completely different reasons to the 'head office' list, being a table comparing the official staff complement with the staff currently in post, giving their maximum salaries, and recommending revised maximums. The official complement was: station superintendent's office, 3; booking office, 11; abstract office, 2; excess luggage, 2; cloakroom, 1; police office, 1; collector, 1; cartage, 2; down parcels, 13; up parcels, 6.

53 Ibid. The next section of this document lists 'maximum staff' at the goods depot in the same way.

54 Ibid. This document lists all of the station's office staff in all stations and, in most cases, recommends that their maximum salary be increased.

55 NA Rail 1149/7, Brunel letter-books, 49. Brunel took considerable interest in the enginemen's welfare: on 18 Jan 1842 he wrote to the board listing the 16 who had given good service and qualified for the £10 bonus.

56 NA Rail 250/8, GWR board minutes 1854–5, 172.

57 Ibid, 173. It is worth pointing out that a GWR policeman was not performing a job we would associate with that title but was something more akin to a

signalman. I am grateful to Mr John Lewis for pointing this out.

58 Ibid, 188.

59 Ibid, 190.

60 Ibid, 249.

61 NA Rail 267/121, report on staff and working expenses at stations, 6 Jan 1863.

62 NA Rail 250/18. The GWR board minutes for the next three meetings after 6 Jan 1863 were examined, but no reference to the report was found.

63 Information from Mr John Lewis.

64 Dodds 1953, 374. Mr Dodds does not give a source for this and I have not been able to verify it from GWR records.

65 NA Rail 1005/212, file on the GWR Literary Society.

66 The Illustrated London News, 17 Dec 1859.

67 The best run of the magazine is that held by STEAM, Museum of the Great Western Railway, Swindon. Other good runs are held by the National Archives (formerly Public Record Office), and by the Great Western Trust, Didcot.

68 NA Rail 253/669, catalogue of paintings etc at Paddington, 89.

69 NA Rail 1005/66, 'Miscellaneous History', document published to mark the company's 91st birthday, 1929.

70 NA Rail 1005/82, copy of Green, F W 1937. 'The working of Paddington passenger station'. Proceedings of the GWR (London) Lecture and Debating Society, Jan 1937.

71 Ibid. The data from here to the end of the chapter is taken from Mr Green's article.

72 Information from Mr Robert Thornton, Network Rail.

Chapter 6

1 Hitchcock 1951.

2 Information from Robert Thornton; NA Rail 1005/82, British Rail press release dated 24 Sep 1968.

3 Information from Robert Thornton. Moving the newspaper services to the new depot enabled British Rail to keep the articulated lorries, which had been loaded at night inside the station, outside.

4 Ibid. The masterplan was produced in-house, the first stage of work designed by Aukett Associates.

5 Fowler 1990; Brindle 1991.

6 I am very grateful to Mr Robert Thornton of Network Rail for much information on recent works at Paddington.

7 Personal communications from Robert Thornton, and Andrew Whalley of Nicholas Grimshaw & Partners; Powell 1999.

8 Buchanan 2002, 221–4.

Chapter 7

1 Hitchcock 1970, 559.

2 Addyman and Fawcett 1999, chapter 5.

3 Turner 1850, 204. Turner's roof was immensely influential and several mid-Victorian stations still have crescent trusses based on this model. His original Lime Street roof did not last long, being replaced by the present 212ft (64.7m) crescent truss roof in 1867.

4 Addyman and Fawcett 1999, 76.

5 NRWRPR roll 13320.

6 NRWRPR catalogue, records roll 102790 as containing 39 drawings of full-size details for the ornamental cast-iron work, all signed off by Brunel, but this was missing when requested in Mar 1992.

7 The Builder, 12, 17 Jun 1854, 322.

8 NRWRPR microfilm 24213–7, formerly roll 52658, drawings for new steel columns between platforms 7 and 8, Cleveland Bridge & Engineering Company, 12 May 1923.

9 Grimshaw 2000.

10 BUL, Brunel Collection, office diaries: on 24 Mar 1851 Brunel met his assistant Charles Gainsford and one William Tapper about 'Paddington Station galvanised iron', meeting Gainsford and Charles Fox later the same day.

11 NA Rail 1005/82, typescript copy of the specification for Fox, Henderson's second contract, specifies 'Patent rolled plate 26 ounce [793gm]' glazing for 'Paxton Glass Roofing – in part,' and No. 18 gauge galvanised corrugated iron roofing for the lower part of the roofs.

12 NRWRPR microfiche 115.

13 Hitchcock 1951; Hitchcock 1972, 558–61.

14 Hitchcock 1972, 561.

15 The Builder, 12, 28 Jan 1854, 41.

16 NA Rail 1005/82, GWR half-yearly reports to shareholders.

17 NA Rail 447.

18 I have not found the original letter: it is quoted in an article in GWR Magazine, Sep 1930, 382.

19 NA Rail 250/187, 53. The Expenditure Committee considered 'paving approach from Spring Street and Bishop's Bridge Road with small stones'. Ibid, 56, 24 Nov 1853, the same committee advised that the inclined road to the arrival side be paved with small stones like the road by the departure platform.

20 NRWRPR rolls 13315, 13315A.

21 NRWRPR roll 13315. The elevation is in a roll of drawings of full-size details for the external treatment of the façade.

22 NRWRPR roll 13328 contains a fine drawing for the ceilings of the vestibule, newspaper and refreshment rooms.

23 NRWRPR 17021, contract drawings, dated May 1876.

24 NRWRPR microfiche 118 and 119, plan and details of Paxton roofing.

25 NA Rail 258/343 contains a detailed specification for this building.

26 NRWRPR 63400, 33 drawings for new departure side offices, 1931; 63588, 6 steelwork drawings.

27 NRWRPR 64611, 14 architectural drawings and 127 steelwork drawings for a further extension of the departure side offices.

28 NRWRPR: there are numerous sets of drawings for the office expansion, which evidently took place in phases. They are somewhat difficult to interpret. 17032, drawings for a proposed new storey over existing offices; 17153, has very useful general plans of the offices with their uses marked on, as well as plans for 'additional offices' referring to the south-eastwards extension; 17840, 'fourth additional offices' refers to the south-east extension; 17841, 'additional offices', again refers to the south-east extension and the additional storeys, which were evidently handled under the same contract, by Messrs Kirk & Randall of Woolwich.

29 NRWRPR 17162, 'Additional Storey of Office'; 17841, 'Girders over Booking Hall'.

30 NA Rail 1008/64, misfiled letter from Brunel to Saunders, 23 Jan 1851.

31 NRWRPR, Microfiche 118, 125.

32 NRWRPR, Roll 13315A contains

numerous coloured full-size drawings for these.

33 NRWRPR 17840, 'Fourth Additional Offices'; 17841, 'Extension of Paxton Roofing'.

34 NA Rail 250/5, GWR board minutes, 262, 4 Dec 1851. Brunel submitted plans for the board and committee rooms and general offices, above the booking offices on the departure side. Surviving drawings of these are held in NRWRPR, rolls 13315, 13328 (dated 1851–2) and 16144 (dated 1853–5.

35 NRWRPR 13328, roll of full-size details for interior ornament, including the cornices and ceiling details for the vestibule, newspaper and refreshment rooms, the first-class waiting room and lobby, for the committee room and Mr Saunders' room.

36 NRWRPR 13315, undated drawing for the lantern.

37 NRWRPR 13607–13626 (formerly roll 52629).

38 NRWRPR 13328, roll of full-size details of ornament for interiors; 16144, designs for offices and fittings, 1855.

39 NA Rail 253/669, D V Levien's catalogue of paintings and works of art at Paddington, 1926, listing well over a thousand objects. The Frith copy was a gift from Frank Bibby, a director, in 1917, while the engravings were a gift from Sir Watkin Williams Wynn. The seals remain in the collection of STEAM, Museum of the Great Western Railway, Swindon.

40 Levien 1908 and 1909. Some of the objects are now in the National Railway Museum, York, and STEAM at Swindon.

41 NA Rail 253/669, see above, note 37.

42 NA Rail 258/243, undated memorandum, filed with documents of c 1916.

43 Matthews 1917a–d.

44 Matthews 1917d; NRWRPR microfilm 29827–29840, formerly roll 51526, drawings for roof over platforms 9–11, contract 12, 1913; microfilm 28719–28739, formerly roll 52131, old number 59968, drawings for contract 14, Apr 1914; 'Steel Structures', Apr 1919, 108–12.

45 I am very grateful to Robert Thornton for pointing these splendid features out to me.

46 NRWRPR microfilm 1344–61, formerly roll 63687, 1932.

47 Ibid.

48 GWR Magazine, Mar 1933, 110–11, anonymous article, 'New offices at Paddington Station'.

49 The most important contender for the title of first grand railway hotel is the North Euston at Fleetwood, designed by Decimus Burton as part of Sir Peter Fleetwood-Hesketh's development of the town, c 1841–7. The scheme as a whole depended on the assumption that the London & North Western would take its Glasgow services from Euston to Fleetwood (hence the hotel's name) and thence by ferry to the Clyde. This was wrecked by Joseph Locke's success in taking the Lancaster to Carlisle line over Shap Summit in 1843–6. Sir Peter was bankrupted. Burton had envisaged the North Euston as a giant circular building, of which about a third was built. It remains in hotel use.

50 Hitchcock 1972, 211–12.

51 Lever 1973, 88.

52 Obituary of John Thomas, The Builder, 20, 19 Apr 1862, 275. The Illustrated London News devoted an article to the pediment on 2 Sep 1854, 217.

53 The Illustrated London News, 18 Dec 1852.

54 Hardwick's perspective of the coffee room is in the Royal Institute of British Architects Drawings Collection, see Lever 1973, 88.

55 The Builder, 21, 10 Jan 1863, 21–3.

56 GWR Magazine, Jan 1914, 17. 'Departmental news – connection of Paddington Station with the "Bakerloo" railway'.

57 NRWRPR 7494, undated plan for the 'London Depot', and another undated plan marked 'GWR London Terminus' show variants of this plan.

58 NRWRPR 14909–21, fine series of coloured drawings for the first goods depot.

59 BUL, Brunel Collection, Large Sketchbook 4, 15, 29 Jan 1851.

60 NA Rail, 250/5, 53, 73, 98.

61 NRWRPR 13324, roll of 17 drawings for the goods station, one dated 17 Oct 1851.

62 NRWRPR 17842, general plan of the goods yard; roll 30658 includes an isolated drawing for 'Roofing to Coal Viaduct' dated Aug 1906.

63 NA Rail 250/49, 230.

64 NA Rail 250/6, 381–2, GWR board minutes for 10 Mar 1853.

65 NRWRPR 16122, roll of 22 drawings, for warehouse and goods sheds; 13304, a number of isolated drawings in a larger roll, including drawing for a raking bowstring truss, tracing sent to Gainsford on 23 Jun 1854, and to Bertram on 24 Feb 1856; details of the warehouse roof dated 30 Aug 1855; 17842, roll of drawings for 'Contract G', relating to the second phase of the goods depot.

66 NRWRPR, 13309, drawing of lifting platforms for goods shed, 1853; 13312, 16 drawings of hydraulic machinery, including hydraulic accumulator towers, capstans and gearing, hoists and cranes for the goods shed, several of them signed as by Sir William Armstrong & Company, Oct 1856; Brunel 1870, 85, note 1, referring to an article by Armstrong in the Report of the British Association, 1854, 418.

67 NRWRPR 17843, plans for 'new goods offices', carried over the far (east) end of the tracks, within the first, northern part of the goods depot.

68 The Railway Engineer, Mar and Apr 1906, has articles on the completion of the building: information from Mr Peter Rance.

69 Bond 1925.

70 NRWRPR 49753, new roof to the Birmingham platform, Dec 1908; 50525, 3 drawings for new platforms coverings, 1911; 50533, alterations to north-west corner of goods shed, undated; 50515, roof covering, extension of platform 1, Mar 1912; 52152, reconstruction of roof to one bay of goods station, Oct 1915.

71 NRWRPR list: 52666 7, contract drawings for goods shed roof, Apr 1925, J C Lloyd; 52667, 10 drawings, goods station alterations, Lloyd; 62034, goods depot, reinforced concrete cellarage, 1925, Indented Bar & Concrete Engineering Co; 62307, goods depot alterations, and approach to high-level yard, May 1927; 62311, goods station cellarage, ferroconcrete drawings by the Indented Bar & Concrete Engineering Co, 1927; 62393, goods shed roof, 45 contract drawings, 1927, Lloyd. Many of the drawings are no longer in the collection and they

72 Bond 1925.

73 I am grateful to Mr Peter Rance of the Great Western Trust for this information. The Trust hope to put these objects on display in a new GWR museum and reference library at Didcot as and when funding is available.

74 NA Rail 250/6, 71. NRWRPR 13306, a roll of drawings headed 'Paddington–Narrow Gauge Engine House', in fact seems mostly to consist of copies of the contract drawings for the broad-gauge engine house. It had a central section, 462ft (140.9m) long and 68ft (20.7m) wide inside, with slightly narrow extensions about 100ft (30m) long and 56ft (17m) wide inside at either end. The shed could comfortably have housed 50 locomotives and tenders (though it would have taken a long time to have got the ones in the middle out), and it is not clear why Brunel wanted so vast a building.

75 NRWRPR 13306, drawings for 'Paddington Locomotive Offices'. Two other rolls have copies of what appears to be an earlier version of the design, with ten bays of workshops framed by symmetrical two-storey wings with bay windows, with the engine-drivers' accommodation at one end and Gooch at the other: 13311, a roll of drawings for carriage sheds and workshops includes an undated plan and elevation of this design: 16137 includes a drawing for a wrought-iron beam in the 'floor to Mr Gooch's Office' dated 14 Oct 1853; 13314, a roll of miscellaneous drawings, another undated version of this earlier design.

76 NRWRPR 13306, has a plan and elevation marked 'Narrow Gauge Engine House' showing it apparently as built, 12 bays long. Curiously, the roll contains an alternative version showing exactly the same design but extended to 27 bays, giving it internal dimensions of 327ft (99.7m) by 42ft (12.8m). The Ordnance Survey 25in. map confirms that it was the smaller 12-bay version which was built.

77 GWR Magazine, May 1906, 85, anonymous article, 'New locomotive depot at Old Oak Common'.

78 Ibid.

79 NRWRPR 13311, undated general plan of carriage department sheds and workshops; 10266, now folder HC 189, contract drawings for the carriage department's sheds, offices, stores and workshops, dated between Aug 1855 and Jan 1856.

80 NRWRPR 13311, undated plan, elevations and roof details for carriage department stores and offices.

81 NRWRPR 13305, plan for smiths' and fitters' shops, signed J W for C S, 20 Dec 1853.

82 NRWRPR 13305, undated, coloured contract drawings for Paddington wagon shops.

83 NRWRPR 16144, an unlabelled, undated plan of the ground and first floors of a rectangular building, is probably of the staff hostel.

84 NA Rail 1149/4, Brunel, letter-book III, 1838, 82–3.

85 NA Rail 1149/4, 95–6.

86 NA Rail 830/6. Board minutes of the Grand Junction Canal Company, 1835–8, 293–4.

87 NA Rail 1149/44, 'GWR Tenders', 35, 'London Terminus – various works'.

88 NA Rail 1149/8–13.

89 NA Rail 1149/9, 'Facts', 1836–40, 96–9.

90 NA Rail 250/48, GWR board minutes, 147, 173. NRWRPR roll 30658, miscellaneous drawings, includes an undated, early 20th-century drawing for widening the bridge carrying the Bishop's Road over the canal, in two spans, of 35ft (10.7m) and 16ft (4.9m).

91 GWR Magazine, Feb 1908, 39–40, anonymous article. 'The engineering department – Bishop's Road Bridge'.

92 No early views or drawings of the bridge have come to light, but NA Rail 1149/44 'GWR Tenders' gives the date of the contract, and an outline schedule of prices, for brickwork, concrete and stonework.

93 NA Rail 250/49, GWR board minutes, 93.

94 GWR Magazine, Aug 1910, 207–8, anonymous article, 'The engineering department – reconstruction of Westbourne Bridge'.

95 NA Rail 1149/44, 'GWR Tenders'.

96 GWR Magazine, Jul 1909, 159; NA Rail 250/49, £403 to E C and J Keay for ornamental cast-iron work for the Ranelagh Bridge.

97 Nicholas 1914. The girders carrying the south span, 15ft (47m) long and 17ft (5.2m) deep at the centre, were reckoned to be, for their length, the heaviest ever commissioned by the GWR: the eastern one was calculated to carry 230 tons (234 tonnes) more than its counterpart.

98 GWR Magazine, Mar 1907, 63, anonymous article, 'The engineering department – reinforced concrete in railway structures'; Nov 1907, 244, article on the GWR's use of reinforced concrete.

99 NRWRPR microfilm 29841–6, formerly roll 63121, foundations and preparatory works on the site between Westbourne Terrace and Bishop's Road, R Carpmael, 1930.

100 NRWRPR microfilm 1306–1343, formerly roll 63506, full contract drawings dated Jan to Jul 1932.

101 GWR Magazine, Sep 1933, 374, anonymous article, 'Structural alterations at Paddington. New offices and store for stationery department and hostel for refreshment department staff'.

102 J Smith 1993, 'Historic building report, former Mint Stables, South Wharf Road, Westminster', typescript report, Royal Commission on the Historical Monuments of England; R Thorne 1990, 'The Mint Stables', Historic Analysis and Research Team files, English Heritage.

103 NRWRPR 10242–6, contract drawings for the first phase of work, 1876; 17029, plan showing the southern part of the site with the first phase built, and the whole intended layout, with a contract specification signed by Owen, Oct 1876.

104 Smith 193; Thorne 1990; Gordon 1893, 50–53; Collier 1909.

105 Matthews 1917a and b; NRWRPR microfilm 3758–3777, formerly roll 50523, 23 drawings for additions to the Mint stables by W Armstrong and the new-works engineer's office, including drawings for the reinforced concrete work by L G Mouchel & Partners.

106 Matthews 1917a, 30–31. NRWRPR microfilm 3758–77.

107 Thorne 1990; Smith 1993.

108 Gordon 1893.

109 Harwood, E 'Paddington British Rail maintenance depot, No 179 Harrow Road, City of Westminster', unpublished historical report, Historic Analysis and Research Team, English Heritage; Killick 1969, 151–7.

Taxis pulled up on the arrival side: a foggy evening in 1950.

BIBLIOGRAPHY

Acworth, W M 1889. *The Railways of England*. London: John Murray

Addyman, J and Fawcett, B 1999. *The High Level Bridge and Newcastle Central Station: 150 Years across the Tyne*. Newcastle upon Tyne: North Eastern Railway Association

Barker, T C and Robbins, M 1975. *A History of London Transport. Volume 1: The Nineteenth Century*, revised edn. London: Allen & Unwin

Beattie, S 1975. *Royal Institute of British Architects Drawings Collection Catalogue: Alfred Stevens*. Farnborough: Gregg International

Biddle, Gordon 1986. *Great Railway Stations of Britain: Their Architecture, Growth and Development*. Newton Abbot: David & Charles

Binding, J 2000. 'The final bridge: the design of the Royal Albert Bridge, Saltash' in Kentley, E, Hudson, A and Peto, J (eds), *Isambard Kingdom Brunel: Recent Works*, 86–99. London: The Design Museum

Binding, J 2001. *Brunel's Bristol Temple Meads: A Study of the Design and Construction of the Original Railway Station at Bristol Temple Meads 1835–1965*. Hersham: Oxford Publishing

Bond, A 1925. 'Reconstruction of Paddington goods station'. *GWR Magazine*, September 1925, 343–6

Booker, F 1977. *The Great Western Railway, A New History*. Newton Abbot: David & Charles

Bourne, J C 1846. *The History and Description of the Great Western Railway*. London: David Bogue

Brindle, S 1991. 'Paddington Station Roof'. *Conservation Bulletin*, June 1991, 19–20

Brunel, I 1870. *The Life of Isambard Kingdom Brunel, Civil Engineer*. London: Longmans, Green (reprinted 1970, Newton Abbott: David & Charles)

Bryan, T 2000. 'Brunel's broad gauge' in Kentley, E, Hudson, A and Peto, J (eds), *Isambard Kingdom Brunel: Recent Works*, 37–52. London: The Design Museum

Buchanan, R A 2000. 'Working for the chief: the design team and office staff of I K Brunel' in Kentley, E, Hudson, A and Peto, J (eds), *Isambard Kingdom Brunel: Recent Works*, 14–24. London: The Design Museum

Buchanan, R A 2002. *Isambard Kingdom Brunel*. London: Hambledon & London

Cattell, J and Falconer, K 1995. *Swindon: The Legacy of a Railway Town*. London: HMSO

Chapel, J 1982. *Victorian Taste: The Complete Catalogue of Paintings at the Royal Holloway College*. London: Zwemmer

Collier, E J 1909. 'Railway horses'. *GWR Magazine*, December 1909, 279–81

Conder, F R 1983. *The Men Who Built Railways*. (First pub 1868 as *Personal Recollections of English Engineers*, London: Hodder and Stoughton) 1983 edn, Simmons, J (ed), London: Thomas Telford

Cowper, E A 1854. 'Description of the wrought-iron roof over the central railway station at Birmingham'. *Proc Inst Mechanical Engineers*, 26 July 1854, 79–87

Culverhouse, P E 1934. 'The alterations at Paddington Station: part iv, the new buildings'. *GWR Magazine*, February 1934, 65–73

Cusack, P 1986. 'Architects and the reinforced concrete specialist in Britain 1905–08'. *Architect Hist* **29**, 183–95

Cusack, P 1987. 'Agents of change: Hennebique, Mouchel and ferro-concrete in Britain, 1897–1908'. *Construction History* **3**, 61–74

Dixon, R and Muthesius, S 1978. *Victorian Architecture*. London: Thames & Hudson

Dodds, J W 1953. *The Age of Paradox: A Biography of England, 1841–51*. London: Gollancz

Ellaway, K J 1994. *The Great British Railway Station: Euston*. Oldham: Irwell

Ellis, C H 1959. *British Railway History: An Outline from the Accession of William IV to the Nationalisation of the Railways. Volume 2: 1877–1947*. London: Allen & Unwin

Ellis, C H 1975. *The Royal Trains*. London: Routledge & Kegan Paul

Evans, D M 1859. *The History of the Commercial Crisis, 1857–8*.

Faith, N 1990. *The World the Railways Made*. London: Bodley Head

Fowler, D 1990. 'Paddington bares all'. *New Civil Engineer*, 15 March 1990, 40–41

Gordon, W H 1893. *The Horse World of London*. London (reprinted 1971, London: J A Allen)

Griffiths, D 2000. 'The Leviathan: designing the Great Eastern', in Kentley, E, Hudson, A and Peto, J (eds), *Isambard Kingdom Brunel: Recent Works*, 112–27. London: The Design Museum

Grimshaw, N 2000. 'Paddington station – project assessment', in Kentley, E, Hudson, A and Peto, J (eds), *Isambard Kingdom Brunel: Recent Works*, 69–70. London: The Design Museum

GWR 1971. *Great Western Railway Timetable for 1865*, reprinted edn, Oxford: Oxford Publishing

Hitchcock, Henry-Russell 1951. 'Brunel and Paddington'. *The Architectural Review* **109**, April 1951, 240–6

Hitchcock, Henry-Russell 1972. *Early Victorian Architecture in Britain.* (1st edn 1954) 1972 edn, London: Trewin & Copplestone

Hobhouse, H 1976. 'P and P C Hardwick: an architectural dynasty' in Fawcett, J (ed) *Seven Victorian Architects*, 32–49. London: Thames & Hudson

Jackson, A 1969. *London's Termini.* Newton Abbott: David & Charles

Kellett, J R 1969. *The Impact of Railways on Victorian Cities.* London: Routledge & Kegan Paul

Kentley, E, Hudson, A and Peto, J (eds) 2000. *Isambard Kingdom Brunel: Recent Works.* London: The Design Museum

Killick, J 1969. 'Paddington Maintenance Depot'. *Official Architecture and Planning*, February 1969, 151–7

Latimer, J, 1887. *The Annals of Bristol in the Nineteenth Century.* Bristol: W & F Morgan

Lever, J (ed) 1973. *Catalogue of the Drawings Collection of the Royal Institute of British Architects: G–K.* Farnborough: Gregg International

Levien, D V 1908. 'Pictures at Paddington', *GWR Magazine*, July 1908, 147–9

Levien, D V 1909. 'Pictures at Paddington', *GWR Magazine*, August 1909, 177–9

Levien, D V 1930. 'Through the Great Western Museum, 2 – Frith's famous picture, "The Railway Station" ', *GWR Magazine*, March 1930, 109

MacDermot, E T 1964a. *History of the Great Western Railway. Volume I: 1833–63.* (1st edn 1927) 1964 revised edn, Clinker C R (ed), London: Ian Allan

MacDermot, E T 1964b. *History of the Great Western Railway. Volume II: 1863–1921.* (1st edn 1927) 1964 revised edn, Clinker C R (ed), London: Ian Allan

McKean, J 1994. *The Crystal Palace: Joseph Paxton and Charles Fox.* London: Phaidon

Matthews, E C 1916a. 'The development of Paddington passenger station: part I'. *GWR Magazine*, 159–62

Matthews, E C 1916b. 'The development of Paddington passenger station: part II'. *GWR Magazine*, 203–5

Matthews, E C 1916c. 'The development of Paddington passenger station: part III'. *GWR Magazine*, 251–4

Matthews, E C 1917a. 'The development of Paddington passenger station: part IV'. *GWR Magazine*, 28–31

Matthews, E C 1917b. 'The development of Paddington passenger station: part V'. *GWR Magazine*, 69–70

Matthews, E C 1917c. 'The development of Paddington passenger station: part VI'. *GWR Magazine*, 175–7

Matthews, E C 1917d. 'The development of Paddington passenger station: part VII'. *GWR Magazine*, 236–8

Meeks, C L V 1957. *The Railway Station: An Architectural History.* London: Architectural Press

Menear, L 1983. *London's Underground Stations: A Social and Architectural History.* Tunbridge Wells: Midas

Mitchell, V and Smith, K 2000. *Western Main Lines: Paddington to Ealing.* Midhurst: Middleton Press

Nicholas, J S 1914. 'The reconstruction of Lord Hill's Bridge at Royal Oak Station, Paddington'. *GWR Magazine*, February 1914, 37–41

Nock, O S 1962. *The Great Western Railway in the 19th Century.* London: Ian Allan

Nock, O S 1967. *History of the Great Western Railway. Volume III, 1923–1947.* London

Owings, N A 1973. *The Spaces in Between: An Architect's Journey.* Boston, Mass: Houghton Mifflin

Pevsner, N 1950. *Matthew Digby Wyatt.* Cambridge University Press, Cambridge

Pevsner, N 1976. *A History of Building Types.* London: Thames & Hudson Pevsner, N 1978. *The Buildings of England: Derbyshire*, 2nd edn, revised Williamson, E. Harmondsworth: Penguin

Pole, F J C 1926. *Great Western Railway, General Strike.* Paddington: Great Western Railway

Powell, K 1999. 'Station masters'. *Architects' Journal*, 30 September, 24–33

Reed, M C 1996. *The London and North Western Railway: A History.* Penryn: Atlantic Transport

Rolt, L T C 1970. *Isambard Kingdom Brunel.* (1st edition 1957) 1970 edn, Harmondsworth: Penguin

Ruskin, J 1849. *Seven Lamps of Architecture.* London: Smith, Elder & Co

Saint, A J, Pettit, S and Irlam, G 1992. *Cragside*. London: National Trust

Simmons, J 1968. *The Railways of Britain*. London: Macmillan

Simmons, J 1986. *The Railway in Town and Country*. Newton Abbot: David & Charles

Simmons, J (ed) 1971. *The Birth of the Great Western Railway: Extracts from the Diary and Correspondence of George Henry Gibbs*. Bath: Adams & Dart

Sitwell, O 1974. *Queen Mary and Others*. London: Michael Joseph

Sutherland, R J M 1975. 'Oxford Midland Station and the Crystal Palace', *The Structural Engineer* **53**, 69–72

Sutherland, R J M 1989. 'Shipbuilding and the long span roof', *Trans Newcomen Soc* **60**, 107–26

Thorne, R 1978. *Liverpool Street Station*. London: Academy Editions

Thorne, R 1985. 'Masters of building: Paddington Station'. *Architects' Journal* **182**, 44–58

Toppin, D 1981. 'The British hospital at Renkioi, 1855'. *The Arup Journal* **16** (2), 2–18

Trench, R and Hillman, E 1984. *London under London*. London: John Murray

Turner, R 1850. 'A description of the iron roof over the railway station, Lime-street, Liverpool', *Proc Inst Civil Engineers* **19**, 1850, 204

Tutton, M 1999. *Paddington Station, 1833–54: A Study of the Procurement of Land for, and Construction of, the First London Terminus of the Great Western Railway*. Mold: Railway and Canal History Society

Tweedie, M G 1906. 'Gordon electric light installation at Paddington'. *GWR Magazine*, December 1906, 282

Vaughan, A 1991. *Isambard Kingdom Brunel: Engineering Knight Errant*. London: John Murray

Vaughan, A 1997. *Railwaymen, Politics and Money: The Great Age of Railways in Britain*. London: John Murray

Victoria County History 1976. *A History of the County of Stafford. Volume XVII*. Oxford: Oxford University Press

Waters, L 1993. *London: the Great Western Lines*. Shepperton: Ian Allan

Weiler, J M 1987. 'Army architects – the Royal Engineers and the development of building technology in the nineteenth century'. Unpublished Ph.D thesis, University of York Institute of Advanced Architectural Studies

White, H P 1987. *A Regional History of the Railways of Great Britain. Volume III: Greater London*. 3rd revised edn, Newton Abbott: David & Charles

Wilson, R B (ed) 1972. *Memoirs and Diary of Sir Daniel Gooch, Transcribed from the Original Manuscript and Edited with an Introduction and Notes by Roger Burdett Wilson*. Newton Abbot: David & Charles

Wodehouse, P G 1954. *Uncle Fred in the Springtime*. (1st edition 1939) 1954 edn, Harmondsworth: Penguin

Wyatt, M D 1850. 'Iron work and the principles of its treatment', *Journal of Design* **4**, 77–8

ILLUSTRATION CREDITS

Figures are reproduced by kind permission as follows:

English Heritage (numbers in brackets are the English Heritage Photo Library reference numbers)
Cover (K030812), Preface (K010979), 1.4, 2.6, 2.7, 3.9, 3.17 (K010980), 5.1 (K010978), 6.3 (K030902), 6.6 (K010975), 7.1, 7.2, 7.3 (K010987), 7.5 (K010982), 7.16 (K010988), 7.26 (K010976), 7.32, 7.43 (K030906), 7.44 (K010993), 7.52 (K010969)

English Heritage.NMR/© Crown copyright.NMR (numbers in brackets are the NMR reference numbers)
Chapter frontis (CC97/01127), 3.3 (FF85/9), 3.13 (R/04042/1), 7.4 (AA98/05430), 7.11 (BB48/1157), 7.27 (BB47/878), 7.28 (B904246)

Photographs courtesy of Network Rail Infrastructure Limited. Copyright Network Rail Infrastructure Limited (numbers in brackets are the NMR reference numbers)
Front endpaper (AA031091), Back endpaper (AA031089), 2.8 (AA031048), 3.14 (AA031066), 3.18 (AA031051), 3.22 (AA031068), 4.17 (AA031078), 5.4 (AA031085), 5.5 (AA031073), 7.6 (AA031088), 7.7 (AA031093), 7.13 (AA031070), 7.14 (AA042114), 7.24 (AA031094), 7.33 (AA031082), 7.34 (AA031052), 7.40 (AA031083), 7.42 (AA042117), 7.49 (AA031059), 7.50 (AA031060)

Source Network Rail
4.19, 6.1, 6.5, 7.47

Hulton Archive/Getty Images
Frontispiece, 3.23, 4.20, 4.21, 4.22, 4.23, 5.13, 5.17, 5.20, 6.2, 6.4, 7.8, 7.48, Bibliography

STEAM, Museum of the Great Western Railway, Swindon
Title page, 1.8, 1.10, 2.9, 2.12, 3.1, 4.1, 4.12, 4.18, 5.2, 5.12, 7.22, 7.23, 7.31

By courtesy of the National Portrait Gallery, London
1.1, 3.12, 3.24

Private collection/Photo courtesy of the National Portrait Gallery, London
3.11

Manchester Archives and Local Studies, Central Library, Manchester
1.2

National Railway Museum/Science and Society Picture Library
1.3, 2.2, 2.10, 4.3, 4.7, 4.11, 4.13, 4.14, 4.15, 4.16, 4.24, 5.3, 5.7, 5.9, 5.10, 5.15, 5.18, 5.19, 7.15, 7.18, 7.19, 7.20, 7.21, 7.25, 7.30, 7.35, 7.37, 7.38, 7.45

Science Museum/Science and Society Picture Library
3.21

© Great Western Trust, Didcot
1.5, 2.11, 4.9, 4.10, 5.6, 5.11, 5.14, 7.12, 7.36, 7.39, 7.41, 7.46, 7.51

Elton Engineering Books
1.6

© The National Gallery, London
1.7

The City of Westminster Archives Centre
1.9, 2.1, 2.13, 4.5, 4.6, 5.16

By permission of the British Library
2.3 (650.c.17/74), 2.4 (Maps sheet 1 3479 (43), 1838 det), 4.4 (OS 25in. (1869) xxxiii det)

By permission of the Director of Information Services, University of Bristol (The Brunel Collection is held in Special Collections, the Arts & Social Sciences Library, University of Bristol)
2.5, 3.2, 3.7, 3.8, 3.15, 3.16, 7.9, 7.17,

© B E C Howarth-Loomes, The Howarth-Loomes Collection (held in the NMR; numbers in brackets are the NMR reference numbers)
2.14 (BB72/450B), 5.8 (BB82/12079)

© D Sherborn (held in the NMR; number in brackets is the NMR reference number)
3.4 (BB81/3058)

V & A Images (Victoria & Albert Museum)
3.5

The Illustrated London News Picture Library
3.6

RIBA Library Drawings Collection
3.10, 3.20, 7.29

RIBA Library Photographs Collection
3.19

From the picture collection – Royal Holloway, University of London
4.2

Applications for reproduction of images should be made to the National Monuments Record. English Heritage has endeavoured to ensure that full permission has been sought and given for all material used in this publication. Every effort has been made to trace the copyright holders and we apologise in advance for any unintentional omissions, which we would be pleased to correct in any subsequent edition of this book.

INDEX

Paxton Gutter
upon Girder H.
(Section)

Corrugated Iron Roofing

Side view

Girder A.

Girder A

Girder A

Girder A

Girder G

Girder I

Girder I

Girder I

Large Columns required
Under Girders A & C   2 with Brackets   with Inlet and
    "   "   6 plain   Outlet pipes
    "   H   1 plain   without
          Total   9

Columns required under
    without
    2   with Bra
    2   without
Total 4.

Plan of Large Column.

Elevation of Large Column.

Level of Platform.

Level of Rails.

Level of Platform.